A
UTERUS
IS A
FEATURE,
NOT A
BUG

ALSO BY SARAH LACY

*Once You're Lucky, Twice You're Good: The Rebirth of
Silicon Valley and the Rise of Web 2.0*

*Brilliant, Crazy, Cocky: How the Top 1% of
Entrepreneurs Profit from Global Chaos*

A UTERUS IS A FEATURE, NOT A BUG

THE WORKING WOMAN'S GUIDE TO OVERTHROWING THE PATRIARCHY

Sarah Lacy

HARPER
BUSINESS

An Imprint of HarperCollins*Publishers*

A UTERUS IS A FEATURE, NOT A BUG. Copyright © 2017 by Sarah Lacy. All rights reserved. Printed in the United States of America. No part of this book may be used or reproduced in any manner whatsoever without written permission except in the case of brief quotations embodied in critical articles and reviews. For information, address HarperCollins Publishers, 195 Broadway, New York, NY 10007.

HarperCollins books may be purchased for educational, business, or sales promotional use. For information, please email the Special Markets Department at SPsales@harpercollins.com.

FIRST EDITION

Designed by Bonni Leon-Berman

Library of Congress Cataloging-in-Publication Data has been applied for.

ISBN 978-0-06-264181-6

17 18 19 20 21   LSC   10 9 8 7 6 5 4 3 2 1

For my babies, Eli and Evie: You've made me better in every way. I'm so glad the patriarchy was wrong about you.

And for Paul: I don't "need" to share my life with a man, but I want to share my life with you.

CONTENTS

CONTENTS

A
UTERUS
IS A
FEATURE,
NOT A
BUG

PROLOGUE

I looked to my left down the long, dark, grey tunnel and saw more people joining the mob that was screaming at us. I looked to my right and saw the same. Usually when this many people are pissed off at me, I have some clue what I've done.

Unless there was some secret escape hatch in the middle of this long tunnel of offices, it seemed clear this situation was going to get a whole lot worse before it got better. The crowd was getting denser and angrier, and the air thicker thanks to the uncirculated 100-plus degree Nigerian heat and the confined space becoming crammed with bodies.

"Why don't we just make a run for it?" I asked Jason. It seemed that there was still enough room for us to push our way out . . . for now.

"Trust me, we are safer in here," Jason said. "Out there anything can happen. Half the people in here are on our side."

I'd only met Jason earlier that day, but I did trust him. I had little other choice.

But it wasn't clear that anyone in this crowd was rooting for us to get out of here alive. Everyone's face was twisted in anger. They were screaming, but in the smooth echoing walls of the tunnel, I couldn't make out anything they were actually saying. For all I knew, they could have been suggesting a lynching or wishing me "Happy Friday!" in an overly intense way. It was one screaming din of vowels and consonants all hurtled directly at me and my husband.

A 250-pound bald man was in my face, alternating between

jabbing his finger at me and turning to thrust it into the air to whip up the crowd. His eyes were bulging. His veins were bulging. A white tank top stretched painfully across his muscles bearing the inscrutable phrase: *Skull Shit.*

I can't say I wasn't warned before heading to Nigeria. There were the usual overcautious State Department warnings that I typically ignored. There was every email I've ever received from a Nigerian prince. There was the dinner the night before I left with a Silicon Valley billionaire who grabbed my arm and said, "You cannot go to Nigeria like this. It's too dangerous."

I don't tend to respond well when someone tells me I can't do something. This was 2011, and I'd spent the previous two years reporting in Africa, South America, Asia, and the Middle East for a book about the chaos and the opportunity found deep within the megacities, slums, and villages of the emerging world. Going into places that most venture capitalists didn't care about or have the stomach for was what I did.

My photographer husband, Geoff, rationed his vacation time to come on adventures like this with me. I knew before asking that this was a trip he wasn't going to miss. He wanted to explore Nollywood, the gritty but lucrative Nigerian film industry. I wanted to meet scammers. This was going to be fun.

Ironically, it was the reporting on Nollywood—not the scammers—that had put us in danger.

The crowd was closing in on us. We'd tried locking ourselves in one of the "offices" of a Nollywood producer Jason was friends with—they looked more like jail cells. There was barely enough room for us to stand amid the piles of DVDs. But the crowd wouldn't disperse.

Hiding and waiting them out wasn't going to work. We were trapped.

They were pissed. They were out for blood. Or money. Or something.

Hopefully money.

Geoff looked into my eyes. I nodded with little more than my eyes. He ducked behind us in the prison-cell-cum-office and slipped the memory card out of the expensive camera he'd stashed surreptitiously in Jason's backpack. He stuffed the card in his shoe. After more than a decade together, a husband and wife don't have to say things to each other like "I'm going to be furious if we lose a finger, AND we lose the fucking pictures and video from today."

You just know.

That's when the vigilantes came for us.

It's not every day you find yourself in a situation where the vigilantes are the safer choice. But Jason was essentially telling me that was the case. Jason was building a business putting Nollywood content online and was one of the only people paying producers to globally distribute their work. This was basically another day at the office for him.

The vigilantes were also pissed at us for reasons we never got to the bottom of, but they were charged with keeping order. They were coming to escort us to our "trial." Going along with them peacefully was our best bet to getting out of this long windowless tunnel with all our fingers and toes intact.

We were taken to see the judge: a man named Bones.

We were marched back into the Nigerian heat of Alaba market, the street hawkers still barking, haggling, and negotiating, the preachers still singing, banging on their electronic keyboards, and trying to "save" everyone. "Save" in that God/eternal soul sense. Only a wad of cash was likely to save us from Skull Shit and his crew.

Hopefully money.

"Don't worry, as long as I have my checkbook, they need me alive," Jason whispered to me.

The courtroom looked—surprisingly—like it could have been the set of an old Western. We stood there formally: the accused. Skull Shit and his friends were on the other side fuming. Bones marched in surrounded by his men and took the bench, such as it was. He didn't wear robes and his bailiffs brandished machetes as they walked him in. They made a show of them without acting as though they were making a show of them, dramatically pulling them out of their belts and putting them on the table with a clatter.

I looked at Geoff. He looked more scared than I was, but then again, I'd faced down more mobs than he had. More often than not, those were just Internet mobs, like the gang of Internet commenters that threatened me with kidnapping and gang rape if I traveled to Brazil as planned. I agreed not to write about my trip until I got back as a safety precaution. My boss at the time clearly felt mixed about that. He made me promise that if anyone mailed a pinkie to Geoff, he'd photograph it for our website. "Just think of the traffic," he said joking/not joking.

Journalists have a sick sense of humor.

In that moment, I thought two things. The first was "I might lose a body part today, but we're clearly going to get out of here alive. Now that we're out of that tunnel, this is just a bribe situation. It's a good thing Jason is here. We're going to be fine. And if we are, it'll make a *great* story. We still have the photos." I probably stifled a grin.

The second was directed at my five-months-pregnant belly. I looked down and wordlessly sent a message to Eli, "Sorry, kid. Welcome to life as my son."

INTRODUCTION: LIES

My publisher wants me to tell you that this book is for everyone. Mothers, daughters, women who never want to be mothers, and the men who work for, employ, or fund all these mothers and daughters.

But let's be real: The bulk of you can't possibly understand the words that follow. If you have never held your own baby in your arms—one that you grew in your very own womb—you just will never understand.

You may think you can imagine the greatest love in the world, multiply it by a jillion, and have a *sense* of what I'm talking about. You can't.

You just don't get it.

You won't get it.

Don't even try to get it.

I see you trying. I'm serious: Stop it.

That is what every woman hears from the moment she starts inching towards womanhood until she welcomes her own child into the world. Worse than being told how much you will never understand one of the most universal things that biologically unites women is how much of that "gospel of motherhood" is an absolute lie.

I want everyone who hasn't had kids yet to know something: You've been lied to. I, too, was lied to throughout my twenties and through half of my thirties. We are all lied to.

The lies weren't always intentional or nefarious. But with a topic as highly variable and highly individual as motherhood, accepting one woman's truth as your inevitability is the same as believing a lie.

Even your best friend's truth. Even your mentor's truth. Even your mother's truth. Take my own truth with a grain of salt, too.

Some of these lies are insidious, the product of a male-dominated culture wanting to turn something almost super-human that only women can do into a disability. But many of these lies are well meaning.

My mother was one of the people who lied to me.

She was a brilliant academic with multiple degrees, but she also looked like Sophia Loren. That was an interesting combination growing up in a Southern Baptist family in 1950s Jacksonville, Florida.

She called off one engagement in part because her dashing, well-to-do fiancé didn't want as many kids as she did. But also because she didn't feel he appreciated her brain enough. When she met my dad—a lanky Mississippi-born philosophy PhD student and the first kid in his family to finish high school—it was like hearing doves cry. They got engaged two weeks later, after late nights discussing philosophy, literature, and the ultimate truths of the world. They both wanted to spend their lives together reading, thinking, debating, and having tons of babies.

But my brilliant mother didn't work after they got married. She just—I dunno—sat around the house waiting to get pregnant. And boy, did she. I was the youngest of five kids. She waited to work until I was in kindergarten—nearly twenty years after they'd been married and she'd finished her degrees.

In many ways my mother was lucky: She was able to have it all. She had a concentrated decade-plus of child rearing—not missing a single adorable, chaotic moment—and then still got to have a twenty-something-year acclaimed career as a teacher.

I idolized her as a strong woman and my female role model. So her reasoning for waiting so long to work stuck with me: "I knew I'd want to do both perfectly, and I wouldn't have been able to be a perfect mother and a perfect teacher at the same time."

It's an innocuous-sounding statement. And many of my friends heard their own version of it. Jessica Jackley is the cofounder of Kiva, a company that by giving out microloans has in turn empowered other women to become founders. She told me she remembers her mom telling her she became a teacher because it was the only option if she wanted to spend summers with her kids. That made a deep imprint on Jackley: "This is the *only option* if I want to be with my kids."

My mom's explanation of work-life balance became a model for my own life; I simply inverted it. I focused on my career first. My dream was to go from a business reporter at a tiny weekly business journal in Memphis, Tennessee, to a reporter at *BusinessWeek*, the *Wall Street Journal*, or *Fortune*, write impressive cover stories, and eventually one day write a book.

It was a very slow start, but at age twenty-eight things started happening rapidly for me. I had moved to San Francisco just as the dot-com bubble was bursting. I managed to stay employed during the savage downturn. Years later, after some nine months of interviewing, I got a job at *BusinessWeek*. Soon after that, I cowrote a cover story about soaring valuations of Internet companies in the aftermath of the dot-com crash. It was one of the first national magazine pieces that dared to suggest that Internet investing was coming back and that burgeoning companies like YouTube and Facebook could be worth real money. I was told it broke *BusinessWeek*'s internal newsstand records for the month of August.

But the idea was so controversial back then that it also infuriated people who'd been burned by the dot-com craze in the late 1990s. It was the first time I found myself in the middle of an Internet mob, the first time I felt the intense hatred of thousands of people who'd never met me. "Well, at least no one here will forget your first cover," my editor offered in the middle of the shit storm.

There was an even bigger silver lining: It led to my first book deal with Penguin. After six years of toiling at small publications no one gave a shit about, here I was at thirty with everything I'd ever wanted. And I'd just gotten married, too.

What was next? Extra career-goal credit? I had an on-camera job with a new show for Yahoo Finance. I helped build a startup, TechCrunch, which was the must-read startup publication of its time. I used my final check from my first book to buy an old Victorian house in a gritty neighborhood of San Francisco in 2008.

A year later, I sold my second book on entrepreneurship in emerging markets, spending some forty weeks traveling all over the world to report it.

Once that book published, and TechCrunch sold to AOL, I thought hard about what else I could do that I hadn't done. I was well beyond what I ever dreamed my career could be. I was playing with the house's money. The answer was just more of the same. I didn't have to put anything on hold any longer. And so, I decided, I could finally *risk* having a baby.

And it seemed like the biggest risk I'd taken so far. Bigger than moving to San Francisco at the peak of the bubble. Bigger than quitting *BusinessWeek* to write my first book. Bigger than going to work at a controversial startup. Bigger than traveling to some of the most dangerous places on the planet.

I was never too scared about risking a paycheck. I'd grown up the youngest of five with parents who were teachers. Having basic cable felt like a luxury for me.

I was never as scared as I should have been about risking my safety. The way I saw it, I was more likely to get hit by a bus in San Francisco than be charged by baboons in Rwanda. (Although, only the latter has actually happened.) When it's my time to go, it's my time to go. Better to die doing what I loved: reporting a story. "I've had a good run," I would always say when my husband expressed concerns about the travel risks I took.

But the risk of having a baby was greater. I felt that it risked *me*. Not my body, but my soul. The lies had all told me I'd change. That I'd be unrecognizable. That all the things I'd cared about before would no longer matter. That I wouldn't be me anymore.

Those words—like so many others from other mothers I'd known—had rung in my ears for more than a decade: *I knew I'd want to do both perfectly, and I wouldn't have been able to be a perfect mother and a perfect teacher at the same time.*

I did my career first. I figured I'd crammed a whole career into about twelve adult working years. If it all ended once I had kids, so be it. I made peace with the lie, which I believed was an immutable truth.

You know that scene in the movies when someone is defusing a bomb and they have no idea if they've cut the right wire or not? They sort of close their eyes and brace. And then slowly they open them. Maybe one at a time. They are alive. The bomb is defused. Nothing changed.

That's what happened when I had Eli. I was still there. Even better, actually, I was me-*plus*.

Everything I'd been told about the great disability of motherhood was a lie.

⌘

Now that I have a six-year-old son, a five-year-old company, and a four-year-old daughter, I've been able to think more about these lies from the other side.

My mom, of course, didn't intentionally lie to me. She told me her own truth, or so she thought.* It was intended to be honest and helpful. A seed of knowledge casually tossed in my direction that burrowed its way into my psyche, growing tendrils that wormed deep into my brain. This has probably happened to you: Maybe it was your mother, a teacher, a boss, a Hollywood depiction of motherhood, advice from a women's magazine. Like dandelion puffs on a windy day, these seemingly innocuous seeds float around us all the time, some passing by you, some landing, burrowing, and growing the preconceived-notion equivalent of weeds.

For me, it was one of thousands. I was also told to "get ready to feel like a failure all the time," as a woman torn between kids and work. I was told that my career would become irrelevant—*biologically*—once I held my children in my arms. That I wouldn't allow myself to take risks anymore. That I'd never be able to risk a paycheck or my life in the same way again. That things I'd done before would be absolutely irresponsible as a mother.

Movies that depict a high-powered CEO with a baby always

---

* My mom opted not to read this book before publication, telling me it was my story and she didn't have any right to control it. (Yes, she's amazing. There's a reason she has been my female role model for forty-one years.) But we discussed this "lie." She seemed taken aback and sorry that this comment had such an impact on me. She said she changed her thinking after spending decades as a working mother; that she, too, let go of "perfection" and believed work made her a better mother. She's never even asked whether I'd stop working or believed I should after having kids. My sister, too, has always worked, becoming a teacher at the same school where my mom taught. One thing so insidious about these comments is how they can be frozen in our minds.

involve chaos—a babysitter who doesn't show on the day of a big meeting; clothes soaked with vomit; running into a boardroom in a tight pencil skirt and heels, frazzled, late, with a shirt misbuttoned; overapologizing while the men exchange knowing "I told you she couldn't have it all" looks.

Now, on the other side of it, I can see that I'm not like my mom, or a lot of those other women. I don't actually *want* perfection. A drawer of perfectly rolled-up matching socks all in a row? That was never going to be my life's work. I prefer chaos.

I'm not sure how I missed this before I had kids, but there's one clear trend in my life: Every time things have gotten comfortable, I have found a way to explode my sweet little nest. I could have stayed at *BusinessWeek* for the rest of my career, a job I'd labored days and nights throughout my twenties to earn. Or I could have kept my Yahoo Finance job, making more money than I thought a journalist could. I could have written a second book about Silicon Valley instead of traveling all over the world barely living off a book deal that was a fraction of my first one.

My best friend and coworker at TechCrunch, Paul Bradley Carr, was the first one who noticed this trend. "Once you prove you can do something, you set an insanely harder challenge the next time," he said.

I spent so many years worrying that getting pregnant would change that. In reality, getting pregnant *played into that.*

I promoted my second book while pregnant, taking Eli to five continents; I organized a three-day conference in Beijing to be held six weeks after my due date; and I decided to quit Tech-Crunch and start a new company while on maternity leave, before I'd even hired a nanny.

Then I got pregnant *again* six months into building that

company. Recently, I pitched this book on motherhood just when my family had digested my divorce, my kids were potty trained and in preschool, my company was finally profitable after a brutal four years, and I wasn't immediately being threatened or sued. Life had gotten too calm.

If I know I can do what's ahead of me, I lose interest and get lazy. This is why I love reporting so much. Each story is a new challenge, a new truth to be unearthed. It's also why I love building a company. You aren't judged on doing every-thing right because you can't. You are judged by doing the right things right. And it's why I love being a mother. Your children multiply in complexity every day. They get harder at the same rate you get better.

And now I'm doing all three of these things at once. It's a chaos-seeker's dream come true.

Is it hard? Yes! That's the fucking point! More please!

Knowing I could do something perfectly was never going to appeal to me. My mom's truth was ultimately irrelevant.

So were those others I heard. These little-engine-that-could thrill issues mean that I don't feel guilty at work and at home because, in my mind, I am already trying to do something nearly impossible. I win if I survive. And if it suddenly seems doable, I'll throw some more "impossible" on.

Getting through every day is like a Lara Croft adventure in my mind's eye. That moment when I drop my kids off at school with full bellies, clean teeth, sometimes-matching socks,* and seminutritious packed lunches, and race back home to meet my

---

* When matching socks got too easy, I went for real working mom extra credit: DAYS OF THE WEEK SOCKS.

morning deadlines feels like I just managed to leap over to the other side of the chasm, grabbing it with my fingertips before the rickety bridge collapses beneath me and then bursts into flames. I sit for a moment, every morning, parked at the white drop-off-only curb and just savor my smug satisfaction.

"I rule," I think. "I've totally got this."

⌘

Sure, this could all change when my kids become teenagers. As usual, I'm told that I can't possibly understand what that's like. But after a point, mothering becomes problem-solving muscle memory. You don't fully know how you'll do any of it, but you become confident you will.

The more I thought about it, the more I realized that my mother's truth wasn't just different from my truth. I've become convinced it wasn't true for her either, based on what I experienced as her daughter.

Her view was that she couldn't be a great teacher and a great mother at the same time. But so many of the reasons she excelled as my mother directly tied into her working. One time when I was sick in kindergarten, my mom had to come get me. My mom—new to working—had to teach her afternoon classes and didn't have a lot of options of what to do with me. So she set me up with a little desk in the corner of her classroom, with markers and some paper, and beseeched me to just color quietly while she transmuted the truths of Fyodor Dostoyevsky to her students for the last period of the day.

The students tried to leverage me for maximum distraction. But my mother politely, quietly held her ground and maintained control of the class. My mom would perch on her stool as her teen-aged kids acted up, smiling wryly and adding in a quiet voice, "This is still going to be on the test." The message: I'm not going to scream at you. I'm not going to send you to the office. It's up to you if you want to listen to me or fail senior English.

It must have made a huge impression on me, because at the end of class I looked at her in awe and said to her, "I want to be in charge of something one day."

Her working didn't just allow me to have a better education; she stayed close to me during my teenaged years because she taught me and all my friends. She showed me that a woman could command a room and be in charge of something. None of this would have happened if she'd been a stay-at-home mom seeking "perfection."

She also set a template for me as a mother, whether I realized it or not. Since Eli was in the womb, I viewed him as my little partner. We promoted my second book all over the world, doing more than thirty keynotes together.

After he was born, I took him everywhere with me in those early months of starting my company. He went fundraising with me. He helped make our first hires. He and Evie would be backstage at our events. Most everyone who has ever worked at Pando has held my children—whether they volunteered or not.

I joined the parents' committee at Eli's preschool to be closer to his school community, the way my mom had been by virtue of working there. I leased a minivan so that I can chaperone field trips. I bring our cats for pet week show-and-tell. I know all the names of the kids at school and most of the parents. Eli's always had some social anxiety, and my involvement has made a huge difference in his confidence level with his friends. I learned it from what my mom did for me.

Her truth as a mother was simply not my truth as her daughter. I was made immeasurably stronger by my birth order dictating that I had a working mother. I was made *me*.

She was wrong. She absolutely was able to do both at once. Working made her a "more perfect" mother.

There's only one thing I can think of in my life that has made me even stronger than being raised by a working mom. That made me an even better version of the best me I could possibly be. That gave me the courage to take even bigger risks, be even more adversarial as a journalist, and push myself even harder.

Becoming a working mother myself.

1

Your Uterus Is Not a Ticking Time Bomb

I STARTED THIS BOOK WITH the "lie" my mother told me in part because it had such an impact on me, but also because it's hard to imagine a better-intentioned lie. My mom, after all, *wanted* me to have children and be successful in my career. If the innocuous, well-meaning lies from people who love us can undermine the power of motherhood, imagine the impact of actual institutionalized sexism.

There's another word for "institutionalized sexism" that you're going to have to get comfortable with if you are going to fight it: the patriarchy.

Data shows that men dominate American politics and business, that they outearn women, that they are the gatekeepers in nearly every industry. We all know we live in a patriarchy, but somehow saying the word "patriarchy" makes you sound like some kind of unhinged extremist.

It has become my new swear word in Silicon Valley, packing

greater shock value than an expertly placed f-bomb. You can use it casually in a meeting—"Yeah, I decided to wear pants because I just wasn't feeling the patriarchy today"—or save it for real full-throated outrage.

Who is the patriarchy? It is a collective of both everyone—to a degree—and no single person in particular. Old white men who don't believe women should have basic reproductive rights are part of the patriarchy. The 40 percent of Americans who believe women working is bad for society are part of the patriarchy, whether they are men or women. Employers who pay women less money because the market allows it are part of the patriarchy. Politicians who blame society's ills on single mothers are part of the patriarchy. Twitter trolls who say you are the "wrong" kind of feminist are part of the patriarchy. Even the nice greeter at Disneyland who automatically refers to your daughter as "princess" is part of the patriarchy.

The patriarchy is the general organizing principle of the past and sadly, the present. It's the backdrop behind everything in American life, and its tentacles reach into every part of your life: how much you get paid, whether you get promoted, whether it's OK if you have sex with someone, how high your heels should be for you to be considered desirable, and whether you get pregnant. You know, the things that simply shouldn't be up to other people.

Not everyone in the patriarchy means ill. But the dominance of the patriarchy makes it impossible for women to be treated equally. And so the patriarchy must be overthrown.

There is only one way to do that: We have to stop asking permission and negotiating with men to live the lives we want to live. Women have to take back their rights to all those very personal things that the patriarchy has so rudely butted itself into. We need to start believing that we have a right to live the lives we want, that having a career isn't a negotiation you win with your "50/50" spouse. That you will be paid equally. That you have the right to have a baby when you want to, or not have a baby at all.

And we have to help one another. We have to stop being our own worst enemy. We are both victims of the patriarchy . . . and part of it. We do the patriarchy's dirty work every time we tell ourselves we aren't enough, every time we lift ourselves up at the expense of other women, and especially every time we allow ourselves to feel *guilt.*

Guilt is the most effective weapon the patriarchy has. It both keeps us from achieving and makes us feel bad about it when we do achieve. Guilt pits us against "patriarchs" like spouses and male bosses. Guilt is so effective because it's self-inflicted. Guilt makes you doubt everything you know in your heart, in your head, in your gut. Guilt is the patriarchy's evil little voice inside you. It has to go.

This book will help you dismantle the patriarchy by exposing what it is and how it works. It will examine my own journey from "cool dude patriarchy enabler" to "badass feminist warrior." It will destroy the idea that something as remarkable as having children makes you weaker. It will make an argument for why you need more women in your company, immediately. And it will explain why single moms may be the most badass, politically transformative force in America's future. It will show you why America is far from the feminist envy of the world.

My story takes place in the tech world of Silicon Valley, a place that is in some ways not as overtly sexist as other industries. Silicon Valley, at least, pretends it's a meritocracy. We'll explode that myth as well and explain why micro-indignities and unconscious bias can be even more pernicious to root out than men chasing women around desks.

Silicon Valley matters as a microcosm on gender equality because it is a young industry. It is an idealistic industry of people who want to remake the world and the way it operates. There aren't centuries of "the way things have been done" in an ecosystem that's only about seventy years old. Silicon Valley rapidly changes leaders as hot young companies devour the old. In Silicon Valley, data and results are supposed to be all that matters. Silicon Valley should be the one place that gets this right.

Motherhood is central to my story because it was only by becoming a mother that I had this badass feminist awakening. But it's also central to all of us taking on the patriarchy, whether we are mothers or not, or even want to become mothers or not. Motherhood is the reason that women have value in a patriarchy. Giving birth is the one thing men can't do. And that's a big reason it's used to hold back so many women economically.

When a woman returns to work—frequently without taking the full maternity leave she was entitled to, if she was lucky enough to get any—she is thrust into a no-win dichotomy: Are you a good employee or a good mother? Pick one.

The patriarchy believes—as fact—that a good mother must be constantly available to her children and a good employee must be constantly available to her bosses. By definition, no one can do both. This belief justifies why nearly half of Americans feel it's bad for society if women have careers: because working women are necessarily horrible mothers. It also justifies employers denying mothers career advancement, bonuses, raises, or sometimes jobs altogether, because you'd be aiding them in becoming bad mothers, and you simply can't expect them to be good workers. This is called the "Maternal Wall."

For their book *What Works for Women at Work*, authors Joan C. Williams and Rachel Dempsey conducted interviews with 127 successful working women, more than half of whom were women of color. They discovered a near-universal playbook to the bias women face at work, falling into four major buckets: the "Prove-It-Again!" bias, the "Tightrope" bias of being too masculine or too feminine, the "Tug of War," and the "Maternal Wall." Of the four, the Maternal Wall bias was the most blatant, in part because many people don't see it as a bias; they see it as biology.

This bias is measurable. Williams and Dempsey cite a study by sociologists that found when subjects were given identical résumés, one identified as being from a mother and one not, "non-mothers got 2.1 times as many callbacks as equally qualified mothers and were recommended for hire 1.8 times more frequently than mothers." They quote one sociologist who worked on the study as excitedly saying, "I have been studying these kinds of gender biases for years and I have never seen effects this large."

The Maternal Wall even affects women who never become mothers, who never want to become mothers. It frequently starts as soon as a woman gets engaged. Your years of being totally devoted to your bosses suddenly have an expiration date.

I faced this when I interviewed at *BusinessWeek*. I was engaged but had no plans to have children anytime soon. Just before they sent me to New York to interview with the magazine's editor in chief, a New York–based editor sat down with me. He admitted that what he was about to ask me was illegal, but he wanted to know if I was planning to have kids. I answered honestly that I had no intention to.

Worse: I so totally believed the lies about motherhood that

I wasn't even offended by the question. My competition for the job was all men. It was clear that if I'd said I was planning to start a family, I wouldn't have been hired. And because I believed the lie, that seemed rational to me. Even fair.

Just as with guilt, women have so internalized this that we even enforce it ourselves. In "The Elephant in the Valley," a recent survey of women in the tech industry, 75 percent of women said they were asked about family or marital life on job interviews; 40 percent reported feeling the need to talk about their families less in order to be taken seriously at work. And of the women who took maternity leave, more than 50 percent shortened it because they felt that doing otherwise would have a negative impact on their career. Sheryl Sandberg called her book *Lean In* because she observed that young women take themselves off their career paths before they have children, in many cases before they are even married.

Why? They believe the same lie I did.

Implicit in Maternal Wall bias are several of the other biases women face at work, according to Williams and Dempsey. Mothers experience a heightened form of the "Prove-It-Again!" bias, frequently having to prove their commitment and work ethic over and over again with each subsequent child they have. Because the idea that motherhood changes you is so deeply accepted in society, employers and coworkers are constantly on guard that this pregnancy could be the one.

Because this form of sexism is so generally accepted, employers attribute anything that might signal a female employee's decreased commitment—even things that could happen to anyone—to her being a mother. Williams and Dempsey cite an example where an attorney became a partner and was able to read all her past performance reviews. In her second year at the firm, she missed a meeting to take a child to the emergency room, and she suffered from it for years afterwards.

After that incident, year after year, there was a question about my ability to become a partner, my commitment to the law, and whether, because I had three children, it would just be too much . . . I traveled all the time, I was in court all the time. I missed one meeting because I had to take my child to the emergency room, and that kept getting highlighted in my evaluation.

I suspect that if she had missed a meeting because *she* had to go to the emergency room, it would have never come up again.

We saw the same thing in 2014 when Yahoo CEO Marissa Mayer overslept and missed a meeting at the annual advertising festival in Cannes. Mayer was doing one of the hardest jobs in the tech world—trying to turn around Yahoo, which five previous CEOs had failed at—and was raising young kids at the same time. The media seized on a rare moment to portray the usually steely, professional Mayer as weak. It's hard to imagine them doing the same thing if Twitter's Jack Dorsey overslept for a meeting. Mayer was pilloried for being jet-lagged and honest.

But Mayer was also widely criticized for not taking maternity leave with her children as setting an unfair standard for women. She couldn't win either way. If she looked too much like a mother, she would give fodder to the activist shareholders who were working to undermine her. If she looked too much like the male image of a successful CEO, she was accused of letting down women everywhere. So we saw her on cable TV— shot from the neck up—defending her position against angry shareholders the day before she gave birth to twins. The image of a female leader she was allowed to portray was literally and figuratively boxed in.

I've noticed that when gossip blogs write something negative about me, they frequently pick a picture of me when I was pregnant to illustrate the story. That's how powerful the dog whistle of a pregnant woman in the business world is: She is weak. She is distracted. She is disabled. You even go on "disability leave" when you give birth.

Mayer's career has been a public master class in this tight-rope working mothers walk: Are you a good mother or a good worker? Because the idea of being both doesn't exist in the patriarchy.

Is it any wonder most women's answer is to pretend their children don't exist?

Sheila Marcelo, CEO and founder of Care.com, actually got that advice from a mentor: Do not tell the people you work with that you have children. Can you imagine hiding something so important from people you work with every day? That goes against every instinct a mother has, which you know if you follow any of them on Facebook. I can't imagine the psychological toll of spending eight hours a day feeling shame over one of my proudest achievements.

Marcelo took that advice, but she was not long for that job. That double standard drove her to excel so much in her career that she could build her own company, which in turn helps other women navigate through their own work-life balance challenges. She is one of the only women to cofound and lead a publicly traded tech company, despite the fact that she got pregnant unexpectedly in college and got her degrees and all her early work experience while raising kids.

There is some progress in reclaiming the optics of motherhood, at least in Silicon Valley. The women who were senior in the tech world when I was building my career—like Carly Fiorina or Meg Whitman—would never have talked about their children the way Mayer or Sandberg do. They took a risk talking about motherhood, even if Mayer was careful never to be photographed pregnant.

Lynn Jurich, CEO of Sunrun, pushed this even further, not only taking her company public while pregnant but also ringing the opening bell while holding her baby. It could have come across as weak. Instead it came across as what it was: completely badass that she did an IPO road show nine months pregnant, went to the hospital to give birth, then brought the baby with her to the New York Stock Exchange to start trading.

It's what the message from working moms to men should be: Can you do what we just did?

Seeing pregnant women and women who identify as mothers achieve matters greatly because we live in a world where pattern matching justifies bias. Managers believe they are serving their companies' interests if they worry about the ROI of investing in a young woman's career when she might at any point decide to have a family and leave the field. Many believe they are *helping* a working mom if they don't suggest her for a promotion that may involve heavy travel.

This is what's so insidious about the Maternal Wall bias. It is so strong and so overt because many people don't consider it sexism. That seems insane since only women can get pregnant, and the Maternal Wall is a justification for discriminating against women whether they have children or plan to or not. But it's true: If you believe that a woman away from her children for any period of time is a "bad mother" and you believe a woman who is not on call for her boss 100 percent of the time is a "bad employee," you are *helping* to deny women economic opportunities. "Discrimination against mothers is often viewed as culturally acceptable [because] it frequently shows up as benevolent rather than hostile sexism," write Williams and Dempsey. "Benevolent bias can be ignored or overlooked because it's grounded on genuinely good intentions."

Like compound interest, a little bit of bias can go a long way over the course of a career. Former executive at Google and Apple, entrepreneur, and expert on management science, Kim Scott has written about the toll unspoken bias can take. In a 2016 essay, she details the impact of "compound sexism":

> *Researchers ran a simulation of what happens to promotions over the course of several years when bias impacts [employee] ratings just a little bit. When gender bias accounts for just 5% of the difference in performance ratings, an organization that starts out with 58% of the entry level positions filled by women winds up with only 29% of the leadership positions filled by women.*

To many women, the existence of Maternal Wall bias is not news. Yet in 2003, there was a popular movement to recast the fact that women with children were leaving the workforce as being simply biological. "The Opt-Out Revolution," it was called in a *New York Times Magazine* piece and subsequent books and articles.

A revolution!

The idea was that previously ambitious, driven women were the ones who had decided on their own to end successful careers, pulled by the strong "biological imperatives" to raise their kids full time.

Of course, the more the women's stories are examined, one thing becomes clear: The "choice" these women faced was between being home with their kids or being in an incredibly unsupportive work environment where advancement and projects were being denied, their face time was constantly scrutinized, and they were constantly having to re-prove their commitment to their jobs. Because the lie is so pervasive, these women were made to feel as though they were the ones with the problem, the ones who didn't fit. And so they quit.

The "opt-out revolution" was so dangerous because it offered a defense—seemingly in mothers' own words—to all the biases mothers faced at work. It was their fault they couldn't balance home and work, not the company's fault for holding them to a different standard. This is a common tool of the patriarchy: *You* are the problem, not the culture. I hear this all the time when Silicon Valley companies are accused of having cultures toxic for women: "Look, this culture isn't for everyone. . . . She just wasn't a good cultural fit . . ."

The original *New York Times Magazine* article quotes one woman who says, "I wish it had been possible to be the kind of parent I want to be and continue with my legal career, but I wore myself out trying to do both jobs well."

Williams and Dempsey quote another woman who "opted out" to take care of her kids: "This was a really, really big deal because I never envisioned myself not working. I just felt like I would become a nobody if I quit. Well, I was sort of a nobody working, too. So it was sort of, 'Which nobody do I want to be?'"

Neither sounds like a woman who lost interest in work because she felt a "biological imperative" to be home with her children, as the "opt-out revolution" suggested. Instead it sounds like the familiar lie of the patriarchy—a good mother has to be fully available to her children; a good employee has to be fully available to her boss. It also sounds like another wording of that same thing I heard from my mom—"I couldn't be perfect at both."

The clever rebranding of Maternal Wall bias as women "opting out" was popular in culture when I was in my twenties. It terrified me. I was convinced that somehow I would just change once I had kids; this "biological imperative" would take over. It seemed to be happening to all these other highly professional, ambitious women. Why would I be any different?

Funny thing about that "biological imperative," it seems to only kick in when mothers work for assholes.

In a 2006 study of Wall Street MBAs, 32 percent of women said they chose to quit because of "family responsibilities." But even more of them—36 percent—also said they'd experienced some form of "pregnancy discrimination" or saw it used against someone else.

Further, consider a study of female Harvard MBA graduates who went on to work in family-friendly and non-family-friendly jobs. Guess what? The ones working in non-family-friendly jobs were more likely to feel this irresistible "biological pull" than the ones working at companies that didn't stigmatize working moms.

And if that's not enough, Williams and Dempsey also point out that only 40 percent of women dropped out after having their first child. The majority—some 60 percent of women—who dropped out of work did it after having their second child. Obviously, they weren't changed immediately once "they held that baby in their arms." They just ran out of patience once they had to prove themselves again with baby number two.

And yet, this myth of the all-consuming biological pull persists today, presented unchallenged and stated as fact. I was shocked reading a *Time* magazine piece about the controversy around Netflix offering unlimited parental leave.

Writer Suzanne Venker actually argued that the policy was *bad* for families because of this "biological imperative." Venker is the niece of the famous conservative antifeminist Phyllis Schlafly. Venker has a whole canon of work about how women can only be happy if they depend on men, why men won't marry you, and the dangers of feminism. Both are basically a walking infomercial for the patriarchy.

Her argument that more generous parental leave was bad for families was outrageous even for Venker. Babies and mothers, she argued, would bond too much as a result of Netflix's "cruel" unlimited leave policy.

By encouraging mothers, who are still the primary parent at home, to bond with their baby for a long period of time with the expectation they'll return to work at the end of the year means the baby will become even more attached to his mother, and separation may become intolerable.

She added that women simply change as a result of having kids, and society would do better to acknowledge that. This is basically every bias Williams and Dempsey explore in their entire book, all in one horrific quote.

If you believe this as fact—as many people do—why would you hire a young engaged woman who could suddenly have a child and stop caring about work at any minute? It helps rationalize an incredibly cruel bias against women, pregnant or not, mothers or not, married or not. It embeds that "bad mother" guilt in the psyche of every mother who *has* to work. She isn't doing something good by providing for her family. She is doing something *bad*. It's a particular "fuck you" to single mothers, lesbian mothers, or any family that doesn't include a man who can keep his head focused on work for the good of all those women and children.

"Working mothers do not change in ambition," says Katia Beauchamp, who hired plenty of pregnant women at her company, Birchbox, before she became a mother herself. "If who you are is somebody who thinks you can change the world, that doesn't change because you had a human. It might be challenging at first when you're negotiating sleep, feeding, and all that, but in a few months, when the fog lifts, you're the same person."

But that's hard to believe if you haven't lived it. And a lot of the men who are responsible for denying women advancement will never live it.

Instead, they offer this: "I just don't know how you do it." It's frequently meant as admiration, but it also normalizes the idea that you probably won't be able to do it. That there's something delusional about you trying. That even attempting to work and have a child is somehow an unnatural act.

And that is where guilt comes in. You feel guilt that you aren't more available to your employer, guilt that you aren't more available to your children, because the patriarchy has set you up to fail.

This guilt, this doubt is effective in silencing and controlling women, even pitting women against one another.

The guilt isn't about getting everything done; it's about a working mother needing to do it all *herself*. The shame of hiring childcare is so great that many professional women feel they can't mention the word "nanny," fearing a backlash for being bad mothers. And when more women don't talk about it, it enforces the unrealistic expectation.

Superstar TV producer Shonda Rhimes owns up to this in her book *Year of Yes*. She talks about how she—and so many others—skirt questions about work-life balance in interviews. No one ever wants to admit they just have a nanny. "I just didn't want to say it," she writes. "Because no one else ever said it."*

She continues:

> *Powerful famous women don't say out loud that they have help at home, that they have nannies, housekeepers, chefs, assistants, stylists—whatever it is they have to keep their worlds spinning—they don't say out loud that they have these people at home doing these jobs because they are ashamed. Or maybe a more precise way to say it is that these women have been shamed.*

This is called concern trolling in the social media vernacular—a way of expressing concern while you put someone down. And sometimes it is well meaning. In 2016 the *New York Times* published a story about a woman named Nathalie Miller

---

* I never felt any guilt about hiring a nanny and was happy I had the luxury to have an amazing one for the first three years I was building Pando. Once Evie started school, our nanny quit, and I haven't had any regular childcare since. It's a major pet peeve of mine when women write books about work-life balance and don't acknowledge the help they had at home. For one thing, that disrespects an entire category of badass working women who help raise our kids. It treats their contributions as invisible, taking credit even for their work, which is what we accuse men of doing in the workplace. I couldn't have survived the early years of work and motherhood without our nanny, Megan McQuaid. She's still a close friend of our family and will be forever. In this book, I've tried to emphasize the times Megan was shoulder to shoulder there for me and my kids, and the times I truly was on my own.

who was fundraising for a new company and discovered she was pregnant. Her mentor—a woman who also told her she had to dress in long skirts, cardigans, and low heels to be taken seriously—gave her this well-meaning but incredibly demeaning advice:

> *Having your first child is just physically hard, emotionally hard . . . I would never discourage you or say you can't do it, because you absolutely can. Just be very clear why you're doing it and what price you're willing to pay, because the price is time with your baby.*

"The price is time with your baby." She would never discourage her, except when she did *right there*. Once again, the message is: You can be a good worker or a good mother, but not both. Miller's trusted mentor—a woman who *had* done both—was telling her that by going forward with the fundraising, she'd be a worse mother. How different is that from a male boss who denies a working mother a promotion as a "favor"? ("You can spend more time with your kids!")

The implication is that sure, moms can work, but they can only do certain kinds of jobs. Definitely not start companies. Even supposedly empowering publications fall into this trap. In 2016 a Hearst-owned working mom blogger wrote about new services to "empower" working moms. One service offered to retrain moms as "social media managers" so they could have more flexible schedules. It's not too different from Jessica Jackley's mother telling her that her only career option was to be a teacher if she wanted to spend summers with her kids.

It may be well meaning, but the assumption that you have to be retrained in a new career simply because you became a mother is more offensive than the idea that you'll lose all interest in work once "you hold that baby in your arms." At least if I lost all sense of self and only wanted to be around my baby, I'd get to be around my baby. The idea that I should retrain for a profession I wasn't passionate about just because I had a child is even worse. A mother's right to work isn't just about earning money; it's about her choice to live the life she wants.

It's not a coincidence that 40 percent of Americans don't think women should work, 60 percent of mothers face blatant Maternal Wall bias, and America also has among the worst parental leave policies in the world.

Only three countries are as bad as the US when it comes to parental leave: Liberia, Swaziland, and Papua New Guinea. And when private companies like Netflix, Facebook, or Google have sought to compensate by offering incredibly generous packages for their employees, they've been criticized. It's almost as if there's a driving force in American culture that just doesn't want women to have this time.

If you don't want women to have economic independence, thwarting their ability to recover and bond with their babies just after childbirth is a great way to make work-life balance seem untenable at a mother's most vulnerable moment. To force her to "opt out."

It's a particular breed of fucked-up bias to both

- assume mothers are so inherently disabled they won't be able to perform as they could before having kids,
- and yet, not allow them to recuperate during their weakest physical moment in what's otherwise an almost superhuman feat of strength.

The Birchbox CEO Beauchamp talks about how overwhelmed she felt returning to running her company after having twins but how quickly that feeling faded once she gave herself time to recover, bond, and acclimate. "When I got back to work, my brain was ready to think differently," she says. "At some point, your feet get under you, and you're doing it and you're like, 'What was I so worried about?' I felt guilty, frankly, that all women don't get to have the time to figure it out, because at first, it's really scary."

Susan Wojcicki—CEO of YouTube and one of the most powerful women in American business—has had five children and taken a long maternity leave each time. "Each of those leaves enriched my career and more importantly, enriched my life," she said in a keynote at the Grace Hopper Celebration of Women in Computing conference in 2015. "They left me with the peace of mind, knowing that I could return after spending time I truly wanted and needed at home with my new baby. . . . I also found that each break gave me a chance to reflect on my career."

She helped craft Google's parental leave policy, one of the most generous in America. As a direct result of that policy, Google has seen the rate at which new mothers quit fall by 50 percent. That has a huge financial impact on any company, particularly one in tech where the labor market is incredibly tight. Companies spend on average six to nine months' salary replacing employees, and executive-level hires can cost several times an annual salary to replace. That says nothing of the loss in productivity as a new employee gets up to speed, according to Deloitte. Offering a generous maternity leave instead is financially a no-brainer.

A small percentage of mothers get to experience what Beauchamp and Wojcicki experienced. That's because in American culture maternity leave is a privilege—like taking a vacation or getting stock options—not an entitlement like Medicare, Social Security, unemployment, or some other policy that we agree makes society stronger. This is to say nothing about the benefit to the child. The same children the patriarchy claims to care about so much they can't allow us to make our own reproductive decisions.

Because of the view that maternity leave is a privilege, even the women who get maternity leave sometimes feel selfish or greedy taking it. In Silicon Valley, more than 50 percent of women surveyed had shortened their maternity leave because they felt taking the full amount they were *allowed* would hurt their career. This guilt over something the rest of the industrialized world considers a basic human right drives women back to work at their most physically and emotionally vulnerable point. And at that point, they are subjected to higher scrutiny than their peers and forced to prove themselves again.

It's no wonder motherhood has been painted as a career killer. In reality, it's the patriarchy killing your career, not your kids.

2

Benevolent Sexism and You

IN MY TWENTIES, I DID not get the whole "sexism" thing. I believed Silicon Valley was a meritocracy that simply didn't have enough women trained in the appropriate jobs, careers, and college majors. I boldly called bullshit on women saying they couldn't succeed simply because they were women, because it didn't match my experience. Sure, I'd experienced sexism. I just wasn't convinced it had held me back. I'd also been supported by many male mentors.

I have tried to excuse this, put it in context, and argue that what I *really* meant was [fill in the blank bullshit justification]. But here's the truth: Although many men have supported me in my career, I was wrong, blind to the depths of unconscious bias in our ecosystem, and in doing so, turned on other women instead of helping lift them up no matter how our experiences or points of view diverged.

One thing helps me forgive myself: I was not alone. This has come up again and again in my reporting.

"Until I hit my thirties, I just didn't see it," says venture capitalist Aileen Lee. "I think there are lots of little microaggressions you just brush off. You are focused on doing a good job. You may be having a very different career experience than a male, because you are not grabbing drinks with your boss after work, and this other guy who is senior doesn't invite you over for a BBQ at his house on the weekends. There is all this stuff and information trading happening that I did not realize was happening for many years, because I was not there."

"It's only since I've been in my thirties that I've had these 'ahas,'" says Michelle Zatlyn, cofounder of tech company Cloudflare.

Marie Claire editor Anne Fulenwider was told by her college professors she could accomplish anything, and she entered the work world convinced that older generations had dealt with sexism. "It's not until the world smacks you in the face with one thing or another, whether it's your maternity leave or when you don't get that promotion at work," she says. "I just remember my first maternity leave, just the reality of it, I literally said, 'I understand why feminism happened.'"

This is so universal that Gloria Steinem said repeatedly that women get more "radical" as they age, while men get more "conservative."

But my denial of sexism wasn't just because of my age. I was also taking cues from the older female role models, at least in the tech and startup industry. It was the norm in Silicon Valley back then for senior women to insist they had not been held back by their gender in any way, to refuse media coverage that featured them among the "top women in tech," or to decline to speak in any way about being a woman versus achieving what they had because of who they were intrinsically. Top women in the Valley back then had mannish haircuts and wore boxy pantsuits. They did not talk about their children in the press or in meetings. They did not talk about work-life balance.

They were aware they'd benefited from the sacrifices and efforts of the previous generation of women, but having benefited, many wanted to avoid reminding the world they were women after all.

The template was clear: You succeed in this industry by being "a man."

In interview after interview with successful women, I've heard the same explanation for why they succeeded: they were more like men than women. It is remarkable in how unremarkable this explanation has become.

Entrepreneur and adviser Julie Hanna is just one example. "I socialize very much like a boy," she says. "[I fit in because] in my twenties and thirties the way I worked was very hard-charging and male."

And at *Fortune*'s Most Powerful Women conference in 2016, senior Intel executive Diane Bryant talked about breaking into the industry in 1985 in much the same way. "The first thing I did was I started swearing a lot—a lot. This one guy throws out the F-word, and then stops and turns to me—all eyes on me, twenty-three years old—and says, 'Oh, I'm sorry.' And I said, 'No effing problem.'"

She continued: "I would literally throw the F-word out every now and then just randomly." She also bought a stick shift BMW and drank scotch in her efforts to "fit in," she said. "It doesn't help to be on the outside of the circle. . . . Somehow you have to get to the inside."

Either I unconsciously parroted this pattern of behavior, or I also excelled because it was simply the mold that I naturally fit. After all, I grew up with three brothers and had a lot of male friends as a kid, even though I went to an all-girls school for thirteen years. I drank like a man. I swore like a man. I could get ready in about fifteen minutes. I could look attractive . . . but in that way where I hadn't worked too hard on it. Whimsical T-shirts and jeans attractive. I followed sports and could rattle off the ERAs of the top American League pitchers in any given year. I prided myself on how rarely I cried. I derived a lot of confidence and self-assurance from these things.

There's one problem with this: I am curvy. I don't really like to talk about my body because I don't think it should be relevant to my career. But many a critic has disagreed. Negative articles almost always include a description of my body type. It's an easy and effective way to discredit a woman's work: sexualize and shame her. And, yes, other women do it, too.

While I've always tried to carry my curves proudly, a lifetime of catcalling and people simply refusing to make eye contact with me, or making even crasser statements, has taken its toll. When you are one of the only female attendees at an event and everyone is hanging out in bathing suits at a pool, it's hard to convince everyone you are "one of the guys."

Julie Hanna acknowledged the same but only later in her career. "I remember I had a boss and a mentor in my twenties, and he was an older gentleman," she says. "And he said to me, 'You have to understand when you walk into a room the first thing guys will see is "babe." And then you start talking and eventually they see beyond that, but that's the natural reflex.'

And I would argue and fight with him. I would say, 'No, no, no, the world has changed.' I had a strong belief he was wrong. Now, I think it was more true than not, and I just wasn't aware of it."

Then there are all the microaggressions. The assumption that you are stupid. The sources who say they'll need to read the article before it goes to press because you couldn't have possibly gotten it right. The questions about how a girl like you could have possibly gotten interested in tech. "Is your husband a VC? Was your dad a CEO?" And on and on.

For all my public bluster that I never cried, that nothing offended me, that I was so masculine and tough, so many nights I came home after industry events, dinners, or meetings and just sobbed. I was angry about the things I had to deal with that men in my position didn't. But more than that, on some level I was angry that I was a woman. As near as I could tell, there was little upside and plenty of downsides.

Whoa. Now that I've admitted it, let's all let it sink in how deeply fucked up that is.

⌘

The thing is I'm not alone. Frequently women are turned against one another and themselves by the pressures of trying to assimilate into a male world. Being a mouthy feminist is a buzzkill if you've gotten ahead by acting like a man. What I didn't realize in my twenties and thirties is that when men uphold and support the "right kind" of woman, she's experiencing sexism, too. It's just called benevolent sexism. And it's one of the patriarchy's most devious tools.

Benevolent sexism lurks behind justifying Maternal Wall

bias as a "biological imperative." Benevolent sexism is woven into why a lot of women vote for politicians who don't respect their rights. Benevolent sexism explains why women came forward to defend Stanford rapist Brock Turner and the overly sexist culture at Silicon Valley companies like Uber. When you hear someone say, "It can't be sexist if a woman is saying it," there's usually some benevolent sexism going on somewhere.

If guilt is the patriarchy's little self-enforcing voice in our heads, benevolent sexism is the tool that causes women to punish one another. I only started to understand it one Friday night in 2016 when I drove down from San Francisco to Kim Scott's Los Altos mansion for an evening of misogyny and the patriarchy. *Cheers!*

The speaker was Kate Manne, an assistant professor of philosophy at Cornell and the author of the forthcoming book *Down Girl: The Logic of Misogyny*. She had just published an article for the *Boston Review* using the crude and obvious example of the 2016 election to explore what's typically more subtle in our culture: what exactly misogyny is, how it differs from sexism, and the universal playbook by which women who threaten a patriarchy are taken down.

This is something "cool dude" Sarah Lacy never would have done with her Friday night. She'd be too busy watching a baseball game at a dive bar in San Francisco's Mission District. But feminist warrior Sarah Lacy was elated.

A lot of people think about misogyny as being a more violent version of sexism, but Manne drew a different distinction. Misogyny is the action that upholds the patriarchy, while *sexism* is the belief system that justifies it.

Misogyny is not imposed against all women equally. It is only used against those who are in some way *a threat* to the patriarchy.

"Benevolent" sexism/misogyny rewards women who hold up the patriarchy's view of women. "Hostile" sexism/misogyny punishes those who do not. It's the carrot-and-stick interplay between the two that pits women against one another without men having to lift a finger.

Think of benevolent sexism as a sort of mafia-like protection racket. You uphold the patriarchy? You get rewarded! The more the "wrong kind" of women are punished, the more effective the benevolent sexism is used on the "right kind" of women.

Having a system for rewarding only certain women at the expense of others is crucial for a patriarchy that also wants human beings to continue as a species. It allows misogyny to be *selective*. It allows men to justify control over women with their seemingly contradictory desire to be in loving relationships with them. To be supportive dads who want their daughters to excel and achieve, while refusing to let their wives work. At the extreme, benevolent sexism allows men to scream disgusting things about women at a Trump rally but genuinely love their wives and daughters and not want them to be "grabbed by the pussy."

It's also why Donald Trump may *believe* he is "sooooo good for women." It's why his daughter Ivanka may even believe that. Trump's comments on women are so unsubtle and shameless that they're almost a handy "My First Misogynist!" primer.

Trump tends to praise women's talents only when they are being used to make him more money or elect him president, Manne pointed out. Trump says things like "I have many executives that are women. They are doing a phenomenal job. I pay them a tremendous amount of money. They make money for me."

Consider Ivanka's defenses of her father in this light. "[She] defended him against charges of misogyny in a way few people found convincing. By saying that her father supported *her* career ambitions, as well as those of his women executives, Ivanka missed the point that she and they represent no threat to her father and are thus unlikely to come under fire," Manne writes. "Misogyny can afford to be selective. . . . Women who know their place do not need to be put in it."

It's also why I was supported and championed by many men when I was in the "cool dude" Sarah Lacy mode of my twenties and early thirties. I wasn't threatening to upend anything. I was defending the existing system. I was contorting myself to fit into it. And if I denied the claims of other women experiencing sexism? Well, then I had even more value. *Good girl!*

Regardless of any of her political positions, what device she may have sent emails from, whether she smiled enough or too much, Hillary Clinton was the wrong kind of woman for many simply because she was the first major female candidate for president. As such, she was the largest threat to the American patriarchy the country has ever seen. Remember: 40 percent of this country believes it is "bad for society" if women work *at all*, according to the Pew Research Center. These Americans are gonna be cool with the entire country and free world reporting to one?

Still, plenty of people argue sexism wasn't a factor in the election, and their argument hinges on the fact that women helped elect Trump.

It can't be sexist if women are saying it!

Let's ignore for a moment the thirty years or so of the press repeating GOP claims that Clinton was corrupt before she ever set up a private email server. Let's ignore that she was hounded in ways that men are not in public life, with conservative leaders even using disturbing sexual language to talk about her.

And let's ignore how the forces that naturally made her mistrust the press—and become more insular, privacy obsessed, and scripted—only reinforced the image painted of her.

Benevolent sexism played a huge role in women not wanting a woman to be president, because while women may not be considered equal in a patriarchy, some—particularly white women—have a valued role. A protected role. They feel the patriarchy is *better* for them than other potential options.

Especially when security threats are played up, as they were in this election. Whether it was tactically brilliant or accidental, by constantly stoking fear of global insecurity and "inner city" (read: African American) unrest, coupled with an "only I can save you" mentality, Trump tapped into one of the main levers for juicing benevolent sexism and turning the female vote. "Voter data going back 50 years suggests that women, more than men, are moved by the anxiety of changing circumstances and external threats," wrote Washington insider Heather Hurlburt, in *Project Syndicate* just after the election.

Peter Glick, a professor of psychology and social sciences at Lawrence University, believes this strategy played into how benevolent sexism works and handed Trump female votes in the election. Glick has conducted more than six studies to assess the interplay between hostile and benevolent sexism, surveying more than two thousand individuals. This election bore out much of his results on a national stage. "Trump's strategy was to ramp up anxiety about a dark, dangerous world," he said in an interview. "When women are under threat, their benevolent sexism scores go up."

This isn't unique to women. It's like a kind of cultural Stockholm syndrome. There have been several historical examples of the oppressed appeasing, going along with, or even supporting their oppressors. There's the so-called Uncle Tom syndrome, where African Americans played into racial stereotypes in order to ease their oppression; the so-called useful Jew syndrome, where Jews in eastern Europe helped implement anti-Jewish rules and regimes; and the so-called colonial syndrome, where colonized people believe they are inferior because of the simple fact that they've been colonized.

It's the psychological impact that comes with the games women have to play to survive and succeed in a patriarchal world. And it's particularly effective if women have limited economic options. As Glick explained to Vox.com in the aftermath of the election, "As long as women cater to men's needs, men will protect and cherish women in return. If women have few good options for independent success, this is a pretty good deal."

Kristen Koh Goldstein runs HireAthena, a company that seeks to employ working mother accountants in red states on behalf of tech companies. She's been a lightning rod for love and hate among them: love because she frequently gives them a way to get out from under financial insolvency, but hate because when she has to fire any of her employees, they lash out at her for taking away their last hope.

She wasn't surprised that women voted for Trump, despite the allegations of sexual abuse and his disgusting defense that some of the women were too ugly for him to have abused. "If you are afraid of financial devastation this year, do you care?" she says. "If it means better employment chances for your family, you will vote for the guy who [says he] is going to get your husband a job. If he allows you to have a better year, this coming year, so that maybe your son can actually go to college, why do you care?"

A lot of women living in a patriarchy are scared of what lies outside of that "protection." For them, going along with a bad situation is preferable to advancing the women's movement or putting their own security, safety, or even dignity and rights first.

Extreme financial instability makes this more pronounced. At one point, Goldstein noticed that a large number of women who worked for her started getting divorces. She got worried that maybe they were working too many hours and it was causing problems in their marriages. She dug into it and found out that finally having financial stability had given several women the courage to leave abusive husbands. "Think about that," she says, trying to explain the extreme financial devastation these women were feeling. "It's like, 'Woo-hoo! He won't hit the kids anymore.'"

The more overtly hostile sexism is on display, the more likely women comply with benevolent sexism out of "psychological self-defense," says Glick. It's an effect just like the mafia torching the business that didn't pay protection down the block.

In fact, Glick says the higher someone scores on benevolent sexism, the more likely they are to *blame the women* when they accuse men of sexual assault. "The protection racket of benevolent sexism gives women a lot of incentive to either forgive men for it, or blame women. The alternative—acknowledging that the system is broken, and that virtue can't protect you from violence—can be too terrible to contemplate."

This was one of many disturbing manifestations of the patriarchy we saw in the defense of Brock Turner, who sexually assaulted Emily Doe while she was lying unconscious behind a Dumpster at Stanford University.

Doe was a rare case of a "perfect victim." She was unconscious. There were witnesses. There was forensic evidence. She did a rape kit that was preserved immediately. His DNA was under her fingernails, his DNA was inside of her along with sharp pine needles. He still had an erection when he was arrested at the scene.

Doe cooperated fully with authorities. She went through the humiliating and brutal experience of listening to Turner's teammates and family defend him and to a well-paid team of experts go after her. She even had to listen to Turner insist she "liked it."

And at the end of it all, the jury believed her. Turner got three unanimous verdicts of guilt on three felony sex crimes.

And then Judge Aaron Persky sentenced him to just six months in jail, less than the two-year minimum for assault with intention to commit rape. Persky's concern was that anything more would have a "severe impact on him." This was a pattern for Persky—giving light sentences for young men convicted of violence and assault.

"This was supposed to be the case where we finally win one," says Michele Dauber, a Stanford Law professor who has spent much of her career working on issues of domestic abuse and campus rape. Dauber actually knew the victim; she was a childhood friend of her daughter's. She was in the room when the verdict was read. "There was no doubt she did everything right as a victim and still at the end of the day, it didn't matter because the judge was biased."

Doe's beautifully written, heartbreaking statement went viral. It was read by some eleven million people, including Ashleigh Banfield, who read it aloud in its entirety on CNN. It's been the rallying cry behind an effort to recall Persky, begun by Dauber.

"The reason the recall campaign is so important is we need

to refute the message sent by that sentence," Dauber says. "The message sent was 'This is not a serious crime.' It tells people, 'Don't bother reporting,' and that's the opposite of what we need. That's the opposite of what I've spent ten years working on."

Doe's experience was hardly a one-off: 43 percent of female undergrad students at Stanford experience sexual assault or sexual misconduct. And Stanford's numbers are in line with Harvard, Yale, Dartmouth, Brown, and other Ivy League schools. "If I told you your child has a 43 percent chance of experiencing a gunshot wound at Stanford, you wouldn't send them there. But for some reason, with sexual assault, it's just seen as the cost of doing business," Dauber says. "If a woman has a few drinks, [she's] fair game."

Here's a shocking stat shared by Dauber: Just by attending one fraternity party a month, a woman's odds of experiencing sexual assault go up by more than 30 percent. And at Stanford, sororities aren't allowed to have parties with alcohol. So if they want to have a party that serves alcohol, they have to throw it at a fraternity house. "They have to go to the location of greatest danger," Dauber says. "I'm sure the intent is not that women experience sexual assault, but that's the effect."

And yet, Stanford doesn't seem unduly concerned, according to Dauber. Those shockingly high numbers aside, Stanford has refused to implement any of the commonsense suggestions Dauber has made to make fraternity parties safer for women: requiring licensed bartenders who can make sure kids don't get overserved, requiring that fraternities hire private security trained in bystander prevention, and having security cameras on the periphery of fraternity houses. Stanford agreed at least to improve the lighting in the area where Doe was assaulted. But after eighteen months, the university still hadn't done it.

This directly affects the culture of Silicon Valley because Stanford is the Valley's "feeder" school. Women arrive eager to get their start in the tech's supposed meritocracy. "The vast majority of sexual assault occurs in the first semester of freshman year," Dauber says. "These women are showing up and going, 'I want to be a founder, I want to be an engineer, I am at Stanford, and I can't wait!' And then they get assaulted and that changes everything. Instead of learning to code or instead of learning to start a company or instead of meeting with people in the Valley who could advance their careers, they are going to trauma counseling and taking incompletes and seeing their grades plummet. They are derailed almost immediately upon coming in the door.

"Then there are these spaces like sports, like fraternities, like STEM that are masculinized," she continues. "Is it any wonder a girl who has been assaulted does not want to enter this space? I have seen this happen personally, where they come in and want to do this and get assaulted and now they are an English major, because they want to do something that has more women and women faculty that will be supportive of them. We are never going to get to equality until we solve the problem of sexual assault."

The widespread scale of these assaults combined with the school's lack of meaningful changes to prevent them normalizes the idea that women are second-class citizens in Silicon Valley. We can—and should—be disgusted with Persky's pattern of letting men off the hook lest one conviction ruin their future. But by refusing to even do simple things that could prevent another assault just like this, Stanford sends the message that somehow this is just part of college life.

So it's not a surprise there were some women who did the

dirty work of enforcing that view. Most notable was a defense made in a letter to the court by a female friend of Turner's. She drew a distinction between Turner being a "rapist" as opposed to a man merely convicted of rape:

> *This is completely different from a woman getting kidnapped and raped as she is walking to her car in a parking lot. That is a rapist. These are not rapists. These are idiot boys and girls having too much to drink and not being aware of their surroundings and having clouded judgement.*

It's just something men do! Boys will be boys! It's locker-room talk! It can't be sexist if a girl says it!

The "wrong kind of women" typically attack these "right kind of women" defenders of the patriarchy even more viciously than they attack the men upholding it, because it feels like a betrayal. We should all be in this together. There is enough to fight without women fighting one another.

It is infuriating. But women like these who defend the worst violent behavior in men are, in part, the messenger. If you think about how these women are manipulated by a patriarchy, how their fears of security and stability are used against them, you can see they are also victims.

⌘

The "right kind of woman" differs according to the situation. But certainly the "right kind of woman" is almost always a "good" mother. There is after all only one reason the patriarchy *needs* women: children. Bearing children is the one thing that men cannot do.

What is the Maternal Wall if not the enforcement of a patriarchal idea that to be a good mother you must be 100 percent devoted to your kids and to be a good employee you must be 100 percent devoted to your job? If you are in a heterosexual marriage and have a male boss, two patriarchs are essentially coming into conflict when you try to have a career and a family. Which patriarch do you owe your allegiance to? The extreme case is the one where the boss asks in the job interview if you are planning on having children or the husband says he just doesn't want strangers raising his kids.

The "mommy wars"—the fight between women who stay home and women who work—is one of the biggest conflagrations lit by benevolent sexism.

But the bigger cultural battle around "right" and "wrong" women happens before children even draw their first breath: the battle over women's reproductive rights. If women are going to have any kind of economic self-sufficiency, they must be able to control whether or not they get pregnant. And if the patriarchy doesn't want women to have economic self-sufficiency, there's a great way to accomplish that: Control her uterus.

The battle for control over those uteruses is ground zero for whether we continue to live in a patriarchy or not. A woman's clearest role in a patriarchal society is reproductive. Her ability to control whether or not she gets (or stays) pregnant is a threat to that order.

It's all about the uterus.

Consider the history of how abortion became the Southern evangelical wedge issue. It wasn't a grassroots movement. Abortion was historically a Catholic issue, not an evangelical issue. Until President Richard Nixon. Nixon set out—consciously—to make it the issue to unify Southern evangelicals behind the

Republican Party, according to Manne. "It was deliberately lit by political leaders, who intended that it be fueled by anxieties concerning women's role within the family," she writes.

As women have steadily gained more rights to their own uteruses, the patriarchy has gone into panic mode. It's not so much women that need to be dominated as it's the uterus that has to be dominated.

Consider the bizarrely conflicting stated motivations behind the extreme antiabortion hard-liners who want to punish women who have abortions. What are they being punished for? It's not simply for having sex, otherwise they wouldn't also oppose abortions for women who are the victims of rape. One in five Americans don't favor abortion under any circumstance—even when the life of the mother is in danger.

It also doesn't seem to be about preventing abortions, because many of the same social conservatives are also hostile to cheap and readily available birth control, notes Manne. "What are women held to be guilty of doing or being?" she writes.

This is why liberals point out that only 3 percent of the services Planned Parenthood offers are abortions but that conservatives still want to defund the whole thing. Focusing on abortion is powerful because it's such an emotional issue. But implicit in defunding Planned Parenthood is taking away access to cheap birth control, which prevents the need for abortions in many cases. For many, defunding Planned Parenthood isn't limited to abortion; it's really about taking control of the uterus altogether and with that, robbing women of their economic advancement.

I don't want to imply that people on the right of American politics hate women. What's tricky about all this is how much we are all influenced by the fact that every breath we've ever drawn has been in a patriarchy. We can't begin to parse how that's affected our views of right and wrong, fair and not fair. Even the best-meaning men. Even the most fearless women. Even Gloria Steinem. Even you. Even me.

I know plenty of well-meaning liberal men who fall into traps of unconscious bias in the workplace or pressure their wives to stay home with the kids while they continue to work but would never support a defunding of Planned Parenthood. I know plenty of Christian conservatives who believe abortion is murder but don't believe women should earn less than men, or who support women's rights to birth control.

But giving the government rights to what happens in a woman's body reinforces the idea that women are only here to be mothers on demand (or "mothers as a service" if this were being pitched to a venture capitalist), and it punishes them if they want a life beyond that. We can never have equality in that world.

3

"Everyone Loves the Angry Bitch"

I WENT FROM SEXISM DENIER to full-throated fierce feminist in less than a decade's time. Getting pregnant was the beginning.

For all my seeming confidence and outspokenness, I'd denied my femininity so much that I was in awe that my body knew how to produce and feed a *human being*. I felt as if I were living in a superhero origin comic. As if I woke up one morning and suddenly I could shoot spiderwebs out of the palms of my hands. This amazing power was here all along just lying dormant?

I felt so strong when I was pregnant. I glowed. My teeth and hair and nails gleamed. Before getting pregnant, I occasionally suffered from panic attacks in certain high-pressure situations, but even those eased while I was pregnant. Eli seemed to somehow *chemically* make me a better me. For the first time in my teenaged or adult life, I didn't care about sucking in my stomach because I was so hugely and obviously pregnant. That was enormously freeing. Talk about embracing your curves. I only added to them those nine months, and yet I became *less* of a sexual object to the world.

I talked to Eli constantly and about everything, particularly on long flights. We went to five continents together. Before a keynote, I would promise him that if we nailed it, we'd share a cookie later. We had our first fight on a five-hour flight delay when that child would not get his feet out of my ribs. A few months later he actually broke that same rib. Even *that* amazed me. I was growing a force of life so powerful that he kicked my rib out of place!

I loved that I got to monopolize him. For those forty weeks, he was all mine. I was the only person who got to hug him, and I got to take him everywhere with me. And he was the first person to know me deeper than anyone else. From his vantage point in the womb, he literally saw a different side of me. A side of me I didn't even know.

When I gave birth, I spent nearly twenty hours in labor, pushing for five of those hours. They told me he had one of the biggest heads in California Pacific Medical Center history. For reference, they deliver some six thousand babies a year. My tiny ob-gyn attached a suction cup to Eli's head and actually put her foot up on the delivery table for leverage. I pushed, Eli wriggled, and she kicked against the table and pulled with all her might to get him into the world.

Eli and I were both exhausted. Every muscle in my body was so depleted that I couldn't open and close my hands afterwards. They laid him on my chest, and I looked down at the puffy face and wild head of curly black hair.

"So that's what you look like," I said and gave him a kiss on his horribly goopy head. People talk about the ecstatic moment of seeing their child for the first time, but I'd become a mother long before this moment. I was nine months beyond love at first sight. We were so deep in this thing together.

I realize not every woman has such a good pregnancy. But in a world where we only hear how horrible pregnancy is, it's important to know not everyone has an awful one either.

It's also worth noting that I didn't get to this supermom point on my own. By far the largest influence during my pregnancy was Jane Austin—not the novelist, but a prenatal yoga teacher with a local cultlike following in San Francisco. I also did prenatal Pilates for nine months, and my ob-gyn credited both Jane and my Pilates teacher, Stephanie, with the fact that I avoided a C-section, given Eli's massive head.

But I'd done Pilates for years. The "cool dude" in me liked the somewhat cold precision of it.

I was not a yoga practitioner before Jane. Cool dudes didn't do yoga. I wasn't into what I perceived as the phony spiritualism of it all. When I first heard that women went around the room and shared how they were feeling for the first twenty minutes or so of Jane's class, I was horrified.

Thank God I went anyway.

It's not an exaggeration to say she changed everything I thought about motherhood and womanhood, and started me on a lifelong yoga practice of full-on embracing the spirituality, the chanting, the everything.

Jane had an obsession with women's pelvic floors. She has dozens of models of pelvic floors and has even had sensors put all over her body so she could see what exercises engaged what pelvic floor muscles best.

She would rail against a culture of "tucking" among American women who feel ill at ease with their sexuality. "Tucking" refers to tilting your pelvis forward. It's a kind of rigid reaction to a woman's sexual appeal, similar to how women walk with hunched-over shoulders to cover up their chest or how they try not to take up too much space in their stance. Cranky women? Tucked pelvic floor. Jane was a firm believer in the emotional health of a woman who could shimmy. "Can't push a baby out through buns of steel!" she'd say.

Yogis associate the pelvic floor with the first or root chakra, which is responsible for your sense of safety and security. Without a strong root chakra, the theory goes, the other chakras cannot unlock—you cannot be creative, you cannot think, you cannot love, you cannot have a voice, you cannot connect to anything on a spiritual level. It's the chakra that helps you let go of fear.

And that was pretty essential given that my body was about to become more of everything I was trying to disassociate from: Rounder, for one thing, but also the very parts of my body that I had spent my adult life wanting to de-emphasize would take on all new life-sustaining importance. It's no small change to go from wanting to hide your chest to breastfeeding a child in a meeting.

Jane hated the fear-based culture around pregnancy and would give her students five dollars for their copies of *What to Expect When You're Expecting*. She has a huge pile of them in her garage and is delighted at each one she can take out of circulation.

Like many women, I bought it the second I found out I was pregnant. If you haven't yet, don't. It essentially describes your body as a death trap for a baby. I remember seeing one drawing of likely ways you could give birth that showed a baby's leg sticking out of a vagina, as if the baby had kicked his way out. "That can happen?" I thought.

Jane instead emphasized how many women have been having babies for centuries in far more challenging conditions than any woman in her class would ever encounter—how you already had everything you needed to be a mom. I stopped reading parenting books of all kinds after taking her class and just learned to trust myself. I still mother that way. As far as I'm concerned, I am the world's leading expert on my kids.

Jane also broke down the view of perfection as a woman and a mother. I remember one class towards the end of my first pregnancy, when I had in-laws in town, this conference in China coming up, a house that wasn't in any way ready, and probably even more stresses that I've forgotten about five years later.

I remember saying frantically to her, holding back the tears (because I was still a "cool dude" then), "I just keep trying to hold it all together, but if one more thing happens, I'm going to lose it!"

She squatted in *Malasana* pose in front of me and said something brilliant in response: "I'm going to invite you to stop holding it all together and instead to let it all go." No superwoman cape. No striving for perfection. No guilt. Just have a happy, healthy baby. If that's not enough for anyone else at this moment? Well, fuck 'em.

The perfection obsession is linked back to what my mom told me about motherhood, but it's also linked back to the tucking culture. It's a rigidity of femininity, of what you have to do to survive as a woman and have it all, how much better you have to be to get the job, how much stronger you have to be to prove you aren't weak, the "Prove-It-Again!" syndrome at work, the double bind of the Maternal Wall, the expectation that you smile or not smile too much, the pressure to be beautiful but not so beautiful that you threaten anyone, the pressure to negotiate but not so hard that you seem too ambitious. All of it. The sum total of what sucks about being a woman in the modern age. And Jane was telling me to *just let it all go.*

It was liberating. I cried. And cried. And I didn't care that people saw me cry. I didn't have to worry if anyone thought I was weak. I didn't have to be a man's version of strong. I was a woman's version of strong. That moment was the beginning of the death of "cool dude" Sarah Lacy and the awakening of badass female warrior Sarah Lacy.

It's not a coincidence that my doctor marveled at how "in touch" I was with the muscles of my pelvic floor by the time I had to give birth to Eli's gigantic head. I was, for the first time, in touch with what it means to be a woman. The power of being a woman. I was proud of being a woman.

I have very rarely wrestled with the guilt thing as a working mom, and in large part I credit Jane with changing my thinking on women's obsession with perfection before my children even arrived.

I mean, really, moms are worried about perfection? *You created life for God's sake.* You grew a human being. You are so beyond "perfection," you are playing with the house's money here. Don't let the patriarchy convince you otherwise.

⌘

All women have this power in them, not just moms. It doesn't matter if you chose to have children, can't have children, or have fifteen children. All women.

Pregnancy awakened me to the power of being a woman.

The unfair advantages that women have. Why I was so lucky to be born a woman. But I know women who have arrived there via different means.

One woman I met experienced it via an all-female pole-dancing class. In one routine, she lost control and kicked holes in the wall of the studio with her long, spiky stilettos. Afterwards she apologized to her teacher, who assured her it was already covered in her security deposit. The woman expressed shame with being a closet "angry bitch."

"No one likes the angry bitch," she said sadly.

Her teacher put her hand on her shoulder. "*Everyone* loves the angry bitch. You just have to learn how to channel her."

The "angry bitch" describes women in the class shedding all their shame and body issues and hang-ups from living in a patriarchal society, even experiencing a sisterhood they hadn't in their day-to-day lives.

Software entrepreneur and investor Julie Hanna had a comparatively boring story. She never had children, but she says she learned to embrace a more feminine way of management once her intense, hard-driving masculine style stopped working.

"I had driven [my team] in a way where we got to a great outcome, but I had this demoralized, burned-out team that was looking at me like they were secretly plotting a mutiny," she says. "It made me stop and I was like, 'Wow, what went wrong here?' We had these objective successes and, yet, we're not feeling it. It made me go inward."

She thought about the companies she had built, which all had this young, masculine culture, where you blew off your family and worked all night, and if you didn't fit into that, then you were dismissed as a bad cultural fit.

Hanna had always excelled in the Valley by being a "guy,"

but mid-career, she started to consider how she could run a company with more "feminine" qualities.

"If we are going to call it 'a family,' how can we do this in a way that's more inclusive?" she says. "We ask people to give 24/7 and they have this invisible leash called the phone but then we call into question their ability to perform when they have to take care of their kid? It's not a reciprocal relationship. If the person feels like they are being taken care of, they are that much more loyal."

She unlocked the power of her maternal, nurturing side without ever becoming a mother. And it made her even more successful.

This book is called "A *Uterus* Is a Feature, Not a Bug," not "A *Baby* Is a Feature, Not a Bug." Whether or not you're a mother or even want to be a mother, you're a sister as far as I'm concerned.

4

"I Just Don't Know How You Do It!"

"ARE YOU IN SIPPING-TEA-ON-THE-COUCH KIND of labor or blood-all-over-the-walls kind of labor?" TechCrunch's founder, Michael Arrington, asked me. Arrington was an abrasive ex-lawyer turned journalist who'd started TechCrunch in the early days of blogging and had come to be feared throughout the Valley. He didn't grow up with sisters, had never been married, and I was one of the rare "cool dude" women who could survive in his orbit. To say he didn't have a lot of experience with women in labor is an understatement.

I was in neither type of labor. I was in walking-around-the-Westfield-mall-in-San-Francisco-trying-to-force-my-half-assed-contractions-to-actually-yield-a-baby-coming-out-of-me kind of labor.

About midway through my pregnancy, I started to wonder if Arrington had ever encountered a pregnant woman before.

At one point our CEO, Heather Harde, noted we should get the glass walls and doors of my office frosted so that I could pump in my office when I came back.

"You are going to do that . . . *here*?" he shrieked.

"Unless you want me to work from home," I said. "I'll have to pump every four hours."

"I'm just not sure I'm comfortable with the idea of you getting naked in the office," he said.

"Getting naked? How do you think breastfeeding works?" I asked.

Conversations like these were par for the course at Tech-Crunch. In fact, it was progress.

When I joined the blog in 2008, there was an online poll placing bets on how long I'd last because the abuse hurled at any woman who dared to write for the site was so vile. I was the first woman who lasted long enough and had enough work-life balance to *actually get pregnant.*

Not only that, Arrington had asked me to take over as editor in chief, once I got back from maternity leave. He wanted to stay involved, but he was worn down by the day-to-day grind of journalism and wanted to become a VC. Because we both believed the lies that a baby would change me, we mutually decided to hold off on announcing it to make sure I had a healthy baby first. And that I was still me.

In the meantime, all hell had broken loose, and TechCrunch was in full-on meltdown. Arrington had foolishly decided to launch his new venture firm—the CrunchFund—while he was still editor in chief of the most influential site that wrote about startups. It was as if the editor of the *Washington Post* managed a presidential campaign. It was outrageous by any definition of journalistic ethics. Particularly because the rest of the world did not know that he was stepping down and I was planning on taking over.

Arrington had a total blind spot when it came to traditional journalistic ethics. That was one of the things that made him so successful as a blogging pioneer and was ultimately his undoing. He didn't think the CrunchFund was enough of an issue to even tell the bulk of the staff, but he told Paul and me.

Conscience nagging at me, I wrote a long email to him explaining why this was not going to go over the way he expected; how this was different from him doing his own angel investing on the side and still writing about startups; how he was throwing the staff's journalistic ethics under the bus without even discussing it with them; and in particular how our new boss since we got acquired, Arianna Huffington, was going to lose her mind over it. The Huffington Post was at that moment poised to win its first Pulitzer Prize after years of being considered volunteer written SEO link bait.

The Huffington Post had sold to AOL for some $350 million—the largest purchase of any digital publication. It had already proven a lot to the world as a company. But paramount to Huffington herself at this point was proving to the New York journalism elite that she was an equal.

That and, as the world knew, Huffington and Arrington under the same corporate roof was a powder keg. Any inevitable showdown would be less about Huffington's great sense of journalistic ethics being upset and more about a clear opportunity to oust her biggest, fiercest rival and critic within the company.

It was obvious who would win the battle, despite Arrington's chummy relationship with AOL's CEO, Tim Armstrong. He'd paid $350 million for the Huffington Post and less than $30 million for TechCrunch. While Arrington could write a sulky blog post and nerds would be furious, Huffington could go on *The Daily Show*, *Real Time*, or CNBC at any given moment, express her concern for AOL, and have real repercussions for its stock price.

Mike thanked me for the feedback, said he'd shared it with Tim, and went right ahead and ignored it.

Guess what? A total shit show ensued when the CrunchFund was announced in the *New York Times*. In an effort to contain it, Armstrong helpfully explained to the press that Tech-Crunch's kind of journalism was simply "different" from real journalism—a statement that threw the credibility of every TechCrunch reporter under the bus even though none of us was participating in this new venture fund.

It was so unpalatable that Huffington got what she wanted: an excuse to fire Arrington even though he represented a huge amount of the value of what AOL had purchased in Tech-Crunch. And while we were upset that AOL was breaking its promise not to interfere with TechCrunch's editorial, neither Paul nor I could really criticize her for the stance. Our loyalty to Mike notwithstanding, he'd been his own worst enemy.

This all went down as my contractions were beginning, about the time Jane Austin invited me to "let it all go." It started on Friday, September 2, which was also my due date. TechCrunch's biggest event of the year, San Francisco Disrupt, was September 12.

I didn't go into the hospital until September 6. That gave me four days to help Mike and Heather pull any sort of power play to take back control of the site. The two of them hatched a plan: What if we buy the publication back?

TechCrunch was such a plum asset, which AOL had picked up for such an astoundingly cheap price, that it seemed far-fetched that Huffington—or AOL's shareholders—would actually allow that to happen. But for some reason Armstrong was leading Arrington to believe it was a possibility. (Or so I was told.) The bromance was trumping a reality that Mike should have been smart enough to see.

Raising the money, on the other hand, wouldn't be an issue. I'd personally talked to several VCs who were happy to fund a buyback assuming Heather would stay on as CEO and I'd be editor in chief.

We had one shot to make this happen, one piece of leverage: What if none of the TechCrunch staff showed up to Disrupt on Monday? Just . . . didn't show up. Thousands of people had bought tickets, and there were millions of dollars committed in sponsorship. Almost all the speakers had been asked by Heather, Mike, or me. If we didn't show up, would they go onstage? There was so much loyalty to TechCrunch, I was sure most wouldn't if we asked them not to. What would AOL do?

This was the conversation Mike and I had as I walked the length of the Westfield mall, all the while having side conversations with a few VCs who'd heard the rumors and were calling me to say they were in should we need the capital.

Mike and Heather stopped talking to Huffington or anyone else at the company in the interim, as a negotiating stance. In retrospect, it was a lousy way to achieve the desired result. A New York–based senior editor named Erick Schonfeld took the opportunity to cut a side deal. I was told he met with Huffington and assured her that he would show up for Disrupt; he would lead the conference and pull the team together behind her in exchange for one simple thing: She had to make him the editor in chief right now. She did. About that time I was pushing for five hours with Eli.

I don't think Huffington was acting maliciously. But the truth is she just didn't understand the internal dynamics of TechCrunch well enough to know any better.

I came out of labor and called Paul for an update on the insanity. This was on Thursday, September 8. By the time I came home, all legitimate hope of buying the company back had been dashed. There was a last-ditch attempt during Disrupt, but even that was scuttled.

So much of what I heard during this time was hearsay that it's hard for me to know for sure what was fact and what was embellishment. But by the end of my first week home with Eli, my sister had come to town to help me out, and Arianna was calling me multiple times a day to do damage control and talk me into another job at the company, effectively offering me whatever title or salary I wanted. She sent me some price-upon-request Italian baby loafers for Eli. "You have a weird life," my sister said.

Indeed. Just nine months earlier, I'd decided to stay in this job because of the stability.

Paul finally quit in exasperation once Disrupt was done, publishing a tell-all article on the ins and outs, and going on TV to dish on the insanity of it and everyone who was complicit: Mike, Tim Armstrong, Arianna, and particularly Erick.

The ball was in my court.

I had the advantage of being on maternity leave. I didn't have to make an immediate statement or make a major decision. But it weighed heavily on me. I committed to Heather, the team, and myself that I was going to mentally table the issue until after Disrupt Beijing, which was a scant five weeks away. I'd worked too hard for too long to pull this conference off, and I wasn't going to let anything jeopardize it.

I faced extreme pressure to stay at TechCrunch. Many members of the staff unfairly put whether they'd stay or go on my shoulders, although I hadn't been the one to sell the company to AOL or decide to be a VC despite inevitable fallout. But I loved the blog, the staff, and the community around it.

It wasn't an easy call.

On one hand, I was sure as shit not going to go back to Tech-Crunch *not* as editor in chief. I felt that would be betraying the high-achieving me that still existed after giving birth, not to mention mothers and women everywhere. As far as I was concerned, the CEO and founder had offered me that job, and it had been unfairly taken during a particularly vulnerable moment. But weeks into my leave, I had discussions with executives about making me coeditor in chief, finding me a different position at Huffington Post that superseded TechCrunch, or eventually "the situation with Erick getting sorted out" and me getting my promised job back after all.

Meantime, Paul had decided to start his own company, an irreverent-political-satire-meets-investigative-journalism outfit called NSFWCORP, and was building it in Las Vegas. It was clear we wouldn't be doing something together. I got several offers to join media properties that just weren't right. I had opportunities to join venture firms in "supporting" roles that boiled down to marketing or being an "entrepreneur in residence." A fancy way of getting a paycheck and saying you are a VC until you decide what to do.

At a dinner with me, Eli, and Paul, Mike encouraged me to start something new. He offered to invest, write for it, and help in any way. It was a seductive idea, and one I had thought about many times before. I'd gotten close to starting my own site in

2008 or so, but had decided to join TechCrunch instead. I told myself I thought I could have more impact helping make the already dominant blog even bigger, but the truth is I also lacked the confidence.

Disgraced or not, Mike was the undisputed king of tech blogging. His endorsement in a period when TechCrunch was in upheaval was not trivial and could go a long way towards silencing those inner doubts I had, and the external doubts I feared others would have.

Around this time I had a call with Erick. I wish I'd been more direct. I wish I'd called him out for how he backstabbed Heather and Mike. I didn't. But I made it clear that I wasn't going to return to TechCrunch and work "for" him. He made it clear he wasn't even going to "share" the EIC title. OK, then.

That was probably the breaking point. This was a matter of pride. On one hand I had greater financial responsibilities now that I had a child, but I also had the responsibility of being Eli's female role model. Did I want to be the kind of woman who had her job stolen while she was giving birth and then went back because of money and job security?

More to the point, as my maternity leave stretched on and I thought about going back to work full time and being away from Eli for some sixty hours, seventy hours, or even eighty hours a week, was it worth doing that to rebuild a property that AOL had destroyed in the matter of a month?

In the wake of basically having nowhere to go and with a growing desire to be able to look at myself in the mirror and look my child in the face every day, I started to seriously consider starting my own company—the one thing that I believed pregnancy would absolutely disqualify me for.

I loved Eli and was enjoying the time at home bonding with him. But he was a pretty relaxed baby. I was still working several hours a day, without any help. I still flew to China to host Disrupt Beijing, leaving Eli with Geoff. I missed him, but it was hardly debilitating. It was early days, but I was still me. I was still ambitious. In fact, I wanted my work life to have even more meaning post-Eli.

The irony is if I'd known I was going to start a company, I would have never gotten pregnant. But without Eli, I may have never had the courage and the conviction that my working hours needed to matter so greatly. I wouldn't have known how strong I was. "I've given birth," I'd tell myself in scary moments. "None of these men have done that. I can do this."

One day, as Eli and I walked down the street to get a quesadilla, I texted Marc Andreessen. Andreessen is one of the most famous VCs in the Valley. I'd gotten to know him as a journalist, back when he was an entrepreneur. He'd long pushed me to start a company, offering to fund it if I did. "OK, I've decided. I'm not going back. What should I do?" He sent a long list of suggestions. By the time the quesadilla was procured, I was starting a new company. By the time Christmas neared, I had verbal commitments from a dozen or so investors—enough that I'd have plenty of capital without giving any single person a meaningful slice of the company, certainly not a board seat.

That was crucial since this new publication would cover the industry. My goal was to spread the investment pool so wide that any company we'd write about we'd likely share investors with, but we'd also share investors with all their competitors. It was a so-called party round. Party rounds were ill-advised for most startups for the same reason I raised one. It would mean no single investor had enough of a stake to truly care if we lived or died, to do the heavy lifting to help us raise more money, or to have the incentive or power to meddle in our business. The same apathy that could hurt us if we needed more capital or guidance would guarantee our credibility.

I was pretty far down this path when Arrington called me one day. He'd been talking to Heather—who'd worked hard to convince me to stay even though I knew she had no intention of staying either.

"Do you know how much they'd pay you if you stayed?" he said.

Huh? Arrington had spent weeks convincing me to leave. He'd committed to invest in and write for the site. By this time, I'd talked to investors. I had a name for the site. An industry veteran, Andrew Anker, had agreed to be chairman of the board. We were already working on a design for the site. A lot of this was due to Arrington pushing me to take this step, telling me he'd do anything to support it, convincing me I didn't need a cofounder. "You're Sarah-fucking-Lacy!" he'd said in one conversation where I was struggling with the confidence gap that holds so many women back.

And now—what?—he was trying to talk me . . . out of it? Was this some sort of test?

"Heather says they'd pay you three hundred and fifty thousand dollars a year to stay. That's their opening offer. You could probably push that even higher," he said. "That's way more than they ever paid me. You might want to think about this. I only want what's best for you and Eli."

What's best for me and Eli. Perhaps more than anyone I'd ever met, Arrington was skilled at fucking with my head. Emotional manipulation was his strong suit. During this period, he spent so much time vacillating between hating TechCrunch and day-dreaming of returning to TechCrunch that I don't know what his intention actually was that day.

But I got off the phone with him doubting myself. After all, I did have a new baby to think of. I knew from fifteen years of covering entrepreneurs just how hard starting a company was. Most founders say that if they'd known what they were getting into, they never would have started a company. I knew. Was this insane? I started to wonder if it was worth going back to Arianna and making a crazy last-ditch demand: *$500K and you fire Erick!* I could still be proud of that, right?

I called Paul. He was furious. He interrupted me, yelling, "You keep talking about TechCrunch and what's best for Tech-Crunch, and I don't give a shit about TechCrunch. What about PandoDaily? I want to read PandoDaily."

I'd love to think I had enough confidence to push ahead with my plans without that conversation. I don't think I did. It was one of many ways Paul was my cofounder from the earliest incarnations, without really being my cofounder. My "faux founder," as I came to call him.

For better or for worse, by the end of my maternity leave I was committed, funding was committed, Andrew was committed, and we were incorporated. I even had found a nanny, Megan, who would start in January. I was hiring people. One thing remained: Andreessen needed to actually return the funding documents so I could send them around to the rest of the investors and start the way-too-long process of actually getting *cash* in the bank.

And he wasn't getting back to me. This was very unlike him. Andreessen didn't sleep and was always online. It was almost impossible not to get some quippy response at any hour of the day or night. I kept asking for the docs, and he kept saying we needed to find a time to talk. I was at my parents' house in Memphis with Eli, and I was totally freaked out.

What the fuck was happening?

I suspected that the problem was the terms. Neither Arrington nor Andreessen wanted to set the terms, and there was an annoying back-and-forth. So Andrew suggested we take the opportunity to go for broke. We suggested something called an uncapped note, which is extraordinarily in favor of entrepreneurs. It's a way of raising money without having to set a valuation until later. Assuming you have any level of success, you'll be worth more money in a year or so when you decide to raise another round and have more to show for the company than just a sketch on a napkin. So notes allow you to get the cash now while essentially charging investors for the company you'll be in the near future.

It shouldn't come as a shock: Most investors hate these deals. While they were in vogue in the Valley at this point, one New York investor of ours said—with disdain—it was the first time they'd ever swallowed one. That's how hot being the Michael Arrington–endorsed, Marc Andreessen–funded successor to TechCrunch was in the winter of 2011.

I was not comfortable asking for something this aggressive, but that's why Andrew was such a great chairman. He was brimming with confident, entitled male ego and demanded I do the same. Like so many other times in my career when I'd asked for more than I probably had earned, I wondered what a man would do and just forced myself to do the same and pretend I wasn't massively uncomfortable. While *The Confidence Code* cautions women not to "fake it until they make it," much of my career has been faking it until I made it, in terms of confidence. If I didn't ask for what a man would, I'd still be working at small regional business journals.

But now I worried that Andreessen must have balked at the terms. *Fuck.* I knew it was too aggressive. Worse: I couldn't get him on the phone with the holidays. He and his wife were really into Christmas. Like, so into it the tree is still up in July.

I finally lost it and emailed him. I said that I needed an answer because I had already quit TechCrunch, and I needed an income in January or I was going to lose my house. That I'd already hired staff and hired a nanny. That he was the one—after all—who had spent years telling me I should start something; he was the one who asked me what I needed; he was the one who told me to set the terms. And now he was getting cold feet?

Amused, he called me saying, "I wanted to talk to you because I don't want to invest two hundred and fifty thousand dollars. I want to invest one million dollars. I think you are going to need it to build what you are building, and you'll never have an easier time raising the money."

Ohhhhhh.

This would represent the largest angel investment Marc—fucking king of Silicon Valley—Andreessen had ever made outside of one of his own companies. No pressure.

5

Not All Moms Have the Luxury to Build a Company, but All Moms Have the Skills

I WAS A WOMAN IN my late thirties with a newborn, no cofounder, and no technical knowledge, starting a company in Silicon Valley. I was also an extrovert. That pretty much went against every cliché, checklist, and ideal of the Silicon Valley founder.

I was the exact inverse of the twenty-something nerdy dropout/Stanford grad with no social life who could work twenty-four hours a day in a dungeon of an office, sacrificing his entire life (well, six years or so) to "make the world a better place." (Or at least make his investors wealthy.)

And yet, my differences from that ideal are what made me good at my job, particularly my age and the fact that I had a baby. Starting a company is the ultimate act of career creation, and pregnancy is the ultimate act of human creation.

But, somehow, doing them both at the same time is totally against traditional Silicon Valley groupthink wisdom. The patriarchy will tell you one of those acts of creation is the purview of men only, and the other is the purview of women. Never mind that the two draw on similar skill sets and pose similar emotional, physical, and psychological challenges, rewarding you with euphoric highs and crippling you with debilitating lows.

There is a reason founders always refer to their companies as their babies. It's ironic that the same tech world that views a pregnant woman as an undesirable hire constantly uses maternal metaphors to explain how devoted and awesome they are at their job.

I am not arguing that every mother—or every person—should be an entrepreneur. The rest of this book will disabuse you of any idea that my job has been fun, glamorous, or has made me rich.

Certainly the vast majority of women don't have the luxury of circumstances I did. Most women—even those lucky enough to be in major economic centers in the US like Silicon Valley—do not have ready access to investor cash. Women are more likely to suffer from a confidence gap that holds them back, even if they do have the opportunity. And many women are struggling so hard to put food on the table that they can't even think of a world where they could step back and take a greater risk on a new business.

Even more women may be in marriages where they aren't

supported in any career at all, much less an entrepreneurial venture. And support is essential because this is a hard, lonely job.

There are very real and serious reasons many mothers aren't able to take a risk as I was able to, especially on maternity leave. But I assure you: If circumstances and luck were different, *you could*. The skill set is the same. Mothering pushes women to become the strongest, most resilient, most creative problem solvers on the planet.

I wouldn't believe this if I hadn't lived it.

I've had so many male CEOs and entrepreneurs look at me with what I like to call "single-mom pity face," shake their heads, and say, "I don't know how you do it." First off, in the realm of single mothers, my life simply isn't that hard. I'm not working three jobs just to put food on the table. I own my own house, and my kids are in good schools.

But this concern also totally misses the point: I am only *able* to do all this because all of it is what has made me so strong, resilient, and resourceful. This may be one reason that VCs who have a single female investing partner are twice as likely to invest in female entrepreneurs. *They get it.*

The skill sets required by motherhood and entrepreneurship are astoundingly similar. I've produced a weekly podcast with female CEOs, investors, and entrepreneurs since early 2016, and the similarities come up in every single conversation.

Some of the biggest ones are as follows:

BOTH ARE THE TOUGHEST JOBS YOU'LL EVER LOVE. You will do things for your company and your children that you would never do for a boss or another human being, even for yourself. And you frequently do it gladly.

YOU ARE IN NO WAY QUALIFIED TO DO THIS. It's a weird feeling when the hospital allows you to take a tiny, fragile human home after just about a day of "training." Similarly, many founders have never managed people—or sometimes have never held a proper job before—much less run a company. Silicon Valley values "fresh eyes"; a CEO who hasn't learned how things have always been done can reinvent things more easily. Although I was in my midthirties when I launched Pando, I'd never directly managed more than a handful of people in my career. I knew as much about running a company as my husband did about changing a diaper. We both figured it out.

COFOUNDERS/CO-PARENTS ARE GREAT . . . IF THEY ARE *ACTUALLY* GREAT. Ideally, both building a company and raising a family should be things you do with another human being for all kinds of reasons, but only if the match is uncannily right. Otherwise, both lousy cofounders and co-parents can make the job far harder. If you don't have the right partner, it's easier to go it alone.

YOU BECOME A TIME TRAVELER. Parents and founders can wring maximum productivity out of every moment. But beyond that, time moves in surreal ways when building a company or raising kids. The cliché is "the days are long but the years are short." Once you get a few years and traumas under your belt, you develop an amazing ability to breathe through situations, knowing they will pass. It's all a phase. You learn how to create more time or simply grind it out until you hit a new phase.

EVERYTHING IS PERSONAL IN THE BEST AND WORST WAYS. You are the leading expert in your children and your company, if you trust yourself to be. You bring your own specific, weird, innate skills to each fight and solve problems like no one else would. Your job as a parent or a CEO is to be whatever your child/company needs most from you at that moment.

But everything is way more emotional than it would be if it

didn't involve *your* child or *your* company, because this is your heart and your legacy on the line. You will do things that don't make rational sense or financial sense at times because this isn't about head; it's about heart.

YOU WILL FAIL MOST OF THE TIME. One of the hardest things about entrepreneurship and parenthood is managing your psychology. Perfect is not possible. And that's the good and the bad news about both.

People who become entrepreneurs are used to achieving, but even the best entrepreneurs fail a good percentage of the time. You have to walk a fine line between taking these failures seriously but not getting so distraught about each one that you can't move on.

Knowing failure is expected and normal can be freeing, but it also takes a psychological toll. It's tempting to look back and say what you could have done better—a risk you shouldn't have taken, money you shouldn't have spent on something that didn't pan out—but each of those things helped make your company and your company's culture what it is. It's impossible to just pull out one thing and have the same company on the other end, as suggested by all those warnings about going back in time and stepping on a mosquito.

It's the same with parenthood. You will absolutely fail. You may lose your kids at the mall. You may forget to buckle a car seat in an exhausted haze. You may drop them. You may do a million things that make you feel like the worst parent in the world at that moment. Your kids will absolutely complain to someone in the future about something you did that totally fucked them up. You have to take these failures seriously but also shake them off and keep going.

Lynn Perkins, CEO of UrbanSitter, has noted that having

twins was great for a type A person like her. "You learn you can't control it all."

YOU GET USED TO BEING THE BAD COP. Part of parenthood is being told how much the thing you love more than anything else in the world hates you and not caving. I've hit a point with Eli where I say, "Your tears only make me stronger, because it tells me you are learning a lesson right now." You're the bad cop when you run a startup, too. You'd bleed for your employees, and they respect you enough to believe in your vision. But they also probably do impressions of you behind your back. Your job isn't to be their friend.

ENTREPRENEURSHIP AND PARENTHOOD ARE BOTH THE ULTIMATE HUMAN ENDURANCE TESTS. Because both are so personal, you will go without sleep, without vacations, without luxuries for your kids/companies. It's the life equivalent to running a marathon. The idea that motherhood makes you weaker is absurd when you step back and think about what motherhood actually demands.

NO MATTER HOW BADLY IT GOES, YOU WILL EMERGE A BETTER YOU. In Silicon Valley your résumé levels up a notch as soon as you convince someone—anyone—to give you money for your startup. It doesn't matter what happens to that startup, just having been a founder is seen as valuable.

And it should be. If Pando went under tomorrow, my investors would lose money, but I'd be immeasurably more resilient, experienced, empathetic, and valuable as an employee to someone else.

Parenting is much the same. You win simply by surviving. Even a half-assed parent grows as a person. Even the Grinchiest Grinch's heart grows a few sizes.

YOU WILL LOOK BACK ON BOTH EXPERIENCES AND GLORIFY ALL THE WORST PARTS OF IT AND IRRATIONALLY WANT TO DO IT AGAIN. I remember one of the first times Eli was sick. I was up all night with him for several days on end. He was crying, coughing, burning with fever, and hallucinating sharks swimming around his room. We slept together on a pallet on his floor because his Lightning McQueen bed only supports fifty pounds, and I have a hard-and-fast rule that I don't ever allow my kids to sleep in my bed. (They would never leave.)

It was a miserable few days. It's heart wrenching when you can't take your child's pain away. I didn't get much sleep. And I could feel his hot breath on my face when he would finally crash. I could almost visualize the germs entering my body. When Evie is sick, it's even worse. She cuddles as though it's something she's only read about in a book—arm slung across my neck pinning me down uncomfortably, elbows jabbing into my side, head-butting me when she rolls over.

Then, finally, the fever breaks, and I feel more bonded to them than ever before. Some of my best memories with my kids are helping them through horrible situations. This is where security and unconditional love are built. This is why they run to me when they are scared or hurt. This is why I still feel more at peace taking a nap on my parents' couch than anywhere in the world.

But that's also because these situations all worked out well in the end. It was just a cold, just pinkeye, just croup, just foot-and-mouth, just slapped-cheek. (Slapped-cheek! I had to Google it to believe that was a real thing! Preschool health alerts read like they were written in the 1920s.)

It's the same with startups. Everyone glamorizes those early years of struggle and fear mixed with limitless possibility. But the truth is those early years are horrible. They are only fun in hindsight once you've made it.

⌘

At this point, I've had five years of this conversation with other parents who are founders, investors, or work at startups. I'm always struck by how the anecdotes all feel personal, and yet they are also universal. That's what entrepreneurship and parenthood also share. Your own experiences and circumstances are absolutely unlike anyone else's. And yet, another founder or another parent can always relate in a way that someone who has never started a company or raised a child can't.

Notice I said "parents," not "moms," above. Research has shown that fathers, too, can benefit from some of the productivity and empathetic enhancements of parenting. The more they actively parent, the more they benefit. There's some of this that is intrinsic to motherhood, but only as much as the buck usually stops with moms in most homes.

Thrillist CEO Ben Lerer told me that when he was going through an extraordinarily stressful time splitting his company in two, spinning half of it off, and raising two venture capital rounds at once, he was playing with his toddler one day and it hit him: *You will never even know I did this.* All at once, he calmed down. "I'm doing my best, and this is stressful, but it will pass and it will be fine," he told himself.

Carl Bass, the CEO of the $18 billion software company Autodesk, says he can tell immediately if someone working for him is a parent or not. The nonparent is the one losing their mind because they've encountered a situation they can't exert control over, he says. "Parents get so used to that."

A single dad would have the same benefits as a single mother, just as an adoptive mother, father, or same-sex couple would. It's not about biology. It's not about growing the baby in your womb or nursing it—as amazing as I found those experiences. It's about putting in the hours, loving the child through the worst, and never giving up.

One of my favorite quotes about entrepreneurship came from an onstage interview I did with venture capitalist Ben Horowitz: "One of the horrible things about being a founder CEO, it's the one job you can't really quit . . . or if you do, you're a punk."

That felt so real to me when he said it that we had it faux-cross-stitched on pillows and gave them away to readers one year. But the truth is, I know plenty more "punks" who quit their own companies than moms who quit their kids. Most startups go under, and many of the good ones eventually sell. You are always a parent.

6

If You Don't Hire More Women After Reading This Chapter, You're Just Sexist

BEYOND THE LOGIC AND THE anecdotes, there is plenty of data to back up why women—including mothers—naturally make great entrepreneurs, managers, and employees.

First Round Capital—a venture firm that has backed hundreds of startups at the earliest stages, including Uber, Birchbox, Square, and Blue Apron—produced a groundbreaking public report of its own internal data in 2015. One of the more surprising findings was that women-founded companies in its portfolio performed 63 percent better than companies founded just by men. The Kauffman Foundation similarly has reported that female tech entrepreneurs generated 35 percent higher returns, on average, than male counterparts.

Another 2016 study by a group called Women VC showed that female VCs also outperformed male VCs on average. This despite most female VCs being relegated to lower-return chunks of the market, like health care and ecommerce.

Across several studies, there is evidence that startups led by women are more likely to survive, are more profitable, and generate more revenue. One, by BNP Paribas, particularly highlighted higher success rates—and ambitions—among female entrepreneurs younger than thirty-five.

Beyond the startup world, McKinsey has found that gender-diverse companies are 15 percent more likely to outperform competitors. An Intel and Dalberg study found that tech companies that had even one female executive had as much as 16 percent higher "enterprise value" than companies with all-male executive teams. A study by Bersin reported that successful diversity programs can yield 2.3 times higher cash flow per employee. Studies from Goldman Sachs, Credit Suisse, Morgan Stanley, Catalyst, and the World Economic Forum have all found similarly outsized financial benefits of companies with gender-diverse teams.

Gender-balanced teams are also more "admired," according to a study using data from *Fortune* 500 and the World's Most Admired Companies list. Weber Shandwick found that companies with the best reputations in their industries had double the women in positions of leadership than those with poor reputations.

On a macroeconomic level, the US Congress Joint Economic Committee found that the US economy is *$2 trillion larger now* than it would have been if women hadn't made such powerful inroads into the job market over the last four decades. Women-owned businesses in aggregate generate some $1.6 trillion in revenue in the US, according to the Census Bureau. McKinsey similarly found that increased gender equality in the workforce could add another $12 trillion to the global economy.

I could keep going. I've got a whole file of these studies. But you get the idea: Data simply doesn't back up Maternal Wall bias, gender bias, the desires of a patriarchy, or any of the lies.

Know this.

Even if you never intend to start your own company, there are plenty of ways the strengths of motherhood can help you in your career. There are four main work "muscles" that motherhood cross-trains and develops that can help nearly any woman in any profession become better: productivity, stamina, creativity, and empathetic management.

These are all vital if you start or run a company, but they are also qualities that can help every mother in nearly any job. Motherhood not only makes you a better leader, but a better employee. No matter if you never intend to start a company or even to work full time out of the house again, know that these four muscles you build from motherhood will make you far better than your peers if you just trust and believe in your own power.

Productivity

This one may be the most obvious. When you have children, you have the same hours in the day, but so much more you need to get done. You become a beast at multitasking, which is a skill that women are typically already better at than men. Research has backed up the obvious: A study by the Federal Reserve Bank of St. Louis found that over thirty-year careers, mothers were far more productive than women without children at nearly every point in their careers. And mothers with two kids or more were the most productive of everyone studied.

If you just had a baby, haven't slept in weeks, didn't have the luxury of maternity leave, and are looking around at the chaos of your home, you probably don't exactly feel like a productivity machine. But this survey should give you hope. Because it found that young children take a temporary toll on productivity, of some 15–17 percent. For women with multiple children, the first child causes a 9.5 percent decline in performance and the second child cuts out *another* 12.5 percent. A third child decreases productivity another 11 percent. However, the declines are temporary, and once the children hit thirteen years of age,* mothers not only become far more productive than any other group studied but also stay that way for the rest of their careers.

Think of those early years like taking time to do an MBA in the evenings. You'll be less productive, sleep less, and be more stressed for a few years, but it'll pay dividends for the rest of your working life.

"I was hyperfocused once I had a child," says Anne Fulenwider of *Marie Claire*. "I was focused on productivity in a way I

---

* This is not to say gains in productivity don't occur *before* the age of thirteen; the researchers only studied "children" and "teens" without further examination of stages like infant, toddler, and elementary school age. In my experience, once my children stopped nursing and entered preschool, I experienced huge bursts of productivity.

never had been before. There was no spending an hour surfing the Internet. There was no shooting the shit for twenty minutes with my colleagues. I just became hyper, hyperaware of how to maximize every minute."

Dads got some benefits, too, according to the study. Fathers with one child performed similarly to childless men, but men with multiple kids were more productive than the rest of the men studied (although the increase in productivity was nowhere near as dramatic as it was with women).

When circumstances—like taking care of children, aging parents, or a sick loved one—force you to become far less productive, you stumble, but you eventually find a way to do the same amount of work you did before with fewer hours. And once you build those skills, you've got them for life.

I used to joke that in the first three years of Pando, I was like Inigo Montoya from *The Princess Bride*. People thought I was working hard, but I was pregnant or nursing the entire time. Once I weaned Evie, it was as if I told the world, "I know something you don't know . . . I am not left-handed!" and then tossed the sword to the other hand and kicked even more ass.

Nicole Farb, CEO of Darby Smart, was pregnant with twins when she raised her first round of venture capital. She remembers those early days of building a company with a baby in each arm. It built her confidence in how much she could handle. "Strangely, it didn't feel out of control, it felt in control," she says. "In entrepreneurship you hear 'focus is everything.' I didn't really know what that meant [before becoming a mother]. It's like, OK there are five plates in the air and which one is really about to fall? Do I really need to shower today? Probably not. Do I really need to work out? Probably not."

"Warrior girl" stamina

There is a reason the whole "crooked Hillary" thing stuck better as an insult than "no stamina Hillary": Even a lot of sexists realize how much stamina motherhood (and grandmotherhood) takes. When it came out during the campaign that Hillary lost her footing because she had pneumonia and wouldn't stop working, pretty much every working mother said, "Yep."

Women simply have to work harder than men to prove themselves—especially once they've had kids. And this isn't only on the presidential campaign trail, nor is it only at the office. Women and girls experience it pretty much their whole lives.

Just look at junior high girls' sports.

In 2008 Michael Sokolove wrote an awe-inspiring and terrifying story in the *New York Times Magazine* that sought to get to the bottom of the higher prevalence of injuries in girls' sports.

Part of the difference is biology, according to the piece. A surge of testosterone in puberty means boys can pack on muscle with less work. Estrogen does the same thing in girls . . . only it has that effect on fat rather than muscle. Girls have to train that much harder to build muscle, and that can wear out ligaments and risk injury.

But part of it is also a "warrior girl ethos," where girls refuse to be sidelined by injuries, indoctrinated by a societal pressure to have to work that much harder to be considered as much of an athlete as a boy. That's right: A girl in middle school recovering from a torn ACL experiences her own version of the "Prove-It-Again!" bias that mothers face coming back to work.

The article quotes girl after girl who spend their athletic careers playing in constant pain.

Said one school's athletic trainer: "I get more compliance from the boys. Boys are actually willing to sit if that's what I tell them. The girls want to get back out there. They want me to tape them up and let them play."

This "warrior girl ethos" puts girls at risk because they come back before they are fully healed. More dangerous, they get "inured" to the constant pain, ignoring warning signs of major problems and just trying to play through them.

Don't think it stops at girls' sports:

There is a fascinating parallel in research on injury rates in U.S. Army basic training, a two-month regimen that pushes recruits to their physical limits. In numerous studies going back more than two decades, women are shown to suffer injuries at substantially higher rates than men, with stress fractures to the lower legs a particular problem. But one large study also suggests that the women are both more frequently injured and tougher. It takes a bigger injury to knock them out of the service. The men, by comparison, are wimps; they leave with more minor ailments.

Cue the patriarchy. The article continues: "In sports, just as in the military, women are relative newcomers. In both venues, there may be an element of 'toughing it out' to prove they belong."

And I thought it was fucked up that a woman who just gave birth is considered "weak." By middle school, girls have so internalized the idea that they have to work harder to be considered equal that they are developing lifelong injuries.

Insane stamina clearly isn't all good, unchecked. That said, there's confidence in knowing you can push your body harder than your mind is telling you that you can.

Women shouldn't have to work harder to be considered equal, but the fact that they've been conditioned since middle school to expect it may be one reason that female investors and female entrepreneurs outperform men on average. They wouldn't have gotten to that level otherwise.

Unlocked creativity

Increased stamina and productivity are great. They give you the ability to push for longer hours and make the most out of those hours. But that's all brute force. The most amazing thing to me about motherhood is that the *quality* of my work also increased dramatically. My voice as a reporter became more pointed, more direct, and more aggressive, and my voice as a writer became cleaner and more convincing. Since becoming a mom, I've done some of my best writing, and I can do it more quickly.

My brain seemed to become rewired to think more creatively. Part of this is that magic of constraints. Creativity is the way you fight back against lacking the time and resources you think you need.

CEO Julia Hartz had her first child in the early days of building Eventbrite with her husband. She was answering customer service emails as she was being wheeled into labor. Soon after, she called her mom in a panic because she felt like no one had prepared her for life after she got the career, the husband, and the baby . . . *How do I actually manage all these things?* "All

she could tell me was, 'What got you here will get you there,'"
Hartz says. "It was so annoying and not the answer I wanted. I
was like, 'Oh, don't pull this Zen Buddhist shit on me.' But looking back, it was the best advice."

What her mother was describing was creative problem solving.

This may be a more valuable skill than the first two. Airbnb
CEO Brian Chesky is not a mother or a father but has used creativity to disrupt the half-a-trillion-dollar hotel industry. On his
first day at Rhode Island School of Design his teacher asked all
the students to do self-portraits. They agonized over them all
week before presenting them to the class, wincing at the cri-
tiques, picking apart what more they should have done, lament-
ing how they all weren't quite perfect enough.

The next assignment was to do two hundred self-portraits
in the same time period. "Clearly there's not enough hours in
the week," he said when he told me this story. "The point was
it was a seemingly impossible solution, but with creativity you
can always find a way."

With all due respect to RISD, I can't imagine a greater creative
battleground than raising children. Try to imagine explaining
concepts like God, sex, war, death, Donald Trump, and why the
sky is blue to a three-year-old who has barely grasped the days
of the week. Or imagine crawling inside the brain of a toddler,
deducing what thing they are planning to jump off when you
leave the room, and troubleshooting it before it happens.

It's not just having to come up with creative solutions with
little sleep and finite resources. There's something about
watching—and encouraging or combating—a child's mind as
it develops that unlocks your own insane creativity.

One of my favorite examples of this is Shirley Jackson, the
author of "The Lottery." A recent biography of Jackson called

Shirley Jackson: A Rather Haunted Life details the creative and professional transformation she underwent after having children, even though she had an incredibly unsupportive spouse.

The book relies heavily on her letters. In one, she drew a cartoon of herself standing in a room holding a baby by his ankle while her husband naps on the couch. "I did three paragraphs all at once and it tired me out," the caption reads. Despite that familiar double standard, it was only after becoming a mother that Jackson's career took off.

Jackson often complained about the mental calisthenics required to be at once a mother and a writer—the "nagging thoughts" about finishing the laundry or preparing meals that often interrupted her creative work. . . . But many writers, especially women writers, learn to derive imaginative energy from their constraints. . . .

Writing in the hours between morning kindergarten and lunch, while a baby napped, or after the children had gone to bed demanded a discipline that came to suit Jackson. She was constantly thinking of stories while cooking, cleaning, or doing just about anything else. "All the time that I am making beds and doing dishes and driving to town for dancing shoes, I am telling myself stories," she said in one of her lectures. . . .

She did it, of course, because there was no other way. She needed the children as much as they needed her. Their imaginations energized her; their routines stabilized her. . . . Jackson could not come into her own as a writer before she had children. She would not have been the writer she became without them.

Empathetic management

Newsrooms are tough environments. The daily grind of filling a news hole is fueled by bad coffee, whiskey flasks stashed in desk drawers, all-nighters, and grizzled editors who scream profanity-laced tirades when you screw something up or miss a deadline. I was trained to think that's just how the news business is.

I worked for five different editors before starting my own company. Two were phenomenal, three were borderline sociopathic. (Perhaps not coincidentally, the two phenomenal ones were parents, and the other three were not.)

Managing by screaming and threats is effective. But it's short-term effective. Managing with empathy and compassion is much more sustainable. The problem is it's way harder. LinkedIn CEO Jeff Weiner talked about "compassionate management" with me in a 2014 interview.

"Acting like an asshole is easy," he said. "And oftentimes I think some of that behavior emanates from laziness, because you don't want to take the time to think about what that person is thinking or feeling or you don't want to deal with their energy or their bad day. . . . It's exhausting. But it's the only way to build a team that scales. Bad behavior is the exact opposite. It's just doing whatever comes to mind."

Leigh Rawdon, CEO of the kids clothing company Tea Collection, remembers getting feedback early in her career that "the good news and the bad news is that people like you.

"There's some insights in there that are important for me, but there's also this idea that there is a different way to be a leader," she says. "It is wonderful to start having these examples of women who are showing a different way. I used to hear all these things, like that consensus building is a terrible idea. Is it, or is it a natural maternal way where you are listening, connecting with people, moving things in a direction with a little different mentality than 'I'm the captain, follow me.'"

Like a lot of women I spoke with, *Marie Claire*'s Anne Fulenwider would have never believed that becoming a mother would make her a better employee and a better leader, and that working would make her a better mother. "If you had told me that, I would have thought you were this Pollyanna feminist, but I've lived it," she says.

As a mother, she's been a role model for her daughter. As an employee, she was more productive. But as a boss, it changed her perspective on "what matters," she says. She has more respect for people's time and less respect for face time. "It made me appreciate the different talents people bring to an office," she says. "I see that just standing there and shouting at people really doesn't work with a six-year-old or a four-year-old, why would that top-down way of managing [work at the office]? The problem I'm facing in my house now is my kids simply don't listen at all. And it's made me a much better manager at work, because that's ultimately a management job."

Amy Errett's company, Madison Reed, is very woven into her experience as a mother—it was her daughter who convinced her to start the company, saying her idea to create nontoxic hair color would "save women's lives." "Mommy, are you going to do it?" her daughter said to her one morning after absorbing months of conversations where Errett was weighing the decision. "Everyone in our family are strong women and you taught me you should do anything you want, so you need to do this."

The moment made such an impression on Errett that she

named the company after her daughter. "This brand is about empowering women; for me it's personal," she says.

She manages in a very personal way, too. "Managing a group of people is very analogous to parenting. I didn't understand that at a cellular level until I had a kid," Errett says. "My job is to meet Madison where she's at. Her job is not to meet me where I'm at. It's validating the goodness in them and putting up guardrails. [My wife] Clare and my job is to help her figure out her genius. It's the same job I have here. It's actually my job to understand that the CTO is motivated by different things. I need to go and create the space for his genius to come out, which is good for him and the company. It's a lot like you're of service. You're trying to find this place in yourself that is unconditional."

⌘

A lot of this may sound obvious. But clearly, most people don't believe mothers possess valuable skills, or we wouldn't see 60 percent of them experiencing workplace bias, nor would we see 75 percent of women in Silicon Valley being asked in job interviews if they plan on having kids. Forty percent of women in the Valley wouldn't feel they need to hide the fact that they are moms to be taken more seriously. Female CEOs would make up more than 3 percent of venture capitalists' portfolios.

During the course of reporting this book, I spoke to a dozen or so men who did get this. Men who actually said they *preferred* to hire mothers. Not to up their diversity stats or to look good, but because they found mothers to be more reliable in getting their work done no matter what was thrown their way. Or just because they believe women bring skills to a company that men don't have.

One example is the venture capitalist Mike Maples, whose firm has invested in companies like Twitter, TaskRabbit, and Lyft. When he set out to hire his first partner, he specifically sought out a woman and found one in a highly inexperienced math PhD candidate at Stanford named Ann Miura-Ko. The firm is mostly female staffed, and Maples likes to say Ann is the one with "the hot hand." Indeed, she is one of just six female VCs on *Forbes*'s annual Midas List, and is on the board of Yale's prestigious investment committee. Beyond returns, the mix of male and female energy has made him more likely to admit when he doesn't know something and to compromise on things.

Andy Dunn, CEO of menswear company Bonobos, describes women as being "just like men only a little bit better." "Women have better judgment, more empathy, and they are shown to be better entrepreneurs in an apples-to-apples basis," he said. "They are financially more astute. And yet we live in a world where men weigh one-point-six times what women weigh, and a couple thousand years of history have weighed women down because of that. That's starting to change. And the rate it's changing is accelerating. The next hundred years will be referred to as the female takeover. And by 'takeover' I don't mean 'Run for the hills, guys!' I mean, 'Your life will be improved by the ascendance of women.'"

This, from a man building a business in menswear. Dunn has no agenda in saying this; it doesn't boost his business or help him raise capital to believe it. He simply does.

The research about gender-balanced teams and women-led teams clearly backs up Dunn's and Maples's instincts.

Plenty of men will never believe that women possess real advantages in the workplace. How about we just agree that mothers develop enough skills doing one of the hardest jobs in the world that they aren't a *detriment* in the workplace? That these skills are not something you have to screen out of the hiring process?

Sadly, that would be a radical enough stance in America today.

⌘

At some point in that fall of 2011, as TechCrunch was collapsing and I was weighing my options, I sat down and asked my husband, Geoff, what he thought I should do. He knew how much harder starting a company would be. That it was likely to be way more stressful and consuming than anything else I'd experienced. And that—of course—it could go bust. We lived more or less paycheck to paycheck as, respectively, a journalist and a photographer in San Francisco.

He was supportive.

Through trial and error we'd hit a point in our marriage where we chose to support each other's careers, regardless of what it meant for hours worked or face time with each other. We figured the opposite—a burgeoning resentment from passing on a great opportunity—would be far more corrosive to our marriage.

We'd only been dating a year or so when I decided to move out to Silicon Valley. Geoff was happy in Memphis, but he picked up and moved, too, because he was so confident we were meant to be together.

A few years later, when I was getting ready to pitch my second book on emerging markets, we had huge screaming fights about it. He was worried that my spending forty weeks traveling while he held down the fort at home would come between us. That I would be forever changed by the experience, and we would become different people. But ultimately, he capitulated. "You need to do it, because if you don't, you'll resent me forever and that will be worse," he said. After that fight, he got completely behind me, using whatever vacation time he had to travel with me and swallowing his concerns as I drained our savings flying all over the world.

Just before we found out I was pregnant with Eli, Geoff got an amazing opportunity: to get a masters in fine art from a photography program at the University of Hartford. The beauty of the program was it was a remote class. But every quarter he'd have to spend two weeks on-site. The first session was just before Eli was due. The campus was remote enough that there was a chance that if Eli was early, Geoff would miss the birth. He'd definitely miss being there for me during that last—I assumed—brutal month of "GET THIS BABY OUT OF ME!" that I'd seen on TV.

He asked if I wanted him to decline it, but I insisted he go. It wasn't fair that his opportunity came up once I got pregnant. I even paid for it, using the money from that speaking gig I did in Nigeria—the trip where we "met" Bones.

I remember my conservative dad disapproving. He said it "went against biology" for a man to leave his wife when she was nine months pregnant. Particularly since I didn't live near any family. He told me about an opportunity he had to study philosophy in Greece when my mom was having kids and how he turned it down.

I remember feeling bad for my father. He and my mother both had spent their lives studying and teaching the works from Russia, Europe, and ancient civilizations. But they'd never traveled over there. They'd never left North America. They were long since done having kids; they'd retired with a decent pension, but not before my mom got diagnosed with Parkinson's. They still haven't traveled there.

I remember thinking my dad *should* have gone, that I wasn't wrong; he'd been wrong.

The week after I got back from doing Disrupt in China, before I'd finalized my plans for Pando, Geoff got another opportunity. Tony Hsieh, the CEO of the $1 billion ecommerce site Zappos, had decided to invest $350 million in remaking downtown Las Vegas. Paul was an early believer, moving there after Tech-Crunch imploded and basing NSFWCORP there. They wanted to build some sort of art community. And they had a shitload of cash. With my encouragement, Geoff pitched Tony on giving him a huge check in exchange for a plan to build a photography community space in downtown Las Vegas.

What photographer gets the chance to quit his job and just "build something"? Geoff took it, obviously. But that meant he'd be spending half his time in Vegas and even more time working on his MFA, just as we were starting our family and I was starting Pando.

It wasn't ideal, obviously. But Vegas was just a short flight from San Francisco. Eli and I would go there one week a month, meaning we'd only really be apart one week of every month. We'd weathered worse, I told myself. We'd be fine.

We weren't.

But well before my marriage started to fall apart, I went through another emotional breakup.

7

You Wanna Be the Hammer or the Nail?

IT'S 7:00 A.M., AND I wake up to the sound of the back door of my house being unlocked, bags tossed down in the kitchen, and the kitchen faucet turning on. Either our nanny, Megan, is here and has immediately started in on last night's dishes, or it's some kind of OCD intruder. I'm so exhausted I'm fine with either.

Geoff is in Vegas, and Eli is either asleep or in his crib enjoying his alone time. The best investment I've ever made was a $50,000 down payment on my San Francisco house in 2008—the final check I got from my first book, and more money than I'd ever held in my hands at once. As tech billionaires have moved in all around me, causing property valuations to soar, this house is more likely to pay for my kids' college education than Pando, this book, or anything else I do.

My second-best investment was the $10,000 I saved up during my pregnancy to afford a night nurse. During the first eight weeks of motherhood, Anna came in five nights a week and answered every panicked new-parent question we had, brought me fresh fruit every night, and got Eli on a sleep schedule where he only got up once a night to eat, and pretty soon not at all. It still pays dividends.

The first few months of building Pando have been a fury of writing, of social media, of editing, of interviewing and hiring, and most of all a ton of stress, interrupted every four hours to nurse Eli or pump. I only shower if I have a meeting, and I save those until late afternoon. My assistant actually puts reminders in my calendar to shower.

My house is always chaotic, but on this day it is toxic. I am facing my first major test as a CEO: Ousting a board member, investor, and our most famous contributor all in one move.

⌘

Have you ever had that feeling that you just knew a relationship was going to end badly the moment it began, but you went ahead anyway? Well, that was pretty much my entire work relationship with Michael Arrington.

Mike was known in the Valley for being brilliant and a great entrepreneur but also a bully. He himself would admit, "I'm a hammer and everyone else is a nail." When I first went to work for TechCrunch, a lot of powerful folks I counted as friends and sources were concerned. They didn't like or trust Mike.

Indeed, I'd watched Mike be incredibly emotionally and verbally abusive to a lot of people we worked with. He once berated an assistant because she couldn't book him on a flight between two cities on his preferred airline. Never mind that the route didn't actually exist.

But Mike had been nothing but great to me. He'd gone to bat for me publicly when it wasn't the easy or obvious thing to do, and if anything, I was loyal for far too long because of that. I deluded myself that I knew him on a deeper level than other people.

But I promised many people close to me—including Geoff and myself—that the moment Mike tried to bully me he was gone. I'd seen this too many times with him: If he treated you like a nail once, you were the nail to him forever.

Mike was brilliant and flawed, and I loved many things about him. There was no question that his being attached to Pando added to our value significantly. But I wasn't going to be his new nail.

This was the day that I had dreaded. Deep in the pit of my stomach, I always knew it was coming. The day I had to cut Michael Arrington out of my life forever. I was sitting there, sweaty and unshowered in my living room just staring at my phone, not wanting to make this phone call. That wasn't because I doubted it was the right move. It was because Mike was so uncannily good at getting inside my head and twisting and turning everything I knew to be true. He preyed on my ability to always want to see the other side, to give someone the benefit of the doubt.

I didn't need or want my judgment clouded. I knew this was right. And the sad thing is I knew it would end this way. When he and I talked about him being on the board and owning 10 percent of my company, it didn't feel right. But I was scared. The confidence gap again. I didn't think I could truly do this on my own. Mike's endorsement was a safety net for me. It was the bulletproof answer I could give to those nagging doubts of "Why me?" that too many women are plagued with. His involvement was a way to hack my own imposter syndrome. To fake it until I could make it.

Ten percent is a shitload of equity in a company; typically a board member would get 1–2 percent of stock. Employees get less than a percentage point. I had made sure we spelled out what exactly he'd do for Pando in exchange for so much owner-ship. One of the key things was that Mike would only write for Pando and would exclusively be onstage at Pando events, unless I waived this.

Mike understood this. He even called me one day early on to brag that a friend had asked him to emcee a new conference, and Mike proudly told that person our agreement precluded that. But that was an easy one to turn down. Mike's loyalty was only tested when it was in the way of something he wanted. And he'd spent months desperately wanting to take back Tech-Crunch.

In the spring of 2012, the Disrupt New York conference was approaching, and TechCrunch was screwed. They had no one who could program the event or sit onstage to go toe-to-toe with leaders in the tech industry. They came back to Mike—hat in hand to the guy they'd previously forced out—and offered him what I later learned was big bucks to host the conference. So much for the major ethical issues they had with him months earlier.

Mike wasn't going to let something as meaningless as a promise to me—let alone his fiduciary duty as a major share-holder in Pando—get in the way of his comeback, or his revenge on Arianna Huffington. Worse still, the first I heard about it was when Mike wrote a post on TechCrunch titled "I'm Back." Not only did he not tell me he was breaking our agreement; he delivered the news in a way that *also* broke the agreement.

Because Pando's entire product was our words, and our primary revenue back then was our events business, this was like a Twitter engineer coming up with a killer new feature and heading over to Facebook on the weekends to develop it. Or the head of sales selling ads for a rival company. It was a breathtaking "fuck you" given he was an investor, a board member, and was set to become one of our largest shareholders.

I'd seen Mike navigate like this before. Ask forgiveness, not permission. Storm off when someone gets upset and come back later assuming they'd cool off. Turn the tables by getting so furious, you'd wind up apologizing to him.

I didn't forgive. I didn't cool off. And I certainly didn't apologize. I fired him.

The easy thing would have been to forgive it, but I'd started this company in part because I wanted to be the best me I possibly could for my kids. Did I want them to see their mother cave to a bully? Would I want them to cave to bullies?

Everyone in the company was behind me, but it was scary. So much of the value of Pando was predicated on Mike being part of it. At least, that's what I thought. What I feared. Now he was re-endorsing the larger incumbent we were supposed to be replacing: TechCrunch. The one who'd fucked us all over. My staff, investors, everyone could have balked after two months, accusing me of luring them under false pretenses.

Firing Mike was the biggest career risk I'd faced yet. A far bigger risk than starting Pando. Sure, that was scary. It could have easily failed. But I was getting paid the same thing I was making at TechCrunch, and I'd raised enough money for a year or so at least.

And failure was a badge of honor in the Valley. Even if Pando flamed out, having tried to build a startup, having crossed over to the ranks of "founder," and having been a CEO—no matter how awful I was at it—would still escalate my social capital and earning potential in the Valley.

The only risk was, if it went under, how quickly I could find another job before losing my house, because we didn't really have savings and had a lot of expenses with a new baby. But I could take that gamble. I could find *something* to pay the bills. Geoff was making decent money in Vegas and controlled a two-year budget. Worst case, he could front us the money for our mortgage, and I could . . . I dunno . . . bartend as I did in college. There were ways.

But I was sure of one thing: Keeping Mike in the company would be fatal to morale and my own sense of self-respect. It wouldn't be my company; I would be his puppet. It would send a signal to my team that one person's ego was above everything else I said we stood for.

I called our major investors and the ones closest to Mike and talked them through my decision. Every single one confirmed it was the only choice I had.

I wrote a boilerplate post for Pando disclosing the news to our readers, without gory details or editorializing. I drafted an email to send to the rest of the investors. We were ready to cut off his email and all access to post anything on our site. I practiced what I was going to say to him.

I would be careful not to apologize. I would not open the door for any discussion. This was final. It was done. I was merely informing him of the decision.

I was pacing. I felt as though I was going to throw up. I wanted it done, but I didn't want to do it.

I called him, got voice mail, and fist-bumped no one in particular because I was alone in my living room. It's embarrassing, but the honest truth was I was thrilled I only had to fire Mike to a recording of his voice. This man knew how to (best case) manipulate and (worst case) abuse people in business and in life. I wanted him gone. I had to tell him that, but that was all I had to do.

I left my message, and that was it. I never spoke to him again, except once in passing at a cocktail party.

This was my first huge test as a CEO, and his betrayal wound up being a blessing in disguise. Within a year, Mike would become embroiled in an even more serious, much darker scandal around his treatment of women. He subsequently retreated from the tech world and public life, investing less, writing less, and not even continuing to host TechCrunch events for the gloating and huge paydays.

Firing Mike may have been the right thing to do, but it started to become clear to the world, our team, and investors that the easy "TechCrunch 2.0" narrative of Pando wasn't going to happen. TechCrunch was aggressively hiring and growing in AOL-directed traffic, even if it had lost all the vociferous edge of its glory days. It wasn't going away as the place tech people scanned every morning to get a basic briefing of what was happening.

Around this time, *San Francisco Magazine* published a profile of me titled "It Ain't Easy Being Queen: Sarah Lacy was supposed to rule the tech-media blogosphere. But there have been a few glitches along the way."

Not everything in the piece was accurate. But that headline was certainly fair. In fact, a "few" was an understatement. But the "problems" they seized on were strange.

There was a huge glossy picture of me in my living room talking to reporters and holding Eli on my hip. The editors helpfully drew arrows on the picture like an NFL announcer, pointing out all the "problems" with my life. "Problems" like "This is not an office. Some days, up to 15 staffers crowd into Lacy's house to work. She claims to love the hubbub, but she has to stay up late to write. Coffee is key." TechCrunch and plenty of other blogs were also run out of their founders' homes. Some might call that good fiscal management not paying San Francisco commercial real estate rents.

My nanny took particular exception to the magazine pointing to Eli and labeling him "problem #1" in the photo. Indeed, that might have been the thing the article got the most wrong. Eli was what had inspired me to do this. Eli was what kept me sane. Eli was my secret weapon. The fact that he was seen as problem number one shows the bias against mothers in our culture. And this article was *written by* another mother.

This piece was ultimately great for us. It positioned us as a scrappy up-and-comer worthy of a multipage magazine profile, without overhyping us. This was, after all, part of an issue about how the tech industry was ruining San Francisco. I expected a cynical angle.

But other "press" was a frustrating distraction. I was getting torn apart in gossip blogs and in anonymous comment threads daily. Mostly for things I never actually did or said. I'd dealt with this kind of thing for years, and I had a simple system for dealing with it: I didn't read any of it. It always went away, and it never mattered much in the end. I don't know a high-profile woman in my industry who doesn't have to live with this kind of stuff. But most of my young staff hadn't experienced anything like this before. On top of everything else, it was exhausting to have to keep explaining why they should just ignore it.

But there was one germ of truth in that *San Francisco Magazine* story. It was becoming clear that if Pando was going to make it, it was going to have to become something distinct and new. And I was going to have to figure that out without any crutches. Even my superstar investors couldn't help much. I couldn't very well expect them to feed me information they wouldn't give me as just another reporter if I wasn't willing to do any favors for them. None of them had a board seat or very much skin in the game by design. That cuts both ways.

Andrew Anker played the single biggest role in shaping me as a CEO during this time. Our board meetings were brutal. He had a keen ability to hone in on my weaknesses and not merely expose them but douse them in acid and tap-dance all over them. I still have anxiety for days before board meetings.

But unlike the anxiety I had dealing with Mike, this was productive anxiety at least. When you are running your own company for the first time, you quickly get over the "Wait, who gave me a company?" feeling the same way you quickly get over the shock that a hospital is allowing you to go home with a fragile little baby days after you have it. You start to make decisions, to do your best, to take forks in the road with little thought of the ramifications that could ensue. And no one inside the company can question you—except the board.

One afternoon during that first summer running Pando, Geoff had just gotten home from Vegas, and I took a break from the chaos to walk around the corner with him and grab some burritos. He was talking about his MFA, his work in Vegas, and how in the near future he hoped he could spend more time in San Francisco.

"Good," I said. "Because your wife and babies need you here."

"Wait, did you say *babies*?" he said.

Yep, I was pregnant again. Evie wasn't an accident. I wanted Eli to have a sister, and I didn't see my life getting any easier anytime soon. And by this point I had no more fear of what motherhood would do to me. Eli had made me so much better than I'd been before.

8

The Tyranny of the Pattern

WHAT I WAS DESPERATELY SEEKING in early 2012 was a new template. Some sort of pattern of female leadership. Something that I'd seen work, that I could believe in and apply to my life.

I no longer wanted to be a man, and so far, the senior women I'd worked for or seen as role models mostly didn't embrace being women.

I felt lost without a pattern. And in that feeling, I was reflective of Silicon Valley entrepreneurship as a whole, much as the Valley likes to pretend otherwise.

Silicon Valley prides itself on being a place that breaks the mold, embracing misfits, disrupting business as usual.

We're so radical that we fund college dropouts who've never held down jobs before to build companies!

That is pretty radical. Or it was. The first time it was done. Once it becomes the new template for the only thing you fund, you aren't disrupting anything. The industry's top VCs have actually copped to this. During a 2008 keynote at the National Venture Capital Association, John Doerr (one of the top VCs in the history of Silicon Valley) said to Mike Moritz (another one), "If you look at [Amazon founder Jeff] Bezos, or [Netscape founder Marc] Andreessen, [Yahoo cofounder] David Filo, the founders of Google, they all seem to be white, male, nerds who've dropped out of Harvard or Stanford and they absolutely have no social life." Doerr took it further saying, "That correlates more with any other success factor that I've seen in the world's greatest entrepreneurs."

The striking thing about these words—other than they ignore the existence of Yahoo's other cofounder, the Asian Jerry Yang—is that they use pattern recognition to nakedly justify discriminating against women and minorities. And Doerr implicitly advises all the other VCs in attendance to do the same. *Here's the secret to becoming as successful as John Doerr and Mike Moritz!*

VCs who've been in the industry for decades will even argue that "pattern recognition" is their singular advantage. And that's not all bullshit. There are some similarities in how great companies are built. There's a reason so many of them come out of a place where people have seen how it's done over and over again.

But this blind adherence to "finding the next . . ." Netscape/Amazon/Google/Facebook also leads to a lot of the unconscious bias in the Valley, and it excuses a lot of bad behavior that alienates women and discourages them from wanting to work at startups.

Think about it. I've already cited a ton of evidence that women, gender-balanced teams, and in particular mothers outperform men and male-dominated teams at multiple levels. Forget fairness. I'd be happy for *greed* to drive more inclusion.

Yet in terms of diversity, Silicon Valley has backslid since all this data started to become clear. Fewer women are general partners of venture firms now than in the dot-com bubble, and across the top nine tech companies, women make up roughly one-third of the workforce.

That doesn't sound too bad until you learn that in the high-earning, high-profile engineering ranks it's more like 10 percent female. And an analysis of over half a million salaries shared via Glassdoor showed that the pay gap for women in tech—particularly at the programmer level—is as high as 28 percent. Compare that to the gender gap for all workers using Glassdoor's data—some 5.9 percent.

VCs pride themselves on making investment decisions based on their gut, and your gut is more comfortable betting on someone that reminds you of yourself. Of the massive $60 billion in venture capital deployed in 2015, female founders got just 7 percent (when surveys break out female CEOs, that number falls), and black male founders received just 2 percent. *Black women did not register.* Not coincidentally, 98 percent of VCs on senior investing teams are white or Asian males.

"My heart sinks every time I read a press release about a VC firm who is so proud they've added another guy to their ranks," says VC Aileen Lee, who left Kleiner Perkins to start her own majority-female firm, Cowboy Ventures. "When I know women at the same levels from those same companies that have had a very difficult time even getting interviews at these firms. But these are small privately held firms where the whole investment team might be eight or ten people. They spend a lot of time together. A lot of these guys are straight, white guys and their comfort level is with people like them. They might be afraid they'll say something that offends women. They think,

'I have a great life and I don't want to feel like I can't be myself at my office.'"

Let's look at Facebook in particular. It's not only one of the most successful tech companies on the planet right now; it's also one of the more progressive and outspoken when it comes to gender issues. CEO Mark Zuckerberg set a dramatic example for men at his company when he took two months of paternity leave in early 2016. And COO Sheryl Sandberg is the most high-profile and admired female leader in tech, particularly given Marissa Mayer's struggles at Yahoo. Sandberg is also by far the most outspoken leader about the importance of supporting and lifting up women.

Facebook has pledged again and again that greater diversity isn't just a goal, but that it is "essential" to the company's mission and future. And Facebook is valued at some $330 billion and is one of the top companies people in tech want to work for.

Combine the message sent by the top leadership, the market position, and the resources, and Facebook should be a leader in this, right? After all, this is a company that has connected billions of people on the planet and pioneered a way to beam Internet Wi-Fi from space to connect even more. Compared to that, hiring more women and people of color should be the easiest thing Facebook does all day.

And yet.

In its diversity report released in 2015, Facebook disclosed that it hired just seven more black people year-over-year compared with an overall increase of 1,231 in head count. In its US workforce, Facebook employed just forty-five black staffers out of some 4,263 workers. Facebook's black female head count increased by . . . one person. To a grand total of eleven.

Clearly, given Sandberg's presence at the company, it had to have done better when it comes to gender diversity, right? Wrong. Over the same period it managed to decrease its percentage of male employees across the company by just 1 percent, to 68 percent. When it comes to the makeup of its technology team, 84 percent were male, down from 85 percent.

At Pando we have a saying: Typically when a tech company complains a problem is "too hard" to solve, what it means is the company doesn't really prioritize solving it.

Think of what tech companies have achieved since the dawn of the Internet. They have deconstructed nearly every industry on earth. They have wired the planet. If you live in a major US city, you can push a button on your phone and get nearly anything fetched for you in an hour. Trillions of dollars in value have been created.

And you are telling me it's harder for Facebook to find more than one qualified black woman a year to hire at any level in the company?

Sadly, a 2016 LinkedIn anonymous survey of six hundred founders, executives, and investors in tech proved my cynical point. Oh, the things white men will say when they don't have to be quoted . . . If the earlier chapters on the power of motherhood inspired you, you may want to go get a glass of wine for this part. I'll wait.

The upshot: White men in tech don't actually give a shit about diversity.

Less than 5 percent of white men who responded to the survey said they considered a lack of diversity a top problem. Three out of four respondents were unaware of any initiatives to make their companies or portfolios more diverse. Forty percent of male respondents said the media wasted too much time harping about tech's lack of diversity.

One white male founder went so far as to call it "silly" for founders to have to commit to building diverse teams. Another white male founder said building a diverse team had "nothing to do with his business." Unless he runs a site aimed only at the KKK, you have to wonder why he wouldn't believe his company should at least reflect his customer mix or user base. It takes a stunning dismissal of women and people of color to assume that there would be absolutely no business advantage in listening to their points of view, or that they simply wouldn't be a good fit.

Despite endless "awareness raising" on this issue, the majority of white men in the survey seemed blissfully unaware that sexism and racism even occur in the industry at all. While 80 percent of female investors said they had witnessed sexism in the tech world, just 28 percent of men said they had. Nearly 50 percent of nonwhite investors said they'd witnessed racism, while just 24 percent of white investors said they had. Forty-three percent of nonwhite founders had witnessed racism compared to just 10 percent of white founders.

How could there be such a disconnect in the same industry? I'm willing to bet part of it is that white men frequently don't realize they are doing and saying racist and sexist things, the same way a boss rationalizes that he's "helping" when he denies a working mother a promotion.

One woman surveyed said an investor asked her how she planned on "leading a company as a married woman." I'm not even sure what that means. An African American founder noted he's had white investors "helpfully" introduce him to African American investors, arguing they'll be "more interested in his company."

When Jess Lee was hired as Sequoia Capital's first female investment partner, the very well-known Aileen Lee was repeatedly asked why she was shutting down her own firm to join Sequoia. The last name wasn't the confusing part. *People simply confused two Asian women in the industry.*

It's worth quoting Aileen Lee's Facebook post in its entirety:

Hmm, should I be flattered, insulted, or just brush off that a number of people have confused me with my friend/great CEO Jess Lee, think I'm joining Sequoia Capital, and shutting down Cowboy Ventures? Do they think what we're doing at Cowboy is not that big a deal; that I'd opt to join a legendary all male firm if given the chance; or that Asian women in VC are not worth telling apart? (because Theresia Gouw, Ann Miura-Ko, and I often also get confused by people . . .) Just wondering.

I know, drink. I'm almost done.

And yet, despite the facts that 95 percent of white male respondents didn't consider this a problem, 40 percent were sick of hearing about it, and 75 percent weren't aware of any programs to address it, investors surveyed guessed that within five years, one-third of their portfolios would comprise female-founded companies and racially diverse teams. Founders similarly expected rapid progress: Somehow in five years, half of their hires would be women and people of color.

Something these men just said that they don't consider a problem or a priority will, just, yunno, work itself out. *Because that's happened ever in the history of the rights of women and minorities.*

Similarly, a majority of respondents in the First Round Capital State of Startups survey believed that—*as if by magic!*—in fourteen years the tech industry would mirror the gender and ethnic makeup of the US. How is that going to happen if the majority of men polled believe it's a "pipeline problem" outside their control and the majority of women polled feel it's an unconscious-bias problem or an issue with a lack of female role models and mentors? What is supposed to suddenly change?

Who knows! In my experience, in the tech world, these questions are answered with the same few words: "You see, Sarah, I'm an optimist . . ."

The experience of Amy Errett, CEO of Madison Reed, demonstrates just how hard it is to make a company more diverse once it's already gone down a homogeneous path. She has worked hard at trying to hire female engineers and has failed to date. Despite running a company that stands for female empowerment with a majority-female senior team, her entire programming ranks are men, and every woman she's interviewed is "petrified they are going to be catapulted into bro-land. . . . If you don't start inclusiveness from day one, it's brutal to catch up later on.

"You have to be a really secure guy to work here, and yet I have to fight bro-land all the time," she says. "You close your eyes and if you aren't paying attention in fifteen minutes on a Friday afternoon, there are Nerf gun wars. It's the bros! They've got their guns out, and they are shooting at each other. I'll be like, 'No, no, no, you're putting the guns down, boys.' It's not malice, it's just letting the testosterone run."

Both of these surveys—while depressing—offer the only real explanation for why diversity is still so lousy in the tech world. If the Valley prioritized this problem, it would be solved by now. It isn't hard. You hire diverse teams early on, and hire and promote women and people of color from the beginning.

The talent is there. The desire on the part of the industry's gate-keepers simply isn't.

⌘

For a long time, the acceptable explanation for why companies don't do better on gender diversity came down to two words that absolved gatekeepers and leaders of any responsibility: THE PIPELINE.

The argument goes like this: More men study computer science. Most founders are technical. And the best VCs are those who have operational experience. So until more women study computer science and found highly successful tech companies, they simply aren't qualified for top CEO jobs, board spots, and VC partnerships.

Mike Moritz of Sequoia Capital argued this as recently as December of 2015, before the firm hired Jess Lee. When asked why Sequoia—the top venture capital firm in Silicon Valley—hadn't at that time ever hired a female partner, he told Bloomberg's Emily Chang it was because they were not "willing to lower [their] standards," and he blamed the pipeline. It was a sign of how empowered female and minority voices have become in Silicon Valley that the entire Internet lost its shit.

Journalist Jessica Nordell threw cold water on apologias that he'd simply "put his foot in his mouth." She pointed out:

> No one had asked, "Are you willing to lower your standards?"
> No: that was the question he heard when asked about hiring
> women. That was the association he made. Here, then, is a
> map of his synaptic firings: women → lower standards.

The comments were particularly outrageous because Moritz doesn't actually have any founder experience or coding experience himself. Moritz was a journalist before becoming an investor at Sequoia.

Indeed, if you go down the list of some of the most revered Silicon Valley VCs—Moritz, Benchmark's Bill Gurley, Kleiner Perkins's John Doerr, Union Square Ventures's Fred Wilson, Greylock's David Sze—you'll find most of them have never founded a company before.

So tell me again: What is this industry-approved "standard" that you would have to lower to include women?

While Moritz got lambasted for making his remarks publicly, privately men in both the LinkedIn and First Round surveys mostly blamed the pipeline for the lack of diversity in tech.[*]

Before reading these studies, I assumed I didn't have to address the "pipeline" myth because the reaction to Moritz's words showed we'd made progress, right? Apparently not. So let's take a moment to debunk the pipeline myth again.

First off, there's no shortage of educated women entering the workforce. In 1981 women outpaced men in earning college degrees; by 2026 it's expected to be at a ratio of 3:2. Plenty of educated women enter companies. At Stanford and UC Berkeley 50 percent of the introductory computer science students are women, according to a 2015 *Forbes* article. On a broader diversity point, a *USA Today* study found that top universities graduate black and Hispanic computer science and engineering students at twice the rate tech companies actually hire them.

The problem is the subtle sexism and racism that continually

---

* Bizarrely, 35 percent in the LinkedIn survey said there was no obstacle. I don't know how to process that. Are they saying they find plenty of women and people of color, they just choose not to hire them?

keeps women and people of color from achieving higher levels of success within companies.

A few examples on how the pipeline simply doesn't self-correct. From a 2016 "Women in the Workplace" study by McKinsey and LeanIn.Org:

- For every 100 women promoted to manager, 130 men are promoted.
- Only 20 percent of women at the senior VP level are in line to become CEOs.
- Women who negotiate for a raise or a promotion are 30 percent more likely than male counterparts to suffer retaliation in the form of negative feedback calling them "bossy," "aggressive," or "intimidating."
- Women are less likely to receive feedback when they ask for it or get access to senior executives in companies.

As detailed in chapter one, the problem is all the more pronounced for mothers.

And then there are the women who simply quit the industry because of the hostile environment. Much like the mothers who appeared to be "opting out" of careers because the Maternal Wall bias they faced was so great, these women are (mostly) silently opting out of tech, and the increased "brogrammer" culture of the Uber, Snapchat, Y Combinator world is making it worse.

One of the most absurd examples of this culture was detailed by a Stanford-educated, best-selling technical author and former Uber engineer named Susan Fowler. The company had promised to get leather jackets for everyone in her organization, measured them, and placed the order. Then one day, the six women in the group were told they weren't getting the jackets because "there were not enough women in the organization to justify placing an order." Seriously—this from a company that has raised nearly $9 billion in venture capital.

"I replied and said that I was sure Uber could find room in their budget to buy leather jackets for the, what, *six women* if it could afford to buy them for *over a hundred and twenty men*," Fowler wrote in a 2017 tell-all blog post about Uber's toxic culture. "The director replied back, saying that if we women really wanted equality, then we should realize we were getting equality by not getting the leather jackets. He said that because there were so many men in the org, they had gotten a significant discount on the men's jackets but not on the women's jackets, and it wouldn't be equal or fair, he argued, to give the women leather jackets that cost a little more than the men's jackets."

This is a company that hired Beyoncé to play at a Las Vegas staff party.

A researcher named Kieran Snyder interviewed more than seven hundred women who left the tech industry after an average of seven years. She found almost all of them said they enjoyed their actual work but couldn't stomach the "discriminatory environments."

A study by Nadya Fouad, funded by the National Science Foundation, surveyed some 5,300 women with engineering degrees over the last half century and discovered that 38 percent of them weren't actually working as engineers. "It's the climate, stupid!" she said in her summary of her findings. "This is a huge, unnecessary, and expensive loss of talent in a field facing a supposed talent shortage," wrote a (then) pregnant engineer named Rachel Thomas about this problem.

Women getting run out of tech matters, because it's where

so much of the wealth creation and opportunity in the economy is right now. And it purports to be more of a meritocracy. So if it's not simply a case of needing more women to enter the tech funnel, what gives? Is the tech industry just full of a ton of sexist bigots?

Some, sure. Trust me, I know them. But the far more pervasive problem is one of unconscious bias and an overreliance on pattern recognition. VCs tend to rely on a gut feeling about an entrepreneur because they frequently don't have a business or product yet to evaluate, or in many cases, even a track record to look at. And when you don't have written-out, quantifiable qualifications to hire based on, bias creeps in.

There is plenty of evidence that unconscious bias exists. In her Medium post on why women quit technology companies, Thomas collected a whole laundry list of them:

- A study by Harvard Business School, Wharton, and MIT Sloan found that investors preferred the exact same entrepreneurial pitches when they were delivered in a male voice versus a female voice by a rate of 68 percent to 32 percent. They were considered "more persuasive, logical, and fact-based."
- A study by Yale found that science faculty at six major universities rated lab manager applicants as "significantly more competent" when they were randomly assigned a male name. They were also offered a higher starting salary than identical applications that had female names on them.
- Harvard and Carnegie Mellon University studied the reactions to men and women reading from the same script asking for higher salaries. Guess what? The women

were rated as "more difficult to work with and less nice" while the men were not perceived negatively at all.

These are just a few examples from a massive canon of research out there that proves the pervasiveness of unconscious bias women face, mothers or not.

The question isn't whether this is "a thing." The question is what white male gatekeepers of an industry do when they are confronted with this research.

Top venture capital firm Greylock, for one, required that every partner go through unconscious-bias training to figure out tools for combating something they may not have realized they were doing. And then there was the reaction of a VC named John Greathouse of Rincon Ventures. Greathouse penned a 2016 *Wall Street Journal* op-ed that cited some of those same studies and used them to argue that women seeking funding should simply obscure the fact that they are women, using initials in any pitch documents or social media profiles and certainly not posting any photos.

That's right: Greylock's male partners took the stance that *they* should change. Greathouse took the stance that *women* should simply adjust to the reality of the patriarchy instead. (He apologized belatedly after a massive outcry.)

These are extremes, but in my experience most powerful men in the Valley fall into one camp or the other: The women should change to adjust to the world, or the world should change to include women. If I were starting my career or company over, I'd ask questions of prospective employers to probe which camp they are really in.

Of course, there's another way to combat this: Change the pattern.

9

"We Need a Sheryl"

MOST OF THE CULTURAL WEIRDNESS of Silicon Valley is explained by a single stat: 95 percent of the money made here comes from just 5 percent of the deals. Simply doubling your investors' money in a few years means nothing to VCs, because the gains have to make up for all the losses or the whole concept of backing something that is just an idea falls apart.

No matter how many women build successful companies that make investors money, the industry will still lionize and obsessively try to pattern match the few people who built those rare "super unicorns" worth $100 billion or more. If we're going to change the pattern, a $100 million company, even a $1 billion company doesn't really do it. Mike Maples of Floodgate lamented this fact to me when he complained that so many women founded ecommerce companies, because—aside from eBay and Amazon—ecommerce rarely yields the largest companies. You can count on one hand the US ecommerce companies that have sold for north of $1 billion since the dot-com bust.

As the pattern matchers will tell you, you need the "female Mark Zuckerberg" to change the unconscious bias that pervades this industry. As far as I can see, she isn't on the horizon, but hopefully that changes by the time you read this.

In the meantime, women in the Valley have Sheryl Sandberg.

In the wake of Sandberg's public profile at Facebook, and Facebook's staggering run as a publicly traded company, a new pattern has emerged in the Valley at some of the most promising pre-IPO companies. Suddenly, a string of them have all hired strong female number two executives.

Of the companies worth north of $10 billion, there is Airbnb's Belinda Johnson; there is Gwynne Shotwell of SpaceX; there is Marne Levine, COO of Instagram; and there is Sarah Friar of Square. Of the "mere" unicorns, there is Claire Johnson, the COO of payments-company Stripe. And at the still high-profile companies worth less than $1 billion, there are even more examples, like Zeena Freeman of Shyp, Kristin Schaefer of Postmates, and Stacy Brown-Philpot who was number two before she took over as CEO of TaskRabbit.

Unlike Sandberg, these women are almost never written about. In fact, the trend itself has been little written about. But once you start to notice it, you see number two women suddenly popping up all over Silicon Valley.

The reason? It isn't all those diversity efforts. It's pattern recognition: The most high-profile, successful number two executive in Silicon Valley just so happens to be a woman.

In that same depressing LinkedIn survey that revealed so many of the biases of white men in the industry, Sandberg was a rare woman who got their respect. Ninety-two percent of the respondents picked a man as the leader they admired most, with Elon Musk, Steve Jobs, Bill Gates, Jeff Bezos, and Mark Zuckerberg ranking the highest, in that order. Sandberg was the only woman chosen by more than 1 percent of respondents.

Sandberg's impact on pattern matchers has been so massive for a few reasons.

First, she doesn't fall into the usual traps of other top female executives. She isn't running a company that's oriented primarily towards women, like Sheila Marcelo of Care.com. Facebook isn't in a little-talked-about field, like Lynn Jurich's Sunrun. Nor is she running a troubled Silicon Valley company, like Marissa Mayer. Or an aging enterprise giant like Safra Catz of Oracle or Ginni Rometty of IBM.

It helps that Facebook was *the* super unicorn of its era. A Sheryl at Twitter or LinkedIn wouldn't have had the same cultural impact.

But Sandberg stands out so much not just because Facebook has been so high profile and so successful. It's also that she's done something I've seen very few women at her level do in Silicon Valley: She has stood up, demanded, and received credit for her contributions to her company, and she has done so while acknowledging and celebrating that she is a woman and a mother. She used Facebook's ascendancy to build her personal brand, and that brand wasn't "cool dude," nor was it Marissa Mayer's brainy glam gal. It was as close as a Silicon Valley leader has come to mama bear, arms linked, feminist. (Although critics say Sandberg is a reluctant radical.)

Sandberg routinely brings women of Silicon Valley together at her home to have dinner and to interact with various entertainment, technology, and government leaders. While a lot of powerful women are on her list, a lot of not-so-powerful women are on it, too. Sandberg is hard on women she mentors, but she also seems to genuinely care about lifting them up.

Kim Scott, who has since started a management software company called Radical Candor, tells the story of when she had just joined Google, reporting to Sandberg. She gave a presentation to the senior management about how AdSense was doing. (Spoiler: great!) Scott thought the meeting went well, because they were impressed by the results and asked what resources she needed to keep going. But Sandberg went on a walk with her afterwards and noted Scott had said "um" a lot. Sandberg asked if this was nerves and even suggested that Google could get Scott a speech coach. Kim kept waving the criticism off. Finally, Sheryl was blunt: "You know, Kim, I can tell I'm not really getting through to you. I'm going to have to be clearer here. When you say 'um' every third word, it makes you sound stupid."

Wow. There are a lot of ways to take that. But Scott tells this story as an example of effective management. Sandberg was honest—painfully so—about something she worried would hold Scott back that could easily be fixed. She could be so honest because Scott knew she cared about her. "Caring personally makes it much easier to do the next thing you have to do as a good boss, which is being willing to piss people off," she says.

That is Sheryl. That is also a very maternal approach to management: loving, but firm. At her dinners, she keeps plying you with food, with the disclaimer, "I'm a Jewish mother!"

Sandberg brilliantly understands the appeal of vulnerability in a way that chiseled women like Meg Whitman and Carly Fiorina never did. And because she came a generation later, she could build on their successes. She had more freedom to be vulnerable. I first met Sandberg backstage at an event just after she was named COO of Facebook. She told me that she was wearing jeans not just because it was kinda what you did at Facebook, but because she could finally fit into her pre-baby jeans again.

It's effective. Sandberg shouldn't be relatable—with her house so clean that children don't seem to live in it, her billionaire net worth, and her impeccably crafted, not-a-hair-out-of-place image—but she is.

When Sandberg's husband Dave Goldberg suddenly and tragically died, she shared her grief openly on Facebook. She even admitted months later that her life as a single mother convinced her that some of the critics of her bestseller, *Lean In*, were right. She hadn't considered or been aware of how much harder things are for single moms.

In being able to be so vulnerable, in being unafraid of the stigmas of being a woman, Sandberg comes across likable, competent, and confident. Those are three boxes that Mayer, Fiorina, Whitman, and so many senior women in the Valley have failed to check.

Should the rumors that Sandberg wants a future in politics ever come true, she will excel. She has an uncanny ability to seem just like you, but also incredibly intimidating. As much as she presents as a girlfriend who has struggled with all the same things you've struggled with, I'm always nervous talking to her. You may relate to her words, but you are also aware of how powerful she is and are never quite sure where you really stand with her.

I don't necessarily mean that as a knock on her as much as a clarification that for all her refreshing ability to present herself as a woman, she is also intimidating and commands respect. No one views Sandberg as a pushover. As far as I can tell from personal experience and what I've heard from those close to her, she manages to be neither a hammer nor a nail.

That she has played such a public role as a major architect of Facebook's success, and that Facebook is on the short list of companies that could one day achieve a $1 trillion valuation, has revolutionized how people in the tech world think of women's potential . . . and in particular, of mothers' potential. She has owned her maternity as a way of appearing vulnerable and tough at once.

I'm a Jewish mother!

And, that's . . . mostly good.

Many people in tech have looked at Facebook, looked at their own young, pattern-matched, inexperienced founder, and told recruiters, "We need a Sheryl." I've heard *those exact words* out of founders' and VCs' mouths repeatedly.

"We need to find *a Sheryl*."

"What he really needs is *a Sheryl*."

"We think this could be *our Sheryl*."

Before Facebook went public, people used to say, "We need an Eric Schmidt," the so-called grown-up brought in to be CEO of Google before its IPO. That the proper noun for *that* person every tech company needs to recruit is now a woman's name is not an insignificant change.

And hence, a new pattern has emerged: the rise of female number twos at powerful and up-and-coming companies all suddenly at the same time. This new pattern puts women in the second most powerful position inside some of the largest companies in tech and the startups that aspire to become the largest companies in tech.

To be clear, this is progress. And any progress is good. Several women I've spoken to about this trend, like Cloudflare's cofounder Michelle Zatlyn, hope that more women serving as COO of high-profile, valuable companies will only prep a next generation of senior women who can be tapped to serve on boards, run major *Fortune* 500 companies, or become partners at top venture firms. "People have long careers," she says. "Maybe in their next role they will be CEO."

Not only that, but as the number two executive, a woman can have a huge impact on diversity within a company. Despite the clichéd image of the "catty woman" who keeps other women down, several studies have shown that more women in positions of power yield more opportunities for women. Firms that have a single female founder are twice as likely to back women; large company boards with at least three female members are more likely to tap women for C-level appointments.

Sandberg and her writing partner, Adam Grant, have even taken on the myth of the "catty woman," writing in the *New York Times* that there is no evidence girls or women are any meaner than men; rather, there's the expectation of how they *should* act. "Women are just expected to be nicer. We stereotype men as aggressive and women as kind. When women violate those stereotypes, we judge them harshly. 'A man has to be Joe McCarthy to be called ruthless,' Marlo Thomas once lamented. 'All a woman has to do is put you on hold,'" they write.

Frequently, token women in very male-dominated environments may dig in and defend their turf, or worry that advocating for another woman will make them look bad. If you are one of those women who has experienced a "queen bee," you didn't dream it. It's just that the behavior isn't inherently female. "It's a natural way we react to discrimination when we belong to a non-dominant group," write Grant and Sandberg.

So, the more women in companies and the more powerful those women are, the less you see the "catty woman" behavior. A great example is Google, which became one of the best places for women to build a career in tech, almost by accident.

Early hires like Marissa Mayer and Susan Wojcicki set a tone for female inclusion and even helped craft feminist policies at what could have easily emerged to be a bro company started by two white Stanford guys.

Katie Stanton worked at Google for six years and had only female bosses. That was meaningful because she had three kids under three at the time. "I remember when I did my phone interview for Google, I was pumping and hiding from my three kids in a closet," she told me. "I remember trying to sound as articulate as possible, and for some reason, I got hired. I remember talking to [my boss Joan Braddi] and saying, 'I really want this job, but I have to leave at five p.m. every day because I have three kids under three and I need to pick them up from day care.' I remember her saying, 'Of course you do, and you should do that.' I remember that gave me so much relief and empowerment."

It's not a surprise that the majority of the female number twos listed earlier in this chapter spent part of their careers at Google.

It's not that Google's diversity numbers are so much better than the industry's; it's that the women there were so senior. There is a big difference between having a female C-level officer in your company as the head of marketing or HR and having one who is the COO of the entire company.

Women need new patterns every bit as much as the men controlling boards and capital do.

There is also the role model factor in Sandberg being so high profile—as opposed to many of the number twos in Silicon Valley who have benefited from her patterns. Women are almost four times more likely than men to fear they won't succeed in their careers simply because of their gender, according to a study by McKinsey and LeanIn.Org. "Pattern matching goes in both directions," says Scott, who's coached or worked with many of these women. "A lot of women are also thinking, 'Oh, I should go be a COO.'"

That's all the more reason that the women I listed previously—number twos at Airbnb, Stripe, Instagram, and other major companies—need to stand up and claim credit and demand attention as Sandberg did. They need to accept interview requests even if they're annoyed it's because of their gender. They need to speak at industry conferences. To hire ghostwriters to pen their feminist manifestos. To write their own op-eds for the *Times*. Is paying it forward so hard?

So yes, *the trend is good.* And yet . . . I couldn't help but notice that Eric Schmidt was the CEO, and Sandberg was a COO. She was effectively brought in to do the same thing at Facebook that Schmidt did at Google, but she didn't get the title. As I talked to various founders and VCs about the phenomenal "Sheryls" they'd hired, a few commented that they were able to get a higher caliber of talent for a number two position because of the industry's unconscious biases against women. It was almost described as . . . a management "hack."

Women in tech were benefiting from Sandberg being the second most powerful person at one of the most powerful companies in the world. But was the fact that she wasn't a founder or CEO also putting them in a sort of high-class executive ghetto? Multiple people I spoke to said they simply believed that women were better at keeping order than at being the visionaries. I mean, it's a step up from barefoot and pregnant, but . . .

I called Kim Scott late one night, once we'd both gotten our kids to bed, to get her thoughts about this. She'd worked closely with Sheryl and knew many of these ascendant number two women, and as a CEO coach to companies like Twitter, Dropbox, and Stripe, she was involved in a lot of these "Get me a Sheryl!" conversations. Plus, she's the kind of person who holds lectures on misogyny in her home on a Friday night. If anyone could be both informed and enraged, it was Kim.

Instead, she groaned at me, pointing out how we'd never make progress if women climbing up a rung was still seen as something to be unhappy about. "As soon as something good happens, we get these kinds of narratives," she said. "Let's celebrate it and not be discouraged." I get it. It's like bitching that Hillary Clinton "only" won the popular vote by millions of votes. There is victory in a woman coming that close. Extra cracks in the ceiling, blah blah.

Others noted that COO was simply the right role for many of these women in particular. They weren't necessarily the product-oriented visionaries; rather, they were people who excelled at operations, the precision of running large organizations and building formidable sales teams. The one and only time the elusive Safra Catz spoke to me, she told me how worthless she found media features and profiles on Oracle, saying she was just all about the numbers.

While they most likely have had to work much harder to get where they are, there is no evidence that any of these women wanted to be CEOs or founders and were denied that opportunity. Scott for one has turned down roles like these at large companies and has started her own company instead.

And certainly at the public company level, being an excellent operator doesn't disqualify you from becoming a CEO. Catz is now the co-CEO of Oracle, while other "visionary" men once deemed Larry Ellison's heir apparent have come and gone. Tim Cook was a "Sheryl" of sorts to Steve Jobs, and he succeeded him. Sandberg is certainly on the very short list of who would step in immediately to run Facebook should Mark Zuckerberg get hit by a bus. To Kim's point, there is a difference between any "C-level female exec" and a female number two.

OK. I grant all those points.

And yet, I'm skeptical it's as much progress as a lot of women hope.

Consider the career of Renée James. She scrapped her way up from product manager to president of Intel. She was considered one of the most powerful women in business. She was so accomplished that she was one of two internal candidates being considered to become the next CEO of Intel once Paul Otellini retired. In fact, she and the other candidate, Brian Krzanich, argued they should be co-CEOs.

The board didn't listen, awarding the job solely to Krzanich instead. James quit two years later. (Natch.) Unlike almost any man with those kinds of accomplishments, James struggled to find a CEO job, according to a *Fortune* cover story on the mixed record of women who had appeared on its Most Powerful Women list over the years. "I was president of a very big company, bigger than most companies out there," James told *Fortune*. "But still people say, 'She would be a first-time CEO.' You know how many people have said that? It's insane."

James wound up taking an "operating executive" role at the Carlyle Group's telecom, media, and technology practice instead. As *Fortune* notes, it's the kind of role that executives "typically sign on for when they're on the downslope of their career."

This is not unique, reports *Fortune*. One hundred and twenty-six women fell off their list between 2000 and 2015 for a variety of reasons. "Just about 13% of the women once on our list, all of whom built incredible careers at large corporations and are of prime working age, had another major role at a big public company."

Of the fifty-plus women who managed to become a CEO of a *Fortune* 500 company, only two ever became a CEO of a *Fortune* 500 company again.

Perhaps it shouldn't surprise us that the most respected woman in tech isn't even a CEO. Even when women break the ceiling, it seems to rematerialize on top of them later. *These are the lucky ones.*

A common fate is Marissa Mayer's. As CEO of Yahoo, to get the top job, Mayer had to succumb to something Michelle Ryan and Alex Haslam of England's University of Exeter call the "glass cliff." Oh, top women can get CEO jobs all right, but they are at companies in crisis. Comparable male candidates have more options, so companies—like, say, Yahoo—can get a better-quality CEO when they hire a woman.

Utah State University studied all the *Fortune* 500 female CEOs and found that 42 percent of them were appointed while their companies were in crisis. That compares to 22 percent of male appointments during the same time. It gets worse: Only 13 percent of those women also got the title of chairman of the board, compared to 50 percent of men. That gives them less power and influence, and it also conveys that fact to the world, notes that same *Fortune* story.

PricewaterhouseCoopers published another study showing that 38 percent of female CEOs were forced out of their jobs over a ten-year period compared to just 27 percent of male CEOs. And a study from Arizona State's W. P. Carey School of Business shows that female CEOs have a 27 percent chance of fighting with activist shareholders, who use a bully pulpit to aggressively push for change in a public company. Men have a less than 1 percent chance of it.

These women are offered worse jobs at companies in crisis, given less power to turn them around, and given a shorter time to show improvement, and their gender means they'll be bigger targets for activists.

From the *Fortune* piece:

> *When they are not able to turn their firm around, it's a confirmation bias: They really don't have what it takes. They couldn't cut it. As former Intel president James puts it, "You're a pioneer. You either get to the promised land or you die."*

This next part is going to shock you: Study after study shows that women are *less interested* in becoming CEOs than men. According to McKinsey and LeanIn.Org, only 40 percent of women are interested in being CEOs, versus 56 percent of men, with both mothers and non-mothers saying they "don't want the pressure." In a survey studying the ad industry, only 11 percent of female executives said they ever wanted the top job.

I WONDER WHY!

"Men tend to have more fragile egos than women," Kim Scott said the night she groaned at me. "The thing that causes people to pursue power is a fragile ego. The CEO role can be a shitty job. I'm not sure a lot of women feel they need it."

In some cases, maybe. But the idea that women simply don't want to be CEOs fails to take into account what women have watched happen to the careers of Google's two female superstars, the more high-profile Mayer who became a CEO and then-lesser-known Sandberg who won much more acclaim as a COO. Which trajectory would you pick? These women may be making a choice, yes, but it's a choice based on the realities of institutionalized sexism. The observation that women don't tend to make "visionary product leaders" is a lot like the one that they don't excel in math and science. It may be based on empirical evidence, but it's also the result of a world that doesn't expect them to.

So, yeah, we can all wish the most admired woman in tech was a CEO and not a COO. But watching what Mayer put up with, can you blame Sandberg for the path she's taken?

I am thrilled that so many women are getting *closer* to the CEO office, becoming the second most powerful executives at some of the largest and most exciting tech companies in Silicon Valley. But all that anecdotal progress still hasn't increased the percentage of tech companies that have a woman in the C-suite or on the board level. And I'm not at all convinced it means a surge in powerful female CEOs is inevitable in a few years as a result.

10

"Are You Having Fun?"

BY THE TIME EVIE WAS six months old, I was well aware of everything at Pando that was not in any way working. Despite having raised $2.5 million, we were low on cash—again—with no real hope of becoming profitable. The entire time running this company, I'd been nursing or pregnant. I was hustling to bring in enough cash—through investors or sales or a miracle—to support a dozen-person newsroom. Some days it felt as though my entire world was living off me; literally my kids, as I was still nursing Evie; and the company figuratively, as I was calling in every favor and contact I'd amassed in my professional life to keep the business running. I felt as if I were groggily waking up each morning, pouring myself some coffee, and then just opening up my veins and draining them out for everyone to share.

On top of that, it wasn't working. During that time, people in the industry would ask if I was "having fun."

Are you fucking kidding me? Not at all. This was a lot of things—rewarding that I was hiring and mentoring talented, young, underappreciated reporters, a rush when we closed a six-figure ad deal, hilarious when we were name-dropped on HBO's *Silicon Valley* after just eighteen months of existence, an adrenaline kick like an angry donkey when we broke a major story. But those things weren't "fun." They were so much more beyond fun. I felt as though my skin was vibrating.

And then there was all the shit, which felt personal and horrible and public and embarrassing and constantly, constantly humbling.

That was the company. Learning to be a mother wasn't exactly "fun" either. The straight-to-the-bloodstream ecstatic love that I felt holding my babies was unlike anything I'd experienced. But there were nights I'd look at the clock and think, "How the fuck am I going to entertain Eli for two more hours before bedtime?" or "Please Evie, GTFTS." Especially since more than half the time, I was alone with them.

My life was a drug-free, totally legal version of a Scorsese movie. Insane queen-of-the-world highs, followed a moment later by sobbing-alone-in-my-room lows. You know how only a tiny part of the light spectrum is visible with the naked eye? It's like that was the emotional range I lived in before my kids and my company. Eli, Pando, and Evie had subsequently exploded those barriers, and I was now living in the fringes of the emotional light spectrum that I didn't even know existed before. That's not where "fun" exists. "Fun" is a slumber party. "Fun" is a day at Disneyland. "Fun" is your first college party.

"No, this isn't fun," I'd snap at people. "And it better fucking work, because I'm never starting another company again."*

---

* A few months after filing this, I did start another company. Just like having more kids, we forget the pain and do it all again.

Not that I had the luxury of wallowing. We were fucked in a quick matter of months if I didn't figure something out.

There was one silver lining: Things were way worse at Paul's investigative journalism company, NSFWCORP.

The only thing that had kept us in the black was a routine every-six-weeks ass kicking by Andrew in our board meetings. (Fuck you, Andrew.) But Paul had raised about one-fifth of the money we had. And he paid his staff more. And he had no board to kick his ass every six weeks and keep him in business. (Thank you, Andrew.) So I was essentially Paul's volunteer Andrew.

We spoke daily, and I'd—obnoxiously—grill him on his burn rate and lecture him about the dangers of running a business based on a best-case scenario. I'd expose his problems the way Andrew did with mine. I was a jerk. But would it have been kinder to hold my tongue and watch it happen? He was my best friend.

Finally, in October of 2013, it was clear: We were going to have to raise more money. Again. This was not going to be easy. Fortunately, a new board member and adviser, Mike Tatum, had an idea. Tatum was also from Tennessee, and he suggested I raise money from a syndicate of Southern investors. Nashville is hardly an international center of venture capital, but this idea was plausible. For one, Southern investors didn't always get invited into deals with investors like ours. For another, we'd decided we were going to do our big annual event in Nashville, so there was a legitimate business advantage to the partnership. Also, as Pando was seeking to become more mainstream as a publication, our investor base should reflect that. Tatum did a lot of heavy lifting to introduce me to Southern investors, including a guy called Vic Gatto, who wanted to do the deal but was leaving his firm and between funds. Good news/bad news.

About this time, I had to go to Dublin. Things that would sound fun any other time seem like torture when you have a one-year-old, a nursing baby, and a company on the ropes. One such thing is an annual excuse to go to Ireland wrapped up in a conference called "F.ounders." Yep, it had a period in its name. In case you didn't think "Yahoo!" was obnoxious enough Silicon Valley punctuational branding. The idea was that you go to Dublin with a bunch of other senior-level folks, drink a lot, and meet Bono, take a selfie with him sporting a peace sign and a smug grin, pick the right Instagram filter, and call it work.

Everyone I knew raved about this event. I'd been invited for a few years but declined. The first time, I had just given birth to Eli, and the second time, I had just started Pando. Also, I typically go to two conferences a year at most. Conferences are for the young, childless, and unconnected who can weather the debilitating hangovers that come from drinking with competitors and colleagues until 3:00 a.m. I was no longer any of these things. I'd done my time. But this year, the organizer wrote and said that few people had turned down three invites and that I had no excuse. Another investor pressured me to go for networking purposes. I was after all raising money and building an ad business.

Fine.

The worst part was that it was over Halloween, and Halloween was Eli's absolute favorite day of the year. He was going to be Cookie Monster that year. It was Evie's first Halloween, and she was going to be a pumpkin. This was Eli's idea. Eli loved pumpkins so much he took them in the bath with him and to bed with him during the months leading up to Halloween.

There were going to be pumpkins everywhere, including wrapped around his baby sister. And I was going to miss it to hang out with Bono and drink with VCs.

Geoff and my relationship was strained at the time. He insisted that if I wasn't going to be in San Francisco, he should be able to spend Eli's favorite day with him and baby Evie. So Megan and the kids picked up for Vegas, and I took off for Europe. This was harder than when I left for China when Eli was six weeks old. The older they got, the harder leaving was.

Paul happened to be in London at the time for his mother's sixtieth birthday. Andrew and I had discussed a few times whether buying NSFWCORP made sense. They had a loyal audience, way better technology, and a lot of strengths we lacked. But it was never quite right. I knew—by virtue of being Paul's unofficial "Andrew"—NSFWCORP was close to the end.

Maybe now?

I told Paul he should meet me in Dublin to discuss. As his friend, I was concerned. As Pando's CEO, I knew it was the perfect time to pounce.

My God, that was a horrible trip. I met many amazing people I've stayed close with today. I laughed so much some nights that I got cramps in my sides. Dublin is a great city. But I was racing between outings—at say, the Guinness Storehouse—to rush back to my hotel and pump milk, write, and continue to run the company. I was devastated over the whole Halloween thing. Poor Evie's costume, which I'd ordered from Amazon, never arrived, and she just hung out as Evie. How did no other adult solve that problem, particularly in Las Vegas . . . a city where people roam the streets in costumes every day of the year? And between all this, Paul and I entered an incredibly brass-knuckled negotiation for Pando buying NSFWCORP.

I shelved any feelings I had as his best friend and was absolutely ruthless in our negotiations. I didn't have much choice.

That was my job as the CEO, and we were a few months away from life support ourselves. This new fundraising effort was far from a sure thing, and buying this company would demonstrably add to our burn rate. My board and the world knew he was my best friend. I did him no favors by treating him any differently than I'd treat anyone else in this situation.

By the time we left Dublin, we had the basics of a deal. I handed the nitty-gritty off to Andrew, who was an even bigger asshole about it all than I could have been. (Fuck you, Andrew/ Thank you, Andrew.)

Paul and I were both flying "home" to Vegas. Paul still lived there; Geoff and Megan and the kids were still there post-Halloween. In fact, we'd combined apartments to save costs, since Geoff was only there two weeks a month, and the kids and I were almost never there anymore.

I was excited to see the kids again and replace a loathsome breast pump with my beautiful baby girl. But things were not at all going well in my marriage. In the latter days of my pregnancy with Evie, Geoff would be in Vegas for two weeks or more, then taking more time to finish his MFA and travel for that. Between the stress of the company, a toddler, and a pregnancy, I was losing it.

But the kids and me spending more time in Vegas wasn't the answer either. My parenting philosophy with an energetic boy was, "We're getting out of the house before you tear it down!" But it was too hot for Eli to play outside, and that made my working from the apartment pretty much impossible. And Evie absolutely hated the heat. I was uprooting all of us—taking Eli out of his swimming and Gymboree classes, taking Megan away from her boyfriend and dogs, and taking myself away from where Pando needed to be based—and for what? We didn't see

Geoff much when we were there. He'd come in for dinner and bath time with the kids and then go out again.

We seemed to disagree about everything. He'd talk about spending great "quality time" with Eli (and later Evie) before bedtime, as if he were an uncle. Night after night, Megan and I would sit on the couch watching *Big Brother* or whatever other reality show was in rotation.

Two houses for a family of four plus the flights and travel and paying Megan a full twenty-four-hour rate was costing us a ton of money, and things seemed to be getting worse in our marriage as a result.

After a point, I looked around at me, Megan, the *Big Brother* contestants on-screen, and I wondered, "Why are we all *here*? We could be doing this in San Francisco for less money."*

One night back in San Francisco just after Evie was born, Geoff and I had a huge fight. It was nine thirty, Eli was asleep (bless him), and barely a-few-weeks-old Evie was screaming. I strapped her onto me, and I told Geoff I was going on a walk to give her some air. Our night nurse, Anna, who'd seen us through those crazy first weeks with both kids was arriving at ten.

I grabbed my house keys, swaying back and forth in that weird-but-soothing way all parents do, trying to lull Evie back to sleep. I said in my most controlled voice possible, "I am going on a walk with Evie. When Anna gets here, you and I are leaving this house. We are getting far away from here and getting a drink. And we are going to figure out what we are doing about this marriage."

Walking around my neighborhood, I was angry and crying. I was so sad Evie was having to be there for all this, but

---

* I might be the first person to utter those words.

I was also comforted I had Evie with me. I could feel the love permeating the Ergobaby carrier and oozing onto my chest, even as my heart was breaking on the inside. Was the trauma of your parents' impending divorce more or less traumatic to a baby's brain development than getting kidnapped in utero in Nigeria?

I couldn't believe how quickly it had gone from seemingly perfect to completely falling apart. Anna saw Geoff and me in our most fragile moments of 2:00 a.m. "OMFG!" frazzled parenting with Eli and always told other night nurses that we were "disgustingly" cute. That Geoff was so attentive to me. That we were one of the only couples she'd ever worked for who would never split up.

Clearly, it was a very different vibe in our house this time around, just eighteen months later. When 10:00 p.m. came, I handed Evie over to Anna, and Geoff and I went to a local dive bar and ordered two shots of Jägermeister and a Miller High Life to split. I gave Geoff three choices: "We are either going to therapy, getting separated, or getting divorced because this is getting worse every day, and I'm not raising my kids in this environment." He agreed with my diagnosis of things but wouldn't accept any of the options.

It only occurs to me now how similar that decision to confront Geoff with the reality of the situation was to my debate over whether or not to return to TechCrunch and my angst over firing Arrington. I knew what the right thing to do was. But I simply didn't know if I could.

Geoff and I spent the holidays apart that year, the kids with me in Memphis. I didn't know what was going to happen. I committed to doing couples therapy, and we did it for some nine months. It was incredibly valuable for getting past the gigantic gulf of mutual resentment that had grown between us over the last year or so and finding a way to communicate again.

But at one point, my therapist asked why I was doing this. I said I wanted to be able to look my kids in the eyes if they ever asked and to tell them honestly that I tried absolutely everything to keep their family together. She noted that was not the same thing as actually *wanting* to save my marriage. She was a good therapist.

I really struggled during that time with one of the core existential motherhood dilemmas: Everyone knows you have to take care of yourself first to be a great mother. But living that—if it means depriving your children of something as big as their parents staying together—is another matter. I simply didn't know where the line was between being too selfish or too selfless.

I would do anything for my kids. But what did that actually mean?

One night, I got my answer. I was rocking Eli before bed. We have an incredibly elaborate pre-bedtime routine called "Eli (or Evie) Rock You" that now includes books, songs, an utterly unrelaxing Sonos playlist of teen pop where I sing "Shake It Off" followed by "Party in the USA" and then leave and burst back in the room on cue for certain segments of "Bang Bang" before Eli finally falls asleep to Kesha. At times, the routine has included whole scenes from *Frozen*, too. By the time you read this, it may well include a hip-hop dance routine.

Even when I had a full-time nanny, I always hogged the privilege of rocking Eli and Evie. I noticed early on: Whoever rocked Eli the night before got the most hugs from Eli the next day. *Good night, Megan! Sorry, Daddy!* Eli and Evie hugs were like seeing the face of God in the hell that was my fall of 2013. I grew weary of that *Frozen* scene until the day Eli never wanted to do it again. Since then, I've thrown my heart and soul into every performance of "Shake It Off" as if I'm Lin-Manuel Miranda on his last night of *Hamilton*. There are a finite number of times he'll want to hear it. I never know what night might be my swan song.

This one night, there was something about the way I was hugging Eli as I rocked him. I realized it was . . . desperate. Clinging. Almost parasitic. I realized that Eli and Evie had become the sum total of my emotional and physical connection with any human being. I was somehow forcing him and Evie into the emotional role my husband should have filled. No child should have the pressure of being his or her mother's sole source of emotional stability and support.

"Holy shit," I thought all at once in that moment clinging to my son. It hit me: What it meant to take care of yourself before you could adequately take care of your children. That cliché suddenly became very real. I was thinking I was staying in this marriage for them, but I suddenly saw that if I stayed in this marriage, I was going to do irreparable damage to them.

I had to find a way to be happy on my own in order to be there for them. I couldn't just live for them. I couldn't just live for Pando either. I had to find a way to live for me. Not capital letters SARAH LACY (™) and not Eli and Evie's mom. Me. Did that person even still exist anymore?

"We have to get divorced," I thought right then in Eli's room as he drifted off to sleep in my lap.

11

Wings, Talons, Fangs

UP TO NOW, YOU MIGHT be with me. Yes, you may be thinking, the patriarchy has poisoned our culture, which seduces men into thinking they have the moral responsibility to be in charge and saddles women with a sense of guilt every time they try to make changes to those systems.

Maybe I've convinced you that your preconceived notions about the disability of motherhood are bullshit, given how much motherhood makes you more productive, creative, and empathetic and increases your stamina.

I've hopefully at least made the case that all the data alone won't change anything. We're awash in studies showing conclusively more gender equality and diversity in the economy makes us all richer. And yet, the numbers aren't changing. Turns out white men won't just give up power because you show them a series of charts and studies.

If we want things to change we have to get more aggressive than just showing people data. We have to call out sexism and misogyny when we see it. We have to blow the whistle when we experience it. Take to the streets, go on strike, vote with our feet and our wallets. And we have to keep doing that no matter how much the patriarchy—and the patriarchy's little voices in our heads—keeps telling us we're being a buzzkill or oversensitive or a troublemaker.

But be prepared: The patriarchy does not like to be called out. On a drizzly London night in November 2014, I was served notice by BuzzFeed editor Ben Smith that Uber, the largest and most misogynistic private company in tech, had reportedly just put a $1 million price tag on shutting me up. Some $18 billion then (now close to $70 billion) was riding on Uber's continued success, and almost no one had been able to sell a share of stock yet because the company had not gone public.

From about 2012 on, Pando had been one of the lone critical voices amid a global business press that was enamored with Uber. There was the company's hypocrisy: Its stated libertarian, disruptive stance on laws when they weren't convenient, but its willingness to outspend other industries in lobbyists and forge its own backroom deals when it needed to. There was the company's mixed record on safety and background checks. One of our reporters walked down to San Francisco's courthouse and pulled a criminal record on a driver accused of assault after Uber swore up and down their background checks would have absolutely caught any criminal record.

But the thing that convinced me to delete the app in 2014 was a disturbing pattern of sexism and misogyny coming out of the company. When we reported that story on passengers getting assaulted in Ubers, executives told our reporter that one of the women attacked was drunk and "dressed provocatively." This from the company that told regulators it should get special treatment because it was helping women get home safely if they'd been drinking. It was the defense of Brock Turner and so many other college rapists all over again.

Then there was the "Rides of Glory" blog post where the company bragged about tracking the aggregate one-night stands of its user base by looking at ride data. Then there was the *GQ* interview where Uber's CEO Travis Kalanick referred to his ability to get women on demand as "Boob-er." Finally, there was a promotion for Uber in Lyon, France, where female drivers were likened to hookers.

I don't know what triggered it exactly. Maybe it was having a daughter. Maybe it was finally being established enough that I could say what I felt without caring about retribution. Maybe it was the power I felt from becoming a mother, or maybe it was just that I was sick of decades of my own micro-indignities.

It was some combination of the world becoming way more openly misogynistic in this hypermasculine "brogrammer" wave and me becoming more radicalized, as Gloria Steinem said women do as they get older. But on this particular day when it came to this particular company at this particular point, I had just had enough.

I was never one of those reporters who thought someone running a company had to be a saint. I didn't even care so much about the company disrupting cabs. But the fundamental disrespect of women at every level of Uber scared me. Women were being told they were getting the safest ride home possible, and the company behind it was so deeply misogynistic that it would victim-shame women who got attacked in their cars instead of taking responsibility. Female drivers were being likened to hookers. And the CEO was joking to men's magazines about how awesome it was that Uber's success off those women was getting him laid.

It wasn't just those offenses. It was the fact that no one was ever fired when these things were exposed. The company didn't seem to care. And that can breed a scary culture. Company cultures are created as much by what you say and do as what you don't say and don't do. I explained in my post why I was deleting the app. I didn't care whether Uber's (never backed up) claim that it was safer than cabs was true or not. I knew from experience: Uber went after victims. It wasn't worth my safety and the safety of the women I loved, particularly when Lyft had a nearly identical product.

Like a lot of our past reporting on Uber, this story was widely picked up. We weren't hurting their downloads meaningfully or their ability to raise money, but we were hurting their brand in the Valley and their ability to hire. And talent is lifeblood in Silicon Valley. Uber finally decided there was only one way to silence me: to try to destroy my personal life and reputation by any horrific means necessary.

Being bros, they looked at me and saw what they presumed was a huge weakness—that I was a mother. In the animal kingdom, everyone knows you don't get between a mother and her young. A mother swan can break a grown man's arm with its wing if that man is threatening her cygnet. A mother squirrel will fly at the throat of a dog many times her size if he goes after her babies. There is a video on YouTube of a cuddly cottontail rabbit disemboweling a snake who crawled into her nest.

But the Uber bros had heard the lie, too.

At a New York off-the-record dinner filled with journalists, Kalanick was attempting to reboot his image in the press. It didn't help that at the other end of the table, an Uber executive named Emil Michael was detailing to Ben Smith a plan he had to silence journalists, starting with me.

From Smith's account:

Over dinner, he outlined the notion of spending "a million dollars" to hire four top opposition researchers and four journalists. That team could, he said, help Uber fight back against the press—they'd look into "your personal lives, your families," and give the media a taste of its own medicine.

Michael was particularly focused on one journalist, Sarah Lacy, the editor of the Silicon Valley website PandoDaily, a sometimes combative voice inside the industry.

... it was suggested that a plan like the one Michael floated could become a problem for Uber.

Michael responded: "Nobody would know it was us."

Michael tried to brush this off later as "blowing off steam" and "a drunken rant." Yet for a drunk man supposedly blowing off steam, he detailed to Smith a pretty precise plan. Michael had a head count and desired background experience for the team he wanted to hire. He had a budget in mind, too. And he detailed to Smith the types of things he would try to spread into the media to silence me, in particular by going after my family. He even said I should be held responsible if women who had deleted Uber got sexually assaulted in cabs.

I paced outside an Indian restaurant in London, my phone pressed to my ear, as Smith detailed all this to me and asked if I had any comment. I had spent my career pissing people off in Silicon Valley and working with other brilliant journalists who did the same. And yet, I had never heard of anyone proposing anything this evil.

I thought of Eli and Evie. Right about now they were covered in kitten and dinosaur pajamas, giggling and running through the house in a last-ditch effort to fight bedtime. Maybe they were looking up at the moon, remembering how many times I've told them I'd always be somewhere looking at the same moon even if I couldn't be there to rock them.

If this "oppo research" plan was what the executives were bragging about at a dinner with journalists, what would they do to silence me that they wouldn't brag about?

In that YouTube video of the cottontail rabbit, a *National Geographic* expert explains that the rabbit didn't disembowel the snake out of revenge for killing two of her babies. She did it because one had lived. Disemboweling the snake was the only way of ensuring he didn't come back and finish the job. It wasn't out of retaliation; it was out of the all-powerful protective love that surges through a mother's body when her children are at risk.

I had two choices when Smith published his story and seemingly every media outlet in the world was hounding me for comment. I could do what I usually did when scandal erupted around me—let my work speak for itself and wait for it to blow over. Or I could go full-on cottontail.

It was clear to me the only way Uber would never go through with this plan was if I extended the news cycle as long as possible and made it so that everyone in the world knew what they had threatened. That was the only way my family would be safe. Be so loud and so obnoxious and so omnipresent that in their war room meetings (yes, they really called their meeting room "the war room") someone would tell Michael, "She isn't worth it! Just walk away!"

I had another motivation, too. Michael had made it clear that I was only the first reporter he wanted to go after. I had also heard the smears executives had made about women getting assaulted in their cars. I wanted it on record as loudly as possible that this was how Uber treated women. I knew I had a megaphone others didn't, and I knew I was lucky that being loud and obnoxious was part of my job. I was also lucky I worked for myself, and I controlled my board. I had no boss who could tell me to stop.

Odds were the next woman this company attacked wouldn't have those luxuries. If another story like this ever came out, I wanted the victim in question to immediately get the benefit of the doubt. My maternal rage extended beyond my family to every single woman this company might target next.

So I went full-on cottontail. I did dozens of TV interviews. My story was written up in *USA Today*, the *New York Times*, the *Washington Post*. I went on the attack on social media whenever anyone would try to defend or normalize this behavior. I called out Uber's investors by name for pretending to support women in our industry and being dead silent now. Some of those were our investors, too. And I made it a story beyond just me: It was proof of the toxic, misogynist culture that had made me delete the app to begin with.

Nothing about this was fun. One of my investors sent his security team to my house as the story exploded in the first twenty-four hours and my face was everywhere as the enemy of Uber. After an initial security assessment, it was determined that armed guards would follow me and my children for two weeks. I even had to take armed guards to *Yo Gabba Gabba! Live*.

A lot of "friends" and even investors turned on me. Some of our mutual investors would not even respond to my emails. Uber's surrogates—including, not joking, the actor Ashton

Kutcher—called me a "shady journalist" and said I was "enjoying" the media attention.

I have essentially spent two years (and counting) in a macrohostile work environment when it comes to covering this company. But I have continued to report on Uber, exposing the depths of the fraud and struggles in their Chinese operation a full year before the company finally pulled out of the country completely. We were one of the first publications to raise questions about whether their core business model even worked.

Anything short of continuing to doggedly report the truth about Uber, no matter the consequences, would have been doing Michael's dirty work for him, the way guilt does the patriarchy's dirty work in women's minds. If my own fears over security, safety, and reputation self-censored me, it would have been just another version of Uber's plan working. You don't get to threaten my company, my children, my integrity, and win.

In 2016 a judge backed up my instinct that this was more than just some drunken rant of a single executive. Despite Uber's denials at the time that they would never hire covert oppo researchers to smear critics, Uber did do exactly this to a guy named Spencer Meyer, who was a plaintiff in a lawsuit against Uber, and his attorney Andrew Schmidt.

Uber hired a private investigative firm with a history of working with the CIA and launched an unethical investigation into the personal and professional lives of Meyer and Schmidt, calling people they knew and lying about who they were in order to dig up information they could use against them. Uber executives were even caught lying and trying to cover it up in court.

It was the fourth time Uber had hired the firm, according to the deposition. As shown in court documents, the Uber contact wrote via email: "Would like to keep any communication about it encrypted over chat to avoid potential discovery issues." The judge ordered that they hand over the encryption keys once he learned that Uber's own executives had lied when asked if they'd hired the firm. US District Judge Jed Rakoff said at discovery, "The court cannot help but be troubled by this whole dismal incident," adding that the tactics were possibly "criminal" in nature.

But a lot of journalists swept that scandal under the rug. It took until 2017 for my original claims of Uber's dangerous misogynistic culture to become widely vindicated. Susan Fowler, a female engineer, exposed systematic and blatant misogyny at the company, from sexual propositions by management to HR cover-ups. It was shocking that one person had experienced so much sexism in one year at a company.

When her story came out, Fowler was absolutely 100 percent believed by the press and the wider public because of Uber's well-known track record when it comes to women. And the next woman who comes forward in Silicon Valley will have even better odds of being believed, because Susan came forward. It was Susan who finally got justice. As a result of a corporate investigation she triggered, the once untouchable Emil Michael was finally forced to leave, and Kalanick was finally forced out.

It's not fun. But this is the only way this shit ever ends. One woman at a time standing up to a hostile environment, and all of us supporting her. There's a pro-woman management theory that's popular right now called "shine theory," where women are encouraged to amplify other women when they make a smart point in a meeting . . . the kind of points men typically take credit for. This is the more aggressive form of counteracting that. When a woman comes forward, you stand up and take the arrows with her. New York single mom and writer Rachel Sklar did that when Uber victim-shamed me; I did it for Susan Fowler and many others. Don't let her stand alone.

When you are working in a hostile environment, you learn quickly who your friends and enemies are. It can be a heartbreaking reveal, but you just focus on those who stand with you. When you are vindicated, don't forget the difference but also accept genuine apologies.

Immediately brush off anyone who says you (a) are being hysterical, (b) are blowing things out of proportion, (c) have a vendetta, (d) are "sooooooo obsessed" with him/them/that company. It's amazing how "you're so obsessed" is used against women in junior high if they talk too much about a boy and later when we become adults and try to hold grown men accountable.

My answers are always the same: (a/b) My family was threatened. (c) When has my reporting ever been wrong? (d) My job is to write about tech companies, and Uber is the largest startup in Valley history; writing about them consistently is my job. I don't get into a back-and-forth; I just repeat those answers over and over and over again.

You have to be a broken record in a hostile environment. Because their plan is just to wear you down eventually, even convincing you that you are the problem ("She just couldn't cut it!" "This culture isn't for everyone!" "She just wasn't a fit!"). They want to convince you that you are crazy. So document everything. Know that people are listening and change is happening even when you can't see it. Surround yourself with a support group who can verify that you aren't crazy in those weak moments when all this starts to get to you. It will. And that doesn't mean you are weak. It means you aren't like them.

Save and cherish those emails, tweets, or conversations from people who tell you how much your standing up against misogyny has mattered to them. Read them when you want to give up. Susan Fowler reached out to me at the apex of her Uber scandal, asking simply how I made it through and when it would all end. I told her the worst of it calms down in a few weeks, but sadly, it never really ends. Even when Uber is long gone, it'll be someone else we're all fighting.

My answer of how I made it through was even less helpful to her: "My kids." Hugging them at the end of a long day was the clearest evidence I had in my darkest hours that there was still good left in the world. I'd spent my life believing Silicon Valley was mostly good and that belief had gotten ripped away from me.

Looking at Susan's face, I was transported back to those days after my own Uber scandal erupted. I was shaken to my core at how mean, how wrong, how evil this whole thing was. Particularly because I wasn't some nameless, faceless blogger to them. I'd been friends with these people for years. Uber's cofounders, investors, and execs had been in my home; some had even held my kids.

They'd been so complimentary of what a fearless, outspoken journalist I was; they even funded us. Until all my fearless reporting affected one of the largest private companies in Silicon Valley history. Then my kids and I were just more of the collateral damage that comes with "disruption"—you know, like taxicab companies or that inevitable rape in an Uber here or there. My kids and I had become those proverbial eggs in the omelet that founders and investors always talk about.

I will never forgive what Emil Michael and Travis Kalanick put my children through those weeks. Eli and Evie were both confused and shaken by the large men with guns who were in our home every day and night and went everywhere with us in the big black cars we now had to ride in. The men who stood at the back of their preschool Thanksgiving Day recital wearing dark suits and earpieces.

I walked in that first night to Eli eating dinner and looking at my face on the TV, which probably shouldn't have been on, but everyone in my house was rattled and scared. It was a very different, more somber mommy than he was used to. He asked why I was on TV so much that day.

"Well," I said, kneeling down next to him, tears starting to remake tracks in my cakey makeup. "Mommy is a reporter. Do you know what that means?"

"No," he said.

"OK, well, you know how in *Frozen* Hans seems really nice at first and a lot of people think he's nice, but it turns out he's actually really, really bad? Part of Mommy's job is finding out when people are like Hans, and then telling the world that."

Eli looked at the armed guard standing in the doorway between our kitchen and dining room, a man so large he had to duck to come through that doorway. "Who are they?" Eli asked.

"They help Mommy fight the bad guys," I said.

A picture of Emil Michael flashed across the TV screen. "Mama, is that Hans?"

"Yep," I said, hugging Eli and looking at the smug face on TV who'd sent my world into chaos. The only thing that soothed the pain of seeing his face was the love coming from Eli in that moment.

Looking at Susan's face was like looking at old video clips or photos of me during that time—a mix of shock, numbness, and just being hollowed out. I was surrounded by a lot of people who supported me, but this was the first time I could talk to someone who knew exactly what being targeted by this company felt like. "You are not crazy," we kept saying to each other.

And that is the best reason to come forward. Hostile work environments succeed when they isolate you and make you feel as though you are the only one who has a problem with the way things are.

Smear campaigns are designed to feel highly personal, but if you step back and look at the way women are attacked, it almost always follows the same playbook:

Incompetent → Slut → Corrupt.

After I was attacked by Uber, I started to notice a pattern with the way other female reporters were attacked when they stood up to powerful men. There was the Koch brothers' smear campaign against Jane Mayer of the *New Yorker*. There was Tinder CEO Sean Rad telling the *Evening Standard* that he had done his own "background research" on *Vanity Fair*'s Nancy Jo Sales, adding "there's some stuff about her as an individual that will make you think differently." There was the intense bullying of Fox News' Megyn Kelly by the Donald Trump campaign and Trump himself.

There were three approaches used. Minimizing the woman: "Megyn Kelly isn't very good." Sexual innuendo: "Some stuff about her as an individual that will make you think differently." Or accusations of corruption: "Jane Mayer is a plagiarist."

That the claims weren't true doesn't matter, just as Uber's claims about me weren't true. In fact, it's almost more frustrating when the threatening narrative against you is complete bullshit, because it still works. People "defending" female journalists get so fixated on why their personal lives shouldn't matter that they spread the original invented fiction about them, and it becomes a link in people's minds.

There is a reason we see the exact same thing happen over and over again to powerful women. It works.

It's only after living through a decade of these three attacks, watching these other journalists get attacked, watching the 2016 presidential election, and reading the work of philosopher Kate Manne and social psychologist Amy Cuddy that I began to see how simple, universal, and effective it is to destroy a woman's credibility.

Incompetent → Slut → Corrupt.

Sometimes all those at once. One of the three will almost always stick. The three can be used to reinforce one another as well.

Beyond Uber, people had used each of these tactics to attack and discredit me for a decade.

When people wouldn't like what I'd write or an interview I'd do at an event, things would always get disturbingly sexual quickly. Threats of gang rape. Allegations that I was flirting with the man being interviewed. Or worse.

And there was always plenty of minimizing me that went along with it, but that got harder the more experience I got. The great thing about being a reporter is your work is out there with your name on it. If you consistently deliver great work, get bigger jobs, sign book deals, travel the world reporting, appear on TV, and get paid tens of thousands of dollars to deliver keynotes, it gets harder for people to keep minimizing you. I was simply not going away.

That's when sexualizing me would come in handy. If someone had to admit my work was good, the question became *why*. *Why* did I get that scoop? *How* did I have access to so many powerful people in the Valley? It's both a smear that I couldn't have possibly earned it (minimizing) and that gaining it must have had something to do with my sexuality.

Decades of these attacks—publicly and privately—had taken a toll. They played a large role in my suit of "cool dude" armor that I felt I needed to do my job, and the hatred and shame I felt in being a woman. Unlike a lot of professional women, I got credit for my work because my name was on it. My brain and hard work just didn't always get the credit for it.

But something fascinating happened once I became a mother. Internally, I discovered the power and strength I had as a woman. Externally, the sexual attacks mostly went away. And when I started a company, raising money from some of the most prestigious investors on the planet, very quickly the minimizing attacks mostly went away.

That left one line of attack: the corrupt woman. It was almost like a choreographed ballet. Overnight, I was no longer stupid. I was no longer incompetent. I was no longer wearing slutty outfits or only getting interviews because I flirted with men. I was suddenly a corrupt titan of industry.

I endured a solid year of constant attacks from the gossip blog Gawker and other unsourced sites insinuating that I was somehow in cahoots with my investors to write favorable things about them or their companies.

Facts didn't matter. It didn't matter that Pando was just one of dozens of tech publications that had raised money from investors. It didn't matter that Pando had raised less money in its lifetime than many of these publications raised in a single round. It didn't matter that blogs like TechCrunch and Gigaom actually had founders *who also were investors in startups they covered.* It didn't matter that we were constantly writing critical pieces about our investors or their biggest companies. I was living in a post-fact microcosm around me before the 2016 election exposed an entire post-fact world around all of us.

At the time, I had no idea this was the playbook. I thought it was just a reaction to *me*. In truth, it only had to do with my gender and my refusal to fit into the box that would make powerful men feel more comfortable and allow them to control me.

Pando continued to focus on doing the kind of adversarial journalism we do and the whole "corruption" meme eventually became laughable. The largest company in Silicon Valley history doesn't tend to threaten the family of someone who is a "paid apologist" for the industry.

By 2016, I was suddenly less attacked online than I'd been for most of my career, and it's largely because I became a mom. But how did that happen? Amy Cuddy—the social psychologist who taught us all to "power pose"—explains it with her "quadrants" in a piece cowritten for *Harvard Business Review* with Matthew Kohut and John Neffinger.

Cuddy has studied perceptions around the two primary traits that define leaders: being feared or being loved. Competence or warmth. These two traits, she says, account for about 80 percent of our overall "gut feelings" about people and shape how we interact with them. And they are typically snap judgments, almost exclusively based on nonverbal cues.

Cuddy's simple matrix showing warm/incompetent, cold/competent, cold/incompetent, and warm/competent explains everything from unconscious bias, the "logic" behind the "motherhood penalty" and "fatherhood bonus," and even what societies are targeted for genocides.

These perceptions are hard-coded in our very survival instinct. Evaluating a person's warmth is a way of assessing: Does this person intend to do me harm? Evaluating a person's competence is a secondary function of their warmth: If this person intends to benefit or harm me, how likely are they to be able to do that?

Warmth is perceived first, says Cuddy, and is more important in someone's overall "evaluation" than even competence.

But few people exist in the warm/competent quadrant. "People tend to see warmth and competence as inversely related," writes Cuddy. "The more competent you are, the less nice you must be. And vice versa: Someone who comes across as *really* nice must not be too smart."

This speaks to the trap I fell into as a manager before I had children: You gain respect by screaming, by being tough. Displaying any warmth, I thought, would lead to a loss of professional respect.

Cuddy's quadrants can explain—and predict—almost all bias and prejudice people face. One of the most interesting ones to study is the "cold/competent" quadrant, which Cuddy says causes envy in others. "Envy," she explains, "involves both respect and resentment."

Guess which quadrant working women, professional African Americans, Asians, Jews, and even the Tutsis in pre-genocide Rwandan society fit into? That's right, cold/competent, which evokes envy.

The warm/incompetent quadrant on the other hand evokes pity. This quadrant may not get respect, but it tends to get compassion and help.

Here's where it gets interesting for working moms: Being a career woman puts you in the cold/competent quadrant, but working *moms* are seen as warm/incompetent. Men on the other hand are perceived as warm and competent after fatherhood—hence the motherhood penalty (incompetence) and the fatherhood bonus (warmth without suffering a downgrade in competence).

Indeed, working mothers are viewed as significantly less competent than any other category. After reading everything I had about Maternal Wall bias, that part wasn't a shock. What struck me was the bonus that Cuddy didn't dwell on: Becoming a mother made me "warm," or likable, and hence worthy of compassion and sympathy, not hate or envy.

If you take nothing else from this book, know one thing: The second you become a mother, you will swap quadrants, and it has absolutely nothing to do with you. The sudden perception that you are incompetent explains the workplace bias that 60 percent of mothers face. It explains the myth of the "opt-out revolution." It's the reason women like Sheila Marcelo are told to lie about being mothers.

It has nothing to do with how well you balance work and home. You are moved to a new quadrant the second you become a mother. When you are pregnant. Before your baby even draws outside breath.

But here's the good news: *If you understand the game, this isn't all bad!*

Remember, "only" 60 percent of women face Maternal Wall bias. If I had been working for a large, very biased corporation, this sudden quadrant swap could have led to prime beats being taken away from me, or my story not making it to the cover, or missing out on a promotion. But as it was, I worked for myself. My biggest problem before having kids was the daily waves of hate I would suffer. So the truth is, my quadrant swap benefited me more than it hurt me.

Cuddy's work also backs this up. Competence, she writes, is

easier to maintain than warmth. Someone who has qualitative achievements—a title or a prestigious degree, for instance—will not suddenly be seen as incompetent because they are bad at, say, playing pool. But kicking a dog once will forever make you the kind of person who kicks dogs. Motherhood dramatically increased my "warmth," but the fact that I achieved more objectively measurable things after having kids—raising money, starting a company, building a media brand—combated the natural inclination for others to view me as more incompetent because of my motherhood.

The more I owned my motherhood—incorporating my kids into every aspect of my life, being seen pregnant onstage, on TV, and in photos for a collective eighteen months, talking about my children and the power of motherhood—the less hate I got. The disturbing violent, sexual hate was almost completely gone by the time I was pregnant again with Evie.

This was what was so tactically dumb about Emil Michael pledging to "go after" my family versus following the "corrupt woman" line the rest of my detractors were using. Not only did he enrage my inner protective mama bear, but by elevating my motherhood, Uber evoked pity for me, not resentment.

Having lived through this dramatic shift in perception, I was fascinated by the way every single speech at the 2016 Democratic National Convention positioned Hillary Clinton as a mother and a grandmother.

The clear risk was she'd be viewed as incompetent. But she was clearly the most qualified candidate by résumé. No one who wasn't already swayed by her competence, compared with a man who'd bankrupted a series of businesses and never held any public office, was ever going to vote for her anyway. To

Trump supporters, her competence was evidence of her corruption. They wanted someone who was incompetent when it came to political office. An outsider.

And the Bush/Gore election had proven another of Cuddy's findings. Warmth is ultimately the more important of the two qualities. George W. Bush was viewed as warmer but more incompetent—the guy you'd want to grab a beer with—while Al Gore was viewed as smart (competent) but cold and robotic. Bush won.

So the 2016 campaign focused on Clinton's (and Gore's) single biggest negative: perceived coldness. And the most effective way to make a cold/competent woman warm is to make her a mother. And it worked, in part. Clinton got one of the biggest boosts that any candidate has gotten coming out of a convention. She won the popular vote. It simply wasn't enough to win the presidency.

There's something liberating about realizing that owning your motherhood could give just as many benefits in public life as denying it. It's not a weakness, it's a weapon. The lie actually helped me in one respect. But it helped me because I didn't believe it, and I didn't report to anyone.

12

From Subject to Sovereign

I WAKE UP TO THE glow of the TV. This happens every morning sometime between 2:00 a.m. and 6:00 a.m. I may return to sleep. What I won't return to is my bed. I haven't slept in my bedroom regularly since Evie was born. It's a big empty room that holds piles of laundry Megan dutifully folds that I rarely find time to put away.

Back in 2013, in the months after Evie was born, I slept in the big bed in her room. Now, a year later, I sleep on the couch. For one thing, I can't fall asleep without the distraction of the TV anymore. For another, my bed is too reminiscent of my marriage.

Even after we decided we needed a divorce, Geoff lived in the house until August 2014 or so. And after that, his stuff was here for another year.

I turn off the TV and either fall back asleep, grab my laptop, which is likely right next to me, or just stare at the ceiling.

Megan will be here soon to get the kids up. I have stress, but for a few more hours, I have silence.

⌘

If Uber *had* started its oppo research campaign, they would have quickly discovered Geoff and I had already beaten them to the task of destroying our marriage. We were in the middle of our divorce. He'd moved out, and I'd stopped wearing my wedding ring, but we didn't yet talk about it publicly. Because Geoff had been spending half his time in Vegas since Eli was a few months old, people didn't particularly notice.

But internally, I was already reeling from the loneliness and betrayal that came with the end of my marriage when the Uber thing came right in and shattered all my illusions about Silicon Valley.

Paul took care of me like I was incapacitated. He slept on my couch at night and went with me to every interview or appearance. I referred every request for my time to him, and he prioritized and booked all of it, while making sure the company functioned during those two weeks after the Emil Michael revelations as well. He'd patiently tell me again and again where we were going, who the audience was. That new reality of my world weighed so heavily on me I found basic functioning almost impossible. I was a corpse who only managed to come to life when a video camera was pointed at me or my kids were near me.

Geoff gave me a bottle of my favorite expensive scotch. He was around as little or as much as I needed in subsequent weeks. He took the kids as much or as little as I needed. But that was about all he knew how to do.

When he stopped by in the aftermath of the news, he was rattled just looking at me. "I've never seen you like this," he said. He'd known me for fifteen years. He'd seen me in labor twice. We'd been kidnapped together. We'd been charged by a baboon. He'd never seen me look that scared.

The three of us were sitting in my living room the first day or so of my cottontail media campaign. The guards were hovering by the doors, waiting on my Indian food. I wasn't allowed to open the door myself. I was crumpled on the floor, and Paul and Geoff were on two ends of my L-shaped sectional couch, on either side of me. The three of us only cared about one thing: the safety of the kids.

Looking back, that crisis was the beginning of a shift in my relationships with the two most important men in my adult life, my two best friends, the two people I'd shared three of the most important things in my life with—my work, my children, and my heart.

In a strange way, I'd spent much of my thirties stretched between Geoff and Paul. After my first book, Geoff couldn't bear another conversation about tech or listen to another chapter. He was thrilled when Paul and I became friends, and he welcomed Paul taking on that burden.

The shift in my dynamic with each of them became pronounced during these weeks of the Uber mess and its aftermath.

It wasn't that Paul cared and Geoff didn't. It was something much more fundamental than that. Paul was the first man including my father who ever understood *how* to take care of me. And in some ways, he was the first man I ever let take care of me.

Even when we were married, Geoff didn't ever really try to

"take care" of me . . . and that's a big reason I married him. When I was living in the South, working in a male-dominated world in my early twenties, this was a feature. I was a "cool dude" then, and cool dudes don't need white knights.

Geoff was totally unthreatened by my success and by the fact that so much of my job entailed hanging out with young, very rich entrepreneurs. I required a partner who would have an almost hands-off respect for my career. I was already fighting so many micro-indignities of sexism and double standards every day; I couldn't also deal with it at home.

But somewhere along the line—after gossip blogs started lying about me on a regular basis, after all the death and gang rape threats I got online, after powerful billionaires started lobbying to get me fired from publications—what I wanted in a partner changed.

After having kids, that intensified. I felt as though I was taking care of so many people, between Eli and Evie and Pando. I needed someone who could take care of me when I broke down. "Cool dude" Sarah Lacy would have seen this as a weakness. "Badass feminist warrior" Sarah Lacy knew that there was no shame in being nurturing and being nurtured, that intimacy, vulnerability, and trust with people you love was strength.

Every time my kids and I came through a horrible flu—me rubbing their backs all night, rotating through doses of Tylenol and Motrin every four hours, giving them baths to cool them down, and just holding them all night as they sobbed—I realized we were that much more bonded to one another. This was how unbreakable, unconditional love is built. Taking care of people and letting people take care of you. There was nothing weak or unequal about it if it was reciprocal.

That week when Uber threatened my family and the world

of TV cameras descended upon us, I needed help. I was terrified. I didn't know if this was as bad as it got or if something far more insidious was coming. If Paul and I hadn't had such a strong connection already, I'm not sure I ever would have trusted anyone at that point.

Before that crisis, the idea of me ever dating again had seemed preposterous. I had trust issues before I met Geoff, and my divorce didn't help. My life as a journalist pretty much made me suspicious of everyone. I'd spent years hounded by gossip blogs, so online dating was way off the table, as was dating anyone in the tech world, which was most of the people I knew.

And beyond that, my kids almost exclusively lived with me during this period, and I ran a company. I had almost no free time. Who would like me enough to work around all that? How would I be able to find the time to get to know anyone if I couldn't introduce them to my kids and I spent all my free time with my kids? There seemed to be so much exposition to my life for someone just now coming into the story.

One night just before the Uber thing exploded, I was listing to Paul all the many things I'd never be able to find in someone. He'd recently broken up with someone as well. After listening patiently, he said, "You realize you just described our relationship except we don't have sex."

Wow. So *that* was out there now.

Paul and I had always had a strange relationship. We never got bored of talking to each other and were informal writing partners, editing nearly all each other's work. We had a strangely intense relationship, talking on the phone every day in periods we got along and fighting viciously in other times.

If I'd been single when we met, I'm sure we would have wound up dating. But I was happily married, and whatever feelings there may have been got shoved somewhere deep inside—for both of us. Meantime, we'd gone through a lot together. I helped Paul get sober, and he helped me with . . . well, most everything I'd faced over the previous eight years.

But despite all this, in the aftermath of my separation, it hadn't occurred to me that we might actually wind up together, mostly because we'd been best friends for eight years. *What would that even be like?* But when he said those words, somehow those long-ago buried feelings started fighting to get out.

This long unspoken *thing* now finally out there, we mostly sat in heavy silence the rest of the night. At the end of it I just said to him, "I couldn't risk losing you as my best friend. You are too important to me. You and the kids are all I have left." We didn't really speak about it again. But something had palpably changed between us.

And then Uber changed everything else. Whatever Emil Michael's intention was, I doubt it was shaking me so badly that I allowed myself to risk being with someone again. It pushed Paul and me together, in a development that surprised everyone and no one all at the same time. Something about the way he took care of me convinced me he loved me more than anyone ever would, or maybe could. And I realized how much I needed him. I didn't need "a man." I didn't need "a spouse." I didn't need a "life partner." I could have done this alone, with friends, with my kids by my side. I needed *him.*

I told Paul how I felt, and then I told Geoff.

Geoff said he felt a lot of emotions, but one of them—strangely—was relief. I think he worried that I would close myself off to ever loving or trusting anyone again, aside from the kids. And he felt a lot of guilt over that. He'd seen how deeply Paul cared about me as a friend and how much he loved the kids. But Paul also had a deep respect for Geoff and my past with him, and Geoff's place as the kids' dad. Geoff and I—despite it all—still loved each other and still wanted each other to be happy.

Even though Paul and I weren't dating yet, that moment the three of us sat in fear and concern surrounded by armed guards, waiting for Indian food, was the moment my new modern family was born. Whatever had gone down between the three of us didn't matter. What mattered was that we were all here for one another and the kids. We were all going to get through this thing.

And here's the shock: I found far more work-life balance in my 50/50 divorce than I ever found in my 50/50 marriage.

⌘

We gotta get into the whole 50/50 marriage thing. For much of the last ten years of empowering working mom nonfiction, the most optimistic ray of hope in having it all has been the idea of the 50/50 marriage. It goes something like this: You and your husband make a pact. You explain to him that both of you will benefit from this. You'll be able to have a career, but it's great for him, too!

The more laundry he does, the more you'll want to have sex!

If you are bringing in a steady paycheck, he doesn't have as much pressure on him to provide!

He'll feel like a superhero if he goes so far as to volunteer to be a class parent. He'll practically choke on all that fatherhood bonus flying all around him!

I'm paraphrasing . . . barely. This was popularized by Sheryl

Sandberg in *Lean In*, but she first got it from *Getting to 50/50: How Working Parents Can Have It All* by Sharon Meers and Joanna Strober.

I struggle with these books. I have struggled with them for years now.

I am all for men doing half of the housework. I obviously believe women should have a career if they want a career. It's just that I take issue with that being predicated on asking a man for *permission*. If we're gonna tell women how to pick spouses, let's not advise that they negotiate for the right to a career. Let's advise that they *inform* men of their career plans.

I've debated this a few times with Meers, whom I like and respect a great deal. She wrote *Getting to 50/50* because she was also horrified by the impression the "opt-out revolution" left with women—the "biological imperative" that justified Maternal Wall bias, the shift of blame onto the woman for not being able to make it work, and the lie that you couldn't have both. "When you tell women they can't 'have it all' you are telling them they can't have what men are having and that's just bullshit," she says.

Yep, yep, yep.

What I have a problem with is these books' position as a sales pitch to men for why women working is in their interest. These books represent a "practical" genre of advice for working moms—how to make the most of the world *we have*. "I certainly want for my children a world where my daughter believes it is every bit her right to have a great career that brings out the best in her, just like my son," Meers said to my objections. "That's the world I want. I want her to pursue her ambitions with joy and without apology. That is what I want. Now, the fact is that even sitting here in 2016, if you look at it, the survey gets a little bit better every year, if not every decade, in terms of men doing a little bit more at home. We have come a long way, but we have a long way to go."

I agree with the diagnosis of where we are. But my problem with these practical guides of making it in the patriarchy is they reinforce the patriarchy. At best, they exclude a lot of women from equality—those who don't fit into an upper-middle-class, married, heterosexual box. And at worst, those in that box are lucky to get to 49/51, because if you are still negotiating to live your life the way you want, you aren't equal. Even if he says yes. According to *Getting to 50/50*, what "frees" women is believing their working *helps* their husbands: "When we stop believing that a woman's job will hurt her husband—and realize it might help him instead—we free women to see the importance of their jobs as clearly as men do."

There are a lot of really valuable things about working moms this book argues—why you shouldn't feel guilty, the benefits of kids with working moms, and practical tips for making dual-income households work. A lot of that was revolutionary at the time. But this argument is happy to continue to live in a world where you have to get men's buy-in to succeed. You could argue that it's just another form of benevolent sexism. If you are *this* acceptable type of working mom, we'll allow you to have it all.

Even for the (probably) white, well-educated, well-off women who can have a cozy life of balance under an enlightened patriarchy, there are limits to how helpful this playbook is.

You may have a spouse who gets it. (Mine did.)

You may have a spouse who is relieved you can pay half the bills. (Mine was.)

You may have a spouse who prefers to do the laundry because you will only fuck it up. (Mine did. I handled the cooking.)

You may not even change a single diaper for the first two weeks after childbirth. (I didn't.)

But most women don't have a spouse like this. Let's start with the idea that you can't exactly pull up Amazon and order a 50/50 spouse. You have to fall in love with one. They have to fall in love with you. What if you fall in love with someone else? Just because the women who wrote these books fell in love with supportive men doesn't mean it's a playbook for everyone else. Meantime, "only" 60 percent of women face Maternal Wall bias. You could argue it's easier to solve your work-life balance issues by finding an enlightened boss than the right man to marry. Especially since you don't have to spend the rest of your life working for your boss.

I asked Meers what she would say if a woman came up to her and said she tried their playbook, she tried negotiating for a right to live her life as she wanted to, and her spouse simply said no. That actually happened, Meers said. And she didn't have much to offer that woman. She suggested she try again, and the woman said she couldn't. It was the end of the discussion. That's the problem with asking permission. Great entrepreneurs ask forgiveness, not permission. Great women should do the same.

Oh, and be forewarned, 50/50 ladies: There is a world of difference between you having a career and you actually *outearning* your husband. Nearly 40 percent of married women outearn their husbands, and guess what impact that has on marriages? It *increases* the odds of divorce.

A University of Chicago Booth School of Business study looked at four thousand married couples in America and found that once a woman began to outearn her husband *by any amount*, divorce rates among those couples increased. In fact, the amount a woman outearned her husband by didn't make a difference. It could have been $1 or $1 million. It was simply the act of a woman outearning. Some studies have shown the very *thought* of a woman outearning a man affects his behavior.

Not only that, but typically American women spent about forty-four minutes more than their spouses per day on housework. When a woman was the primary earner, that gap widened *even more*. The more women outearned their husbands, the more they compensated by . . . doing even more housework. "A high-earning woman is trying to make sure that her husband doesn't feel threatened," said FiveThirtyEight's Mona Chalabi in an NPR interview. "The idea is basically that men might feel a bit emasculated by a woman that earns more than them."

Separate research from Cornell University shows that when a woman outearns her partner, it affects his fidelity. A male partner (married or simply in a committed relationship) is more likely to cheat on his partner if she supports him financially.

Let. That. Sink. In. The 50/50 canon of advice is about appealing to men's rational self-interest and hoping equality is the result. But cheating on someone who supports you isn't in your rational self-interest. There is more at play here than economics that is keeping women subservient in many marriages. (Fragile male ego, for one.)

And the balance will likely get worse when you have children, because by default so much of the very early infant care falls to the mom. "You do the dishes, and I'll cook the dinner" rapidly turns into "I'll just do this because I can do it better, and you don't know how." Before he knows it, dad is an outsider.

Sure, do the whole checklist before you marry someone. And consider how the person you marry will impact your career. Set expectations that they will do half the chores. Inform them— don't ask them—if you intend to keep building your career.

But acknowledge that everyone changes what they want and need in a partner over an entire adult lifetime. (I certainly did.) And, let's be honest, we all make a lot of idealized promises in our twenties that we don't keep once life gets messy. A study of Harvard Business School grads showed that a majority of women assumed their careers would be treated equally to their spouses'. In practice, 40 percent later said their spouses' careers took priority. Sixty-five percent of the Gen X women in this study and 72 percent of the boomer women in this study said they take primary responsibility for the children.

This is how the 50/50 "negotiation" frequently turns out a decade or so into marriage.

I never once had to negotiate with Geoff for my right to a career; it was an assumption because *he knew me.* We never even discussed the possibility that I wouldn't work when and if we had children. Yet even we fell into the pattern of the buck stopping with me when we became parents. *I'll just do it, it's easier and faster!*

You know what made us true equals? Our divorce. I wish I'd known in marriage what I learned through my divorce.

This shocks no one more than me, because I bought all the lies about divorce, too. That any marriage was better than a divorce. That divorce was somehow selfish. That divorce with young children was so much worse than a divorce without kids or a divorce with older kids. That divorce is a "failure." The words "you have to work at a marriage" imply that if your marriage ends, you somehow didn't work hard enough. You gave up. And then you are "damaged goods."

"Divorced woman" is about as high on the aspirational list as "stepmom." The worst of all the "faces" I've gotten in the last five years is "Southern divorce face." When someone grabs your hand, or shoulder, or puts a hand on your knee, and says in a barely audible whisper, "How's it going?" The assumption is we're all in mourning and will be for some time.

It was only after a ton of therapy that I genuinely came to see my marriage not as a failure but as a really successful fifteen-year relationship that enabled me to become a way better me, to build an amazing career, to buy a house in San Francisco, to have the confidence to start a company, and to give birth to Eli and Evie. Those are the defining things in my life, and I shared them with Geoff. And we'll share Eli and Evie forever.

What of that is failure?

Don't get me wrong. There was a lot of anger, a lot of scream-ing, and a lot of pain. During the worst of my divorce, I worked out *nine times a week* to manage my stress and anger. There was one time I walked into my regular Tuesday night yoga class after my kids were in bed and asked my teacher, Estee, hypo-thetically, if I killed Geoff and went to prison, would she con-sider coming to teach special classes in jail.

Not only did she say yes (*namaste*), but she also on the fly changed the theme of that class to one in celebration of Kali. "You don't hear about Kali a lot in yoga classes . . ." Estee began class that night.

With good reason: Kali is a form of *Durga*, which is pretty much the most terrifyingly badass female goddess in Hindu mythology. Kali vanquishes foes that male gods can't and then drinks their blood in celebration, doing sort of a drunken vic-tory dance. Kali is basically the patron saint of a woman going through divorce.

When I'm telling you I was put into a Zen state by hearing

about an angry goddess drinking the blood of the vanquished, you know that Geoff and I didn't get to this happy place overnight. But by the fall of 2016, our divorce was downright idyllic.

I talk to Geoff more regularly these days than the last few years of our marriage. We share more about our lives, too. We get along better and do nice things for each other without being asked.

At Eli's fifth birthday party, I suddenly realized that I had just been sitting around talking to other moms instead of *doing things*. It's like that nightmare when you realize you haven't gone to a class all semester and now there's an exam. I looked around in a panic and found Geoff manning the bounce house and taking pictures of kids, and Paul refreshing all the foods and snacks, handing out birthday hats and even pushing someone else's kid on a swing.

A few weeks later, when I was suddenly called out of town on work, I realized my red-eye fell on a "mommy night" that also happened to be Geoff's birthday. Typically, we leap at the opportunity to grab another night with the kids, but Geoff had plans to go out with friends.

So Paul picked the kids up at school and did their baths, dinner, and rock-yous. Geoff came over the next morning just as Paul was getting them up and dressed, fed, and ready for school, and Geoff took over lunches and the drive to school. Later that day, Eli had an early pickup at his new school's spirit day at the same time Evie had the trike-a-thon at her preschool. So while I focused on work guilt-free halfway around the world, Geoff went to Eli's school, and Paul went to the trike-a-thon to cheer for Evie.

More recently, Geoff was rocking Evie at his house one night, and she dreamily said, "I love Daddy and Mommy and Apple Paul.* I love all of my parents." More remarkable, Geoff shared this story because he thought this was adorable and sweet, not threatening to his position as their father.

Even though our kids don't live with either of us full time, we both have more quality time with them. Since breaks are built into our schedule and we both have flexibility in our work schedules, neither of us has any regular childcare. Geoff has never hired a babysitter since we split, and I have maybe a dozen times. Between me, Geoff, and Paul, there are three adults whom the kids are always happy to be with, and one of us is almost always available to pitch in if something comes up for the other.

We came up with our own custody schedule, rather than following the templates of others. We don't do one week on/one week off because neither of us wanted to be away from the kids for more than a day or so. There are only two days a month I don't see them at all, and Geoff sees them most days, too.

Even better, we both get time for ourselves. Geoff and I—obviously—don't vacation or go on date nights together anymore. I always have every Wednesday night away from my kids. I always have every other weekend away from my kids, but I

---

* I should explain "Apple Paul." Back when I was pregnant with Eli, I would refer to Paul as "Uncle Paul" when discussing him with my belly. Paul took exception. "I'm not your brother," he said. "If I am going to have an honorary title I didn't earn, I should be able to pick the title. Why would I pick 'Uncle'? That's rubbish."

"OK, what do you want?" I said.

"Captain! No, admiral! I want to be Admiral Paul."

Paul had never been around children and didn't realize they couldn't say "Admiral." Eli settled on "Apple Paul" and introduced him to Evie as such.

This was lucky. Can you imagine "This is my mommy and her boyfriend, Uncle Paul"?

still take them to school Friday morning and tuck them in Sunday night so it isn't too devastating. I always have a week away from my kids at the end of the year to relax and refresh.

At the beginning of this process, I hated this. It felt unnatural to spend any time away from them; like I was getting punished all over again. But a few years into the routine, it has absolutely made me a better mom.

We all appreciate the time together more, and no matter how exasperated I am with my kids, I know a break is coming up. If they are being monsters on Tuesday, I tell myself how much I'm going to miss them on Wednesday night, and it somehow makes me appreciate them even in those frustrating moments. I rarely feel that I "need" a break, because breaks are just worked into my schedule regularly, whether I like it or not.

Forced time alone has also made me work on myself and my adult relationships. My kids can't be my only sources of emotional strength; that isn't fair to them. I have way more friends now than I did when I was married, even married before kids. It's made me do what everyone says moms should do: take time for themselves and take care of themselves.

I go on mini-vacations because multiple days alone in my house are super depressing. I've started going on quarterly yoga retreats that I can't really afford, where I've gotten to know an amazing gang of powerful women (and a few dudes who aren't threatened by our power) of all ages, all incomes, and all walks of life. It's the closest to my fantasy of being part of a Wonder Woman–like Amazonian tribe that I've ever gotten. And it's one of the few groups I've ever found in my adult life where I am just *me*, not SARAH LACY (™) or Eli and Evie's mom.

I never would have found any of that without divorce. Most

Americans get so few vacations, who would *only* go on trips without their spouse and frequently without their children?

I've had to let go of the way I think things should be done when it comes to Eli and Evie. "How good were you at controlling what Geoff did when you were married?" my therapist spent a year asking me before it actually sunk in.

We still have some interdependence on each other. We have to compromise on things like what schools they'll attend and clear it with each other when one of us wants to take a vacation. I can't just suddenly decide to take a job in another city. But other than major changes, our lives are ours to live.

As long as they aren't in any danger, it's none of my business what the rules are at his house. It's none of my business what goes on in his personal life either. I make a point never to ask if he's seeing anyone. I assume he'll tell me when he's ready to tell the kids. I spent so much time worrying that he planned to freelance instead of working a full-time job. My concern was whether he'd be able to pay for half of the kids' school as agreed. It took a lot of therapy for me to fully internalize the reality that his finances were *his* problem, not mine.

Once you get there, it's freeing. My kids will tell me they're allowed to say or do something at Daddy's house, and I shrug and say, "I don't make the rules at Daddy's house. Get it out of your system there, because you can't here." Geoff is responsible for his own relationship with them. There's no "You know, your father loves you . . ." or "Here's what your father meant to say . . ." that you hear from other families where the mom does the bulk of the parenting. I don't have to momsplain anything to the kids about their dad or anything to Geoff about Eli and Evie. The three of them know way more about their relationship than I do.

These were the lessons I wish I had when I was married: That your life is ultimately *your life*, even if a handful of major choices require discussion with the people you share your life with. That every parent needs to take ownership of their relationship with their children and regularly take care of them alone for days at a time to make sure they are fully checked into that relationship. That every parent needs regularly scheduled breaks—mandatory breaks, even. That I am always here if Geoff asks for help, but it's not my job to grab the ball proactively if he drops it, or if it looks as though he *might* drop it. It's his ball.

In divorce, our co-parenting became boiled down to two questions: Is each person doing their best? Do they have the right intentions? Then anything else is fine.

Even the 50/50 experts say dads must take ownership of their relationships with their kids. Meers and Strober quote Stephanie Coontz, the author of *Marriage, a History*, on this: "[When women quit their jobs] not only does it reinforce women's second-class position in the work force, but it reinforces dad's second-class position in the family. She becomes the expert and he never catches up."

Divorce forces dads to catch up quickly, with no safety net. I know "engaged dads" who have never taken their kids alone on a plane, never had them solo for a weekend, or never even done their evening bedtime routine. Divorced dads, on the other hand, frequently have to take total ownership of everything their kids need, because there's no one else around when they have them.

Dads learn to do things in their own ways, which they don't always get the chance to do when the parents are still married. One of my kids' favorite dinners is "Daddy spaghetti." Do I even want to know what that is? They have it once a week and every doctor's checkup shows growing, healthy kids. I don't really care if it's Pixy Stix and lard.

Divorce forced Geoff to step up where he needed to and forced me to stand down where I needed to. In a sense, it gave him the space to become more selfless and me the space to become more selfish.

After watching the movie *Sing* recently, Eli remarked to Evie how lucky they were that they didn't have a dad like Norman. Norman is a daddy pig who goes to work all day, comes home exhausted after the kids are in bed, and crashes in front of the TV while the mama pig, Rosita, does all the child rearing, cleaning, and cooking. She has to devise a Rube Goldberg machine to find time to follow her dreams because Norman falls asleep when she even tries to ask him to step up. "Norman doesn't even *know how* to take care of them," Eli said to Evie. "Some people have a dad who is great, some people have a mom who is great. We are so lucky we have a daddy and a mommy who are both great."

It's fascinating that his takeaway from watching a "traditional" family was that he and Evie *gained* something in having an engaged dad, not *lost* something by having a mom who isn't at her children's beck and call.

I AM NOT ADVOCATING YOU GET DIVORCED. (I have to put that in bold.) But damn, do we make divorce look good. I went on a moms' retreat about a year after my kids started going back and forth between houses and was stunned at how little the other moms' concerns resonated with me. It took me a few days to realize that so many of their concerns—never having a break, never taking time for yourself, always feeling you have to do everything because you simply do it better—I used to struggle with. It was divorce that forced me to get past all that.

There's this, too: If we didn't have kids, I never would have spoken to Geoff again. We wouldn't have done all that therapy to get past things. I wouldn't have forgiven him. I'd be carrying around anger and hate. Perhaps one of the most surprising things my kids did for me was force me to get to a good place with the person I shared most of my adult life with.

⌘

I'm not the first woman to react uncomfortably to the promise that the right husband can solve gender inequality. There is an astounding increase in single women—both divorced and those putting off marriage longer—who are terrified of falling into a trap where their lives and choices are no longer their own, as chronicled in Rebecca Traister's best-selling *All the Single Ladies: Unmarried Women and the Rise of an Independent Nation*.

Marriage has a lot of baggage as an institution. It is rooted in a legal construct just a hair better than slavery. It is based in the British idea of "coverture," which maintains that a woman's identity is essentially suspended during marriage, as she is "consolidated" into her husband "under whose wing, protection and cover she performs everything." Coverture even meant there couldn't be contracts or agreements between men and women, because the married couple is one unit, and you can't have a contract with yourself.

It was only in 1972 that the Supreme Court ruled that both parties within a marriage were separate entities with their own individual rights. *Just three years before I was born.* "When people call single women selfish for the act of tending to themselves, it's important to remember that the very acknowledgment that women have selves that exist independently of others, and especially independent of husbands and children, is revolutionary," writes Traister.

Feminists have predicted this era of the single woman for more than a century. Susan B. Anthony said in 1877 that the "journey toward gender equality would necessarily include a period in which women stopped marrying." She didn't mean that you were a bad feminist if you wanted to be married, simply that it was a necessary transition "from the position of subject to sovereign." "There needs to be an era of self-sustained, self-supported, homes," she wrote.

"King of the house" cold turkey.

The rise of single moms is either terrifying or thrilling depending on who you are. Men are for the first time faced with the fact that women may not *need* them. This isn't bad news for a lot of amazing men, because their wives and families want to be with them. Sharing your life with someone you love and co-parenting with someone who shares your values is a wonderful way to live. The point isn't that women *need* to be single or they are bad feminists.

The point is that men can increasingly no longer count on the patriarchy—its control over women's economic freedom, its lies that mothers are weak, its denigration of single mothers as what's wrong with society—to keep them warm at night. They have to earn their place next to us, and in some cases next to their children.

The rejection—or at least resetting—of that baggage that comes with marriage is all over the statistics: In 2009 the percentage of married American women fell below 50 percent. Up until 1980 the median age at which women first got married was between twenty and twenty-two. Now, it's twenty-seven.

Forty-six percent of adults younger than thirty-four have never married, up 12 percent in less than ten years. Only 20 percent of Americans are married by age twenty-nine. There are nearly four million more single women in 2014 than in 2010.

It's happening at both ends of the economic spectrum. There's an acceptance—and even glorification—of single moms among celebrities and top businesswomen in major cities, a surge in single moms among the poor, and an increase at every economic level in between. There is almost nothing rich and poor single moms have in common except neither will be with a man unless he is an absolute, unequivocal value-add to the household. Simply being a husband no longer guarantees that.

It's much the same as with cofounders. When it's a good fit with a great complement of skills, it's far easier to build a company with a cofounder than to do it alone. When it isn't, it's far harder.

There is a subtle distinction between the patriarchy telling you that you need a man in your life if you want social standing, economic stability, and children and you *choosing* to share your life with a man or a woman whom you love. It should come from desire and something extra in your life, not fear of a void or need for a master.

There is so much well-meaning advice I'm glad I didn't listen to. "Don't make a dramatic decision about your marriage while your kids are still young!" "Stay together until the kids are eighteen!" "Don't date your business partner!" My personal life is, on paper, a cautionary tale of a million things you "shouldn't" do. But in practice it's one of the most balanced, supportive co-parenting arrangements of anyone I know.

It's the empty seduction of pattern recognition once again. Thank God I didn't heed it.

The answer isn't that you have to have a 50/50 marriage. The answer isn't to be a single mom. The answer isn't to get divorced and start dating your business partner. The point is there isn't *an answer* and women need to stop looking in books like this for "an answer." The "answer" is a woman believing she is entitled to whatever life she wants to live. Or as Traister writes, "The revolution is in the expansion of options."

Given it's only been about forty-five years that the US government has allowed us to legally retain our individuality within a marriage, I'd say women are overdue for a period of "selfishness."

13

The Single-Mom Penalty and the Single-Mom Bonus

I OPEN MY EYES IN a panic.

Where am I? What time is it? What day is it?

Pretty quickly, my mind flicks through the answers.

The first is invariably in my bed. Alone.

It's sad when waking up alone in bed represents progress in your personal life, isn't it? I decided—after more than a year—sleeping on the couch every night was depressing and unhealthy. So I bought a new bed. A bed that only I have slept in. A bed with a tall padded headboard so that my kids can crawl into it in the mornings, and we can comfortably sit up and talk, cuddle, and read books. This is the bed for my new single-mom life.

I cleared Geoff's stuff out of my room. I took down the wedding photos. The stack of his photo books on our dresser has been replaced with a neat row of my favorite boots.

Paul has mostly taken my old spot, sleeping on the couch in my living room. We are together enough at this point that he is here most nights, but not quite together enough to explain the situation to Eli and Evie. And Eli likes to wander into my room unannounced.

For the answer to the second question, I reach into the side of my bed frame and feel for my phone: 6:50 a.m.

I can *feel* that it's Monday, because my thirty-nine-year-old body aches more than usual from the weekend. My back doesn't lie about my stress level, and a weekend of two toddlers is like a wrecking ball on top of it. I lie in bed and mentally scan myself to see how bad my back is going to feel when I get up. I wonder if I can make it to the chiropractor sometime today but know I won't until it gets so bad I can barely walk.

Then I think about the day's stories. Monday is always the roughest day of the week. By the time we hit Friday, our reporters all turn into grasshoppers. But on Mondays I take my kids to school so that's Paul's problem for the next hour or so.

I drag myself vertical before 7:05; I load a Keurig pod. Once there was a time I'd actually clean a machine, grind beans, and measure out coffee and water. Ho ho ho. Eli helpfully loads the unused pods in trays for me each night. It's his "chore," and he approaches it with ritualistic precision. He's the first to remind me when we're running low. Thankfully, today, we are not.

I clean off the table from the night before, put away any last feather boas, hats, Lightning McQueens from the weekend while my coffee brews. I put some sausages and Eggo waffles in the toaster. I get some plates and forks and put them on the table. I get fresh waters "with a big ice." I take a slug of coffee and head to awaken the krakens.

I knock quietly on Eli's door. He likes a warning. I enter cooing softly, "Good morning, baby." I kneel at the foot of his race car bed. He groggily looks up, climbs out of bed and into my lap, kneeling on top of my knees, clasping his arms around my neck.

He smells like sweaty Froot Loops.

Without fail, this is the best moment of my morning so far. I can't believe I used to let Megan wake him up. Was the extra hour of sleep really worth missing this? The quiet of his dark room, his sweaty, groggy little four-year-old body kneeling in my lap. His forehead resting on my shoulder with total trust, safety, and surrender.

Eli and Evie are mine in a way nothing ever has been before. My proudest achievements, and the hard part is *done*. They are here. They were born healthy. I just have to manage not to fuck it up from here.

Just like that, the cobwebs are gone, and I'm in the mommy zone.

The day ends much the same way. That moment when I'm singing the last song to them, the stalling is all done, and Eli and Evie just surrender to the fact that it's bedtime. They lean into me with total assurance that I'll always be there and always protect them. I feel as if my heart has been pierced like a perfectly poached egg and love is oozing out all over them like a warm yolk. No matter what has happened this day, no matter how bad they've been, no matter what fights started or lawsuits were threatened, no matter how close we are to going out of business on that day, no matter how many stories I have to write once this moment is over, *this moment* is worth it all.

I am making enough money; we have a roof over our heads, barely. And yet, I am able to spend enough time with them that we have *this*.

Just before I lay Evie in her crib every night, the last thing I whisper to her is the one thing I hope she internalizes well before the world tells her she's too much or not enough.

"I think you're perfect," I say.

"I tank yur puwrfect," she groggily whispers back.

Eli is emotional and dramatic but steady Evie excels at giving me whatever I need at any moment.

Her Chinese astrological sign is a water snake—the most manipulative and resourceful combination possible. The snake actually jumps ahead in the order by grabbing ahold of the horse's heel. And water is basically unstoppable. It weaves through rocks and crevices adapting for any size, shape, or form of obstacle, other than maybe extreme ice or heat. But even then, water can go back to its original form. Water is both brutally devastating and essential for life. Since she was a baby, I've thought of her when bullies have threatened my company. *Evie wouldn't take this . . .*

I wasn't going to discipline a tiny bit of that fierceness out of her, because the world would take too much eventually.

I walk squinting out into the brightly lit kitchen. Pots, pans, cutting board, and grated cauliflower are everywhere. This fall we are testing out the many meal kit services like Plated, Blue Apron, and HelloFresh for Pando, and Paul is using that as an opportunity to learn to cook. As a result, nightly takeout has suddenly turned into nightly gourmet home-cooked meals.

"Hello, Supermom, dinner is almost ready," he says, kisses me, and hands me a glass of wine.

My life is pretty good, I think, in that moment. And I don't let myself fast-forward from that moment. I just loll around in it feeling totally happy. This moment is going to go quickly enough, and I'm not going to be the one to rush it out the door.

I tell myself, in the harder moments, that I'll hit a point where the stress and work will decrease. The company has had ups and downs, but it's getting stronger. Even our near-death experiences have a longer warning time, and we're better at solving them. At some point, I won't have the constant nagging stress that we could still go out of business if the next ad deal doesn't close.

Likewise, the kids will grow up. They'll need me less.

Life will get easier.

But in those euphoric blasts, I'm not ready for that to happen anytime soon. Moments like these, moments of pure bliss and accomplishment, only happen because the daily struggle is so great.

⌘

I love to refer to myself as a single mom almost as much as I enjoy talking about upending the patriarchy. I find that somehow I've co-opted the fatherhood bonus along with the motherhood penalty.

Mention it casually on a flight. You will get something for free, I guarantee you. You will skip lines. People will soulfully tell you what a great job you are doing, even if your kids are going nuts. People have a reverence for the badass stamina and dedication of a single mom . . . that is, if you are a white, successful businesswoman living in a city like New York or San Francisco.

That's less the case when you are living in poverty or are a woman of color. In fact, single moms in poverty are casually referred to as the cause of many of society's problems.

Don't get me wrong: The patriarchy hates us all. It only takes it out on the poor mothers because they are the vulnerable ones.

If anything terrifies the patriarchy more than women having control of their own uteruses or women getting true economic equality, it is the normalization of the single woman. When women can make ends meet, it's the ultimate expression of a woman having economic self-sufficiency without giving up children. When she can't, that woman has to be made an example of.

For the first time in the history of this country, there are more single women than married women. The year when marriage began to get statistically decoupled from motherhood was 1992. It was the year that the average marriage age rose above the average birth age for the first time. And white male politicians *lost their shit.*

In the same speech where Dan Quayle attacked the fictional Murphy Brown for having a baby without a husband, he also answered a question about the 1992 LA riots by saying, "Lawless social anarchy that we saw is directly related to the breakdown of the family structure."

And you thought it was racist cops! Nope, all those single moms. Especially the fictional ones.

Two years later Rick Santorum said, "We are seeing the fabric of this country fall apart, and it's falling apart because of single moms." In 1994 Jeb Bush bemoaned that there was "no longer a stigma attached to" having children out of wedlock. At one point Rush Limbaugh expressed in exasperation, "What is with all these young, single, white women?" Marco Rubio said the "greatest tool to lift children and families from poverty . . .

[is] called marriage." In 2013 Republican state senators in North Carolina proposed a bill requiring couples to endure a two-year waiting period before they could get divorced, and a Republican state senator from Wisconsin tried to pass a bill that declared being a single parent was a factor leading to child abuse.

In 2012 Mitt Romney said that a "major step" in curbing violence in the United States was "[telling] our kids before they have babies, they ought to think about getting married to someone."

In 2013 Romney also issued this masterful concern troll: "Some people could marry, but chose to take more time, they say, for themselves. Others plan to wait until they're well into their thirties or forties before they think about getting married. They're going to miss so much living, I'm afraid."

Amazing. From the casual "they say," which seems to imply these women (and men) have a more secret, nefarious agenda, to the belief that you are not "living" if you are single. This was three years ago, not decades ago.

While marriage used to be essential for women to rise in economic and social status—let alone to have a family that wasn't shunned by society—that is changing. In fact, a 2015 study published in the *American Journal of Public Health* showed that *men* even get more health benefits from marriage than women.

No. Shit. Almost half of American households are majority paid for by women *and* women do the bulk of the housework.

You can understand why this shift is terrifying to men who are comfortable in a patriarchy. It's like waking up one day and realizing the laws of gravity that have ruled your life, your dad's life, and your grandfather's life no longer apply. You are going to have to *work* hard to keep your feet on the ground. It will no longer "just happen."

If you don't need them to pay the bills, and you don't need them to realize your dreams of motherhood, men have to earn their place as a father and a husband the same way women have been having to earn their place as an equal at home and at work for generations.

And this is the *only thing* that's true for many single moms in affluence and single moms in poverty: If a man isn't a value-add beyond sperm, life is deemed easier without him in a way it wasn't even twenty years ago.

⌘

Jennifer Justice is one of those women for whom the whole shtick about the 50/50 marriage was more of a deterrent to getting married than an incentive. Sex for laundry? That's supposed to be a selling point? How about just pay someone to do your laundry?

She grew up the daughter of a single mom living off food stamps and in and out of bad marriages. By her thirties, she was dating rock stars and celebrities and magnates of industry, hardly the same kind of men who rotated in and out of her home growing up. And yet to her, marriage was the same: "A prison."

"I want nothing to do with [marriage], unless I can find somebody who is equal and lets me do whatever I want to do," she says. "That had not been my experience in my dating life, ever."

Amazingly, Jennifer *Justice* is a lawyer. In fact, she was Jay Z's lawyer and business manager for seventeen years, helping build Roc Nation, his label, talent agency, and production company, whose artists include Rihanna, Demi Lovato, DJ Khaled, T.I., and more. Her friends call her "JJ."

Her big break came when she was interviewing to be an associate at a major entertainment law firm. They mentioned they represented a young hip-hop artist named Jay Z, and she was a fan.

This was during a golden era of musicians hiring female lawyers. It was common in the grunge scene in Seattle, where JJ grew up. A lot of these artists had grown up poor, were largely uneducated, and felt like outsiders to a rigged game. A lot of them had also been raised by single mothers. "[Female lawyers] represented Nirvana and Pearl Jam and Alice in Chains and Sublime, too. It's like this motherly thing," JJ says. "Female lawyers are very efficient because we can multitask. Our egos don't get involved in arguing things. We usually get a lot of things done very quickly. I just think it really resonated with the bands."

JJ and Jay Z clicked because they were both outsiders to the white, male system fraught with labels and middlemen. He would ask questions about why the system was a certain way; she wouldn't have a great answer. Not being invested in the system herself, she'd push to change the rules for him.

"It was this connection," she says. "In watching him grow, I grew. I came in with this fresh set of eyes. When ignorance is bliss kind of thing. We just started creating a lot of different ways to do things in the business together, because the thing about Jay is: He's fearless. He will do things based on his instinct. He doesn't care what everybody thinks."

Jay Z was soon taking up at least 50 percent of JJ's billable hours, and she made partner in three years. She was soon playing a significant role in changing the very economics of the music business, particularly in the hip-hop world, where some of music's greatest entrepreneurs reside. After eleven years in the trenches together, Jay Z wanted her full time.

Every New Yorker I know hates when you compare their lives to *Sex and the City*, but tell me the story of Jay Z offering her the job couldn't be a scene in the show:

"I was with all my friends. We'd just started a vacation, a short mini-vacation around a three-day weekend in Malibu. First glass of rosé, sitting out on the balcony watching the beach. And I got a text from Jay saying, 'Can you call me?' I was like, 'Oh shit, what did I do?'"

"He was like, 'Look, I'd really like you to come work solely for me. You have the weekend to think about it.' We both started laughing, and I was like, 'OK, I'll get back to you.'"

"I got off the phone and I went out to all of my friends, who were all in the movie business. I was like, 'Oh my God, Jay Z just offered me a full-time job working solely for him.'"

"This was the exact quote of what they said: 'Bitch, please, you're doing it. Can you pass me that rosé?'"

The next few years were a whirlwind of the glamour that comes with mixing in those circles—"I'm dating probably way too many of them and having a really good time"—and the grind of being part of a six-person team building Roc Nation—"How do we order letterhead?"

At some point, all that felt hollow. JJ wanted kids. "I've come this far," she says. "I've flown all over the world. I've had this great life. How many more bags and shoes can I get? It's not going to make me happy. I'm not religious in the slightest, but it was like this weird spiritual . . . 'How did I get this far? Why am I here, versus anybody else in my family? There's got to be more to it.'

"The only thing is really children and passing whatever knowledge that I've learned on. It was more that and less having children because that's just what you are supposed to do. It was a very calculated thing: There's more to this life, my life and how I got here, than just me. I really wanted kids."

It didn't occur to her that was a reason to get married.

"I was never scared about doing it by myself," she says. "Because everybody I knew growing up had done it by themselves. Even in my adult life and career here, most of the women I knew were still doing it by themselves, whether they were married or not. That never scared me at all."

Women like JJ had moved to New York in their twenties, lived in shitty walk-ups, and steadily conquered the city in the *Sex and the City* era, when women were taking control of their lives in a city rich with endless dating options.

In real life, women in New York in this era didn't necessarily obsess over shoes, and a lot of them didn't wind up with their own "Mr. Big" in the end. And that wasn't necessarily a tragedy. Many lived in gorgeous apartments and had dream jobs and powerful networks of friends. The only thing they hadn't quite done was get married. Why should that stop them from having a baby? New York had never stopped them from achieving anything else. They didn't want you to feel sorry for them. This was another *accomplishment*.

If men were single moms, this is exactly how they'd brand themselves. As some sort of life hack or endurance sport. *Oh, you needed a man to do that? I didn't.*

Becoming a mother wasn't the hardest struggle JJ had faced. She was the first person in her entire extended family to go to college, let alone law school. She picked the legal profession out of a fixation on making sure she could earn a decent living. She wasn't worried about any stigma either. I asked how she navigated dating so many musicians and remaining a respected woman in business. Didn't she face the same haters and double standards as the rest of us? "I just said, 'You know what? Guys do it all the time.' I was like, 'You're a hypocrite, and I'm not going to put up with it.'"

JJ was way post-50/50. If that was as good as marriage got, that was the pinnacle, no thank you.

She had her twins, Nico and Jack, on her own, using IVF. "Being a single mom without a dad, I was like, 'At least they'll always have each other,'" she says. "I'm glad I have both of them. It's hard, obviously, but I don't know any different."

Like so many women I spoke with for this book, her kids changed her, but not in the way society likes to make us think. Her life, her priorities, and her sense of what she wanted to accomplish in the business world sharpened into focus. "I needed to see if I was good outside of Jay, and if I could have that career without having that safety net," she says.

After many conversations, she quit. She took three months off, her first adult vacation ever. She'd worked forty hours a week since she was fourteen years old, with the exception of when she was studying for the bar and took two months of semi–checked out maternity leave.

She wound up becoming the president of corporate development for Superfly, producers of major music festivals like Bonnaroo and Outside Lands. Superfly had been a cozy all-male partnership, and JJ gave them a shot of aggressive, unapologetic estrogen and ambition. Within her first year there, she had a dozen new major festivals and events and partnerships in development.

In 2016 I flew to New York to get a closer look at the lives of several of these new power single moms. Were stories like JJ's as effortless as they sounded? Did power New York single moms have armies of help? Did they live in the kind of chaos that I did underneath the placid image of "I got this"?

I started with JJ. She opened the door one morning with wet hair, no makeup, and a silky robe. She introduced me to Nico and Jack with a wave of her hand as she scooted off to her room, emerging about ten minutes later completely polished in an easy black pantsuit, hair brushed, and just enough makeup. She spoke as her arms and legs did a dozen different things efficiently, as if disconnected from her body. She interrupted herself every few moments to tell her kids to put on their shoes or hurry up.

The apartment was full of pictures of celebrities and two massive—*massive*—teddy bears that a grown person could sleep on. Jack and Nico's first gifts from Jay Z and Beyoncé. They took up almost half of her living room. "They are huge, but I have to keep them," JJ says. Her nanny got Jack and Nico in shoes finally, as JJ piled everyone onto the stroller and leashed a yappy dog. "Can you imagine if Frank Sinatra had given me a baby gift and my mom threw it out because it was too big?"

She walked her kids to school, greeted the other kids and parents by name, and had a quick powwow with the teacher, then handed the dog to the nanny to take back home. She moved from mom mode to power mode almost immediately, stopping for coffee on a route that passed half a dozen powerful and famous people in New York, whom she vowed to have drinks with *very soon*, before explaining to me who they all were. Every moment of her day was optimized.

Most women who decide to have a baby on their own will never do it with such comfort and ease, and no one appreciates that more than JJ. The only thing Jack and Nico have in common with her childhood is the lack of a reliable father. And this gulf of experience dominates her mind-set. She is unapologetically *obsessed* with money, because she is so afraid of not having it again.

"Having money is not only a luxury in terms of what you can do with it, but in your head space," she says. "When you are poor, and you have no money, all you are thinking about is eating and how you are going to pay your rent. You're not thinking, 'Do I really like this person? Do I really want this job? Where should I vacation?' You're thinking, 'How can I get gas in my car? How can I keep my car running? How can I eat? How can I feed my family?' I didn't want those issues. I wanted to be able to live life.

"I wasn't scared of doing this by myself, but I was scared of being poor again," she says. "When you have been really poor, as poor as we were, where food is an issue . . . you just still have a poverty mentality. I'm worrying that I don't have enough for them."

Despite the nanny, the New York apartment, the massive teddy bears Beyoncé—*Beyoncé!*—gave her, somewhere deep inside she is still that little girl living in poverty, unsure of where her next meal might come from. And beneath the incredible confidence and swagger, you see inklings of those confidence issues that plague so many women. "Women are terrible at negotiating for themselves," she says. "But you know what? I'm a great lawyer, and now I have two new clients named Nico and Jack."

I spent several days in New York shadowing power urban single moms like JJ. Stephanie Rudnick represents high-powered female athletes and is raising two young kids on her own after a marriage gone bad. Rachel Sklar had gotten pregnant unexpectedly during a summer fling, but decided to have the baby anyway and bravely wrote about it publicly.

Vanity Fair reporter and author Nancy Jo Sales wanted to have a baby so badly that she convened a dinner of would-be baby daddies she'd had relationships with in the past to discuss who could be the father. "I didn't have $50,000 to spend on a sperm bank, and I had man friends who would be good donors," she said. (She wound up getting pregnant via a fling instead.)

Not all these women had the baggage around marriage that JJ described. They certainly didn't "hate men." Rachel had just never found *that* person and when at forty she found herself pregnant, she realized becoming a mom didn't have to hinge on it. Stephanie never expected her marriage to fail when she had kids, but here she was. Nancy Jo was married twice—even promised the whole 50/50 thing the second time. But it just didn't work out that way.

"I love men but something happens when you get in a relationship with them and you are suddenly talking about jobs and money and who is to blame and all this crap that women have to go through," Nancy Jo says. "They just do not see it as a gender equality issue. I like hanging out with them. I like having sex with them. I just don't like being in a relationship with them. So I thought, maybe I could split-screen my life, and I could just have the relationships that work for me."

It was the men—not the kids—that had proven to be a net negative on many of these women's careers. Sales said she did the worst work of her career while married. Her marriages detracted from who she was and what she could do, but like Shirley Jackson, Sales's career accelerated once she became a mom. She interviewed with Graydon Carter at *Vanity Fair* eight months pregnant and dressed in "ridiculous" teen-skater clothes because they were baggy. She was hired on the spot to do a profile of Paris Hilton. She has since written two best-selling books, one of which was made into a film.

"When I had my daughter, I became myself fully," Nancy Jo says. "I no longer filter my existence for men. I am not somebody's wife or girlfriend or looking to get married or hoping you'll have a baby with me. I know I am the most myself in my relationship with her. I am the most comfortable and at ease."

Every New York single mom I met approached the challenge with the same one-day-at-a-time tactical problem solving that had allowed them to build careers and lives in New York City. They weren't about perfect; they were about getting it done. Rachel greeted me wearing jeans and a white V-neck T-shirt smelling of ammonia. "I started to pick up for you, and I got carried away!" she gushed when she opened the door.

When faced with a spare hour in which she didn't have an immediate child or work task to do, she grabbed the rare window to scour her bathroom. If studies have shown that a married mother becomes more productive the more children she has, imagine the productivity of the single mom.

The circumstances—and levels of comfort—for each of these women were different. But they were unapologetic in their love and gratitude for their children . . . and in their belief that they were entitled to experience that love whether they'd been lucky enough to find "the one" or not. They were so natural as their kids' "everything" it seemed strange to think anyone could view their families as "incomplete."

And while none of these women had family nearby to help out, their corners of New York operated like a big family for them. The grocery deliveryman, the doorman, the preschool in their neighborhood, the woman who is walking her dog every morning as they walk to school, all the parents at the park where the kids stop and play after school in the afternoons.

And then there was the New York sisterhood of single moms itself. "When I was pregnant [we hung out all the time] but then it was like we all got busy and went on with our lives," JJ says. "We all know we're still there for support. We all look at each other and wink, and we're like, 'Yeah, we got this.' It's not like this thing where we have to get together and be like, 'Oh my God! What are we doing?!' It's just moms being really confident moms that don't have free babysitting."

They may have men in their lives, because they want them, but they don't *need* them.

⌘

The affluent single mother doesn't want a husband for fear he might endanger her career or sense of self.

The single mother in poverty doesn't want a husband for fear he might endanger her children.

Yet it's the single mothers in poverty who are vilified as not only "bad mothers" but also responsible for most of the ills in society. The gulf in perceptions of well-off single mothers of New York and single mothers living in poverty is also summed up in Amy Cuddy's quadrants. Career women are viewed as cold/competent, evoking envy. Working moms are viewed as warm/incompetent, evoking pity. But the homeless or mothers doing their best in poverty are viewed as cold/incompetent, evoking *contempt.*

That is hard-coded in how we react to people. Think of how cruel that is for a moment. Not only do the New York single mothers have the confidence that they can feed and clothe their children, they at worst inspire *pity*, while a single mother doing her best in poverty inspires *contempt*.

The single most transformative book I read on motherhood in the last two years was called *Promises I Can Keep: Why Poor Women Put Motherhood Before Marriage*, by Kathryn Edin and Maria Kefalas. These two sociologists studied 162 low-income women, roughly a decade ago, all having had children outside marriage. Their research began as that switchover—where the average marriage age was older than the average age women became mothers—was taking place. When they started their project, one-third of American children were born to single moms, and in just twenty years that grew to some 40 percent.

Edin and Kefalas wanted to understand why there had been such a dramatic decoupling of marriage and motherhood, calling it "perhaps the biggest demographic mystery of the last half of the twentieth century." Forget "Is it good or bad?" They wanted to understand *why* poor women were three times more likely to have a child while single.

The sociologists did something radical. *They actually got to know them.* They even lived among more than a hundred of these women, centering their research on eight poor neighborhoods in Philadelphia, Pennsylvania, and Camden, New Jersey.

Half of the women they spoke with hadn't graduated high school; one-third hadn't worked in a year; and first-time unwed mothers were on average twenty-one. But compare that to the men they spoke to: Half of them hadn't finished high school either; 25 percent didn't have a job, with half of the ones who did making less than $10,000 a year. And 40 percent of these men had already been to prison or jail before the baby was born.

Most of these women did not set out to become single moms. At the time they had their children, 80 percent of them were still with their partner and 40 percent were living with them. By the time the children turned three, two-thirds of the couples had split up.

Part of that was financial stress, but that was hardly the whole story. One-third of these mothers said crime, drug dealing, or jail time was behind their split. More than one-third blamed their partner's drug addiction or alcoholism. Forty percent said it was the father's chronic infidelity. And nearly half of these women cited ongoing physical abuse as the cause.

Story after story shows that parenthood changed these women, but not the men. So many of these women chose to be single mothers as a supreme act of protecting their babies.

Said one mother, named Monica: "He's in jail, I have two kids, I'm raising them, I'm working, I'm doing this, I'm doing that. What was his *purpose?* I started thinking, 'I don't need him.' He was just like an extra burden. It was actually easier without him."

Said another mom, named Toby: "He's not going to take food out of my daughter's mouth for [drugs]."

And in doing that, these women felt redeemed. The mothers didn't see their children as a burden. Their children saved their lives. "[They] almost never see children as bringing them hardship; instead, they manage to credit virtually every bit of good in their lives to the fact that they have children," Edin and Kefalas write.

For some women, it was a path to greater standing in society, since paths like college weren't an option for them. For other women, it was the first time they'd experienced unconditional love. "I think [I got pregnant] mainly because I wanted to be loved," said one woman, named Pamela, who had seven children. "I went through my childhood without it. Somehow I knew that . . . I would grow up and have kids, and it was something that was *mine.* Nobody could take it away from me. It was something that would *love* me. I would be able to love it unconditionally. There was no strings attached to it."

These women describe their children as forcing them to grow up, to think about the future, and thus saving their lives.

"I'd be dead or in jail."

"I'd be still out partying."

"I'd be messed up on drugs."

And from one mother in an abusive relationship: "I wanted to kill myself—I really wanted to kill myself, but my children are what's kept me alive."

The authors note that there is research showing children raised in single-parent homes "learn less in school, are more likely to have children while they are teens, are less likely to graduate from high school and enroll in college, and have more trouble finding jobs as adults." Only "half of the disadvantage" is income related, they argue, giving some credence to politicians who blame these women's choices as weakening society.

But when you consider the redemptive power that motherhood has had on these women, how can you begrudge them their right to love? To feeling a sense of value and importance in the world? Do we really live in a world where the government should get to control whether middle-class women are allowed to abort babies and at the same time tell women in poverty they aren't allowed to have them at all?

Because having children is seen as so redemptive and being married frequently comes with abuse, the two milestones are completely decoupled in poor communities. These women couldn't fathom that middle-class women choose to wait until their thirties to have kids. Meanwhile, these women couldn't imagine getting married before thirty-five. Motherhood was something they needed to do to feel valued, to achieve their potential, to give back to the world, but marriage was considered a luxury.

That sentiment is almost as old-fashioned as it is radical.

While middle-class women get married for love and wait for the perfect time and circumstances to have a baby, poor women do the opposite. Many said that after forty was the ideal time to get married, citing their fear of "rushing into something." "Marriage to these mothers represents not only the end of one's youth, but also the end of one's dreams for social mobility," Edin and Kefalas write. Meantime, these women don't feel having kids will dent their potential in the future unless "they let it."

It's exactly inverse of how marriage and pregnancy are viewed in middle-class life. Marriage is a way of joining adult society and having kids is what might derail your career mobility or spoil your youth.

What explains such a disconnect? Pattern recognition, once again. These women know more "good" single mothers in their neighborhoods than "happily" married couples.

They dream of their kids being the exception—the one to get out, go to college, move to a good neighborhood, and buy a home. Unlike the New York power moms I met, for the poor moms, it's the schools and neighborhoods that typically drag their kids down, not become their de facto spouse.

But while the odds are stacked against them, that elusive success story does happen. Tristan Walker was one. He grew up in the projects of Queens, one of three boys raised by a single mother working three jobs after his father died. Today, he's the CEO of Walker + Company, which has raised millions in venture capital. This after early stints at Twitter and Foursquare and an entrepreneur-in-residence job at Andreessen Horowitz.

He hustled his way out via luck, smarts, scholarships, and his mother continually kicking his butt, he says. "[She gave me] every value that I have. My mother worked three jobs at the same time. I cannot even fathom—fathom!—how that's possible. Three jobs, three children as a single mother in the 'hood. You know? That is superhuman to me. And I always believe my mother is indeed superhuman in that regard.

"To come from where she came from, to come from where we came from, and to see where I am right now is a testament to her strength. It is a testament to her loyalty to me. It is a testament to her conviction in her own values to make sure I was on the straight and narrow. Without her I don't think I'd be here right now."

⌘

I was so moved reading about the moms in Edin and Kefalas's book, the feeling of empowerment and redemption they got from their children in impossible situations. How giving can save you, even when you have so little to give. It's infuriating that the world believes joy is somehow a drag on society. That only certain people have rights to have that kind of love in their lives.

I was even angrier that so many white male politicians insist the answer for them is marriage to *anyone*, seemingly, as long as it is a man. Even though nearly half of these women leave their partners because of chronic physical abuse. The answer can't be tying them to men who put their lives and their children's lives in danger. It needs to be programs that help these mothers.

Writ large, this is benevolent sexism once again. Affluent

single moms are "the right kind" of single moms. The patriarchy may not like us, but we can at least pay our way in society, without depending on the government. By tolerating us, the patriarchy can vilify "the wrong kind" of single moms who raise kids in poverty.

The patriarchy wins when women are divided. We need to fight for single mothers living in poverty if we believe anything we say about equality. We can't enjoy the increased social and economic freedom of being single moms at the expense of women born in less advantageous circumstances.

"This is the way the country is going, and we are going to see more and more and more single moms," Nancy Jo says, aware of the comparative privilege she has next to most single moms. "How are we going to be this without supporting them? Right now we just blame the mom. We don't look at the whole system. Let's blame these women, not the man who isn't there.

"Being a mom wasn't that hard for me because I had resources," she continues. "Journalists don't make a lot of money, but I made enough, and I borrowed on a credit card for a while. But a lot of people don't have that as an option. I could enjoy it because I had those resources. I want all moms to be able to enjoy their children."

14

You Don't Fuck with the Women of Iceland

AS I DUG MORE INTO Maternal Wall bias and single-mom stigmas, I kept wondering about something Kate Manne said during that lecture on misogyny at Kim Scott's house.

Someone asked her about so-called male and female traits in business, the kinds of things we all observe. How women are less likely to negotiate for a raise, are plagued with confidence gaps, don't go into fields like math and science in big numbers . . . you know all the stereotypes. This person asked if Manne had seen any new research that said conclusively whether this was the fault of DNA or society.

Manne said this was the single hottest area of funding in gender studies at the university level. And she also said she thought most of it was a waste of money. "We will never know how much is society and how much is nature, because we have never had a control group," she said. "We have never had a society where women are truly equal to men to compare to."

Whoa.

That stuck with me throughout the fall of 2016 as I read the modern canon of empowered, thoughtful feminist literature, whether *The Confidence Code* and its grappling with how to make sense of women's inherent insecurity; or *The Pie Life*, which begs and begs women not to quit careers when they become mothers because 70 percent of them will never get full-time jobs again; or even *Getting to 50/50*, with its frustrating sales pitch to men for why women should work. Even Sallie Krawcheck, the author of *Own It: The Power of Women at Work*, argues we shouldn't use the word "empowered" anymore because the definition of the damn word is "to *give* power or authority to." It's my same objection with 50/50, and I use it *all the time*.

For all the hundreds of thousands of words written by empowered women trying to make sense of why empowerment (OMFG, you are right about that word, Sallie) came so hard to us, Manne's comments were the ultimate leveler: We would never really know how much of each of our struggles was us and how much was the patriarchy.

And that's when I started getting obsessed with Iceland.

Iceland is not that idyllic control group that Manne referenced where men and women are equal. But it's a damn sight closer than the US. The *Economist*'s "Glass-Ceiling Index" ranks Iceland as the best country in the world when it comes to gender equality at work. The United States ranked twentieth out of twenty-nine countries measured.

Women in Iceland are more educated than men, they hold 41 percent of management positions, 44 percent of board seats, and 47 percent of seats in parliament. Childcare costs are just 6.5 percent of average wages, compared to nearly 40 percent in the US.

And Iceland is a single-mom paradise, even compared to the single-motherhood-bonus women I met in New York. Some two-thirds of the children born in Iceland are born to single moms. Blended families are the norm in this small country where grandparents help out, older siblings pitch in, five-year-olds are given the autonomy of walking to and from school on their own, and unmarried co-parents swap their kids every other week, even if they were simply the result of a one-night stand in a bar. It's the rare Icelandic kid whose siblings are all full brothers and sisters.

People have kids young, in their early twenties on average. Because of that, families are bigger and it's common for a successful woman to have had kids by multiple partners, never marrying any of them. And those rare children who do have all full-blooded brothers and sisters, whose parents are still together? Odds are those parents either never got around to getting married or did it after their children were born. Many homes look like a sort of modern family square dance, where one group of kids rotates out to the other parent while the others rotate in. Kids regularly go from classmates one year to brothers and sisters the next.

The more I read about Iceland, the more I had to see it for myself. Was it possible that there was a country where the story of a Jennifer Justice or a Nancy Jo Sales didn't represent insane social progress and a liberal blue-state outlier? Where there simply was no stigma to working moms or single moms or parents living together and raising kids despite no document making it socially OK?

If you asked me to connect you with single-mom entrepreneurs in Silicon Valley, I would have to sit down and think to even come up with five. But in Iceland, these women were remarkably easy to find. I happened to know one person in Iceland via a conference I'd attended years ago. Within hours of reaching out to him on Facebook, I had three days of meetings booked with women who worked in government and education, had built companies, and most of all mothered the shit out of their kids, husband or no.

As I was preparing for the trip, I was introduced to Brynja Gudmundsdóttir, a single mom to *four kids* starting in her early twenties. She'd also built a software company along the way.

I thought of every person in America who found it so remarkable that I could juggle two kids and a company—of how often I got sucked into my own single-mom martyr syndrome. Were Icelandic women just stronger? Or was this all mental? Just the product of all the shame and concern trolling of American society?

In meeting after meeting with women of all income levels and of several generations, I found three major consistent themes.

The first was these women were incredulous when I told them my go-to stat: 40 percent of Americans believe it is bad for society if women work. Indeed, the idea of a stay-at-home mom is bizarre and unimaginable to women in Iceland. I asked each of them if they'd ever known any stay-at-home moms when they were growing up or raising their own kids. The answer was almost universally no. A few women gazed into space for ten minutes and recalled there was that one woman who was disabled and couldn't work.

I asked one woman, Ragnhildur Arnljótsdóttir, how she would

react if her teenaged daughter told her she didn't want to have a career. *This had never occurred to her.* There are no mommy wars in Iceland. "I think I would never believe her," she finally said. "I think I would always fear that she was missing out on something, and I would feel very sorry for her."

It's worth noting Ragnhildur is the permanent secretary in Iceland's prime minister's office, one of the highest ranking civil servants in the nation. Even in Iceland, she sometimes felt guilt for working too much, having too ambitious of a career.

Every woman I spoke with was even more shocked when I said I took no maternity leave after Evie was born. When women in Iceland talk about taking a "short" leave, they still mean at least three months.

The second theme was that each woman insisted there was no moral or religious stigma whatsoever to being an unwed mother in society. You aren't damaged goods. You aren't a slut. You aren't representative of the moral decay of society. You aren't reckless and irresponsible. You aren't pushed into a shotgun wedding. You are simply . . . a new mother.

Ragnhildur only got married two months after her first child was born, and her husband didn't so much propose as her mother suggested one day at the kitchen table, "Maybe you two should get married, you know?" The priest who did the ceremony had himself been divorced four times. The big reason to get married is your legal status is stronger should your husband die. But it is in no way tied to when you have children.

That stigma, that fear, that shame was so ingrained in American society, politics, and popular culture, it seemed almost Kate Manne–like to imagine a world in which that stigma of being pregnant out of wedlock simply didn't exist. It was even stranger to actually encounter it.

One of the most extreme stories I heard was of a woman who had a one-night stand, got pregnant, and didn't even consider having an abortion. No one in her family or friend group pressured her to have an abortion. She never wound up dating the dad, but to this day they have a 50/50 co-parent relationship, and the child goes back and forth between each family regularly, with loving relationships with all the cousins, aunts, uncles, grandparents. It was just something that happened in a society where . . . you know . . . *people have sex.*

While in America, conservatives want to make sure that middle-class women don't have abortions and that poor, unmarried women are shamed out of having children, the government of Iceland doesn't seem to have either obsession with its nation's uteruses. *Don't those belong to you ladies?*

Similarly, there are few hang-ups in Iceland around gay and transgender issues. One LGBT activist, Kitty Von-Sometime, told me that her partner actually hates living in Iceland because there is no "gay community," because there is no ostracism of gay people to rally around. Gay bars are just . . . bars.

The third theme—which is all the more surprising given the first two—is that women in Iceland are overall more pissed off about inequality than women in America. Woman after woman told me not to believe the hype that Iceland is a "feminist nation," even though no one pressures mothers not to work, even though there is no stigma against unwed mothers, even though the country has far more enlightened parental leave laws, even though there are quotas for gender representation on boards of companies a certain size, even though that gap in pay is one of the lowest in the world.

The women happily granted each of these points. They happily granted that Iceland is better than a lot of places. But these women were insistent—to a one—that sexism is alive and well in Iceland. And they were pissed about it.

Women in Iceland describe the same kind of sexism we see in the US. "There are so many men who want my chair," Ragnhildur said at one point, exasperated. She convenes a regular meeting of eight permanent secretaries, and for the first time in history, five are women. The remaining men were so destabilized by it that she replaced the conference room table with a round table "to try to make them feel better." Fragile male ego is an international language.

But the difference is, to these women, talking about sexism isn't playing some "gender card." It is a fact that there's still a wage gap. It is a fact that men try to undermine them. It is a fact that not enough women get the top jobs, and it is a fact that it is unacceptable. Young women, old ones. It didn't matter.

That simply didn't match conversations I had in the United States with women who lived with far less ideal circumstances. Women who didn't feel they deserved these things. Women who truly did think they had to negotiate with their husband to have a career.

To me, that is what makes Iceland such a feminist country: the expectation that things need to get a lot better. These women had internalized that they deserve it, whether it fully exists yet or not.

Around the time I visited, women in Iceland staged a protest, marching out of their offices early in reaction to the country's remaining 14 percent gender pay gap, compared to 18 percent in the United States. That protest translated into action. In early 2017 the country became the first in the world to require employers to prove they are paying women equally to men. "We may rank number one in the world at the moment, but the job is still not done," said Iceland's *male* prime minister, Bjarni Ben-ediktsson.

No stigma against working moms, no stigma against single moms, and an outraged and universal sense of unfairness that things aren't equal enough and something has to be done about it. That's a powerful and alluring combination when you've spent a lifetime terrified that becoming a mother would destroy your career, your autonomy, your standing in the world, and that a divorce would render you "a failure."

⌘

There are a lot of explanations I got for these cultural distinctions in Iceland. That it is a small and not very diverse nation. When you want to force change, a relatively small number of people can shake up the electorate. People never move far from where they grew up, so grandparents can help single mothers in a way they can't in major urban centers in the US. That it is safe enough so kids can have more autonomy and take care of themselves more. That it is an isolated country that didn't interact much with the world until World War II. That you have to be hearty to make it in Iceland—whether you are a man or a woman. One legendary winter destroyed one-third of the population, and another third left. Iceland needs everyone to make the country function.

Like most cultures it's likely a mix of all this and more. But one of my favorite explanations came from Halla Tómasdóttir, whom I met with on my first full day in Iceland.

Halla is only seven years older than I am. Like me, Halla started her career in the American South. Like me, Halla did well because she could drink like a man and swear like a man, and people accepted her as a man. Like me, Halla wasn't super aware of or concerned about sexism back then. "Early on, I didn't believe we needed to do anything about this. I just thought it would sort itself out," she says, as we sip wine in the lobby of a Reykjavík hotel.

Yep, yep, yep. I nod.

"I thought it was a question of time because when I was seven, women took the day off in Iceland and they brought the country to its knees, so from 1975 people started saying, 'OK, life doesn't work in Iceland if women don't show up to work.'"

Wait, back up.

That's right: The year I was born, 90 percent of women across Iceland walked off the job and took to the streets. Contrast that to America in 2017. Even in an era of social media and even in the wake of the highly successful Women's March, the attempt here at "A Day Without a Woman" wasn't anywhere near as successful. There were few places in America where life was truly disrupted; the message around why the strike mattered was muddled, and many people saw it as divisive. Only a subset of affluent women *could* strike without retaliation, people argued. In liberal San Francisco, I joined in, but almost no women I knew did. The teachers in my kids' schools had either not heard about it or thought it was less supportive of moms to strike and close down school for the day.

But the women of Iceland in 1975 didn't let any of that stop them. They were upset with the country's inequality and wanted to send a strong message: The world didn't work if women didn't work. They walked out whether their "job" was driving a bus or working at a bank or even taking care of newborns at home. For that day, Halla says, kids didn't get fed, buses weren't driven, banks didn't get opened, schools didn't open.

"Nothing worked, because ninety percent of women in Iceland did this," she says. It took a year to organize the walkout. Some women's husbands left them because they'd helped organize it.

But do you know what happened five years later? Iceland elected the first democratically elected female president in the world, and she was a single mom. Halla puts it down to that women's strike.

"I'm raised with women who have the courage to do that, and we do change the world, because five years later we have that first female president," she says. "She was not only a single mom, she was a breast cancer survivor. She was asked during her campaign, 'What are you going to do as president? You're a woman.' Someone added, 'You're even half a woman,' because she'd had a mastectomy. She answered, 'Well I was intending on leading the nation, not breastfeeding it.' She took the high road and she won.

"This impacted me profoundly, and not just me, but the men of this generation. They thought it's normal that a woman is president."

Wow.

This happened in Iceland before 1980, and I sat there talking about it a month before America voted overwhelmingly for its first female president, though she lost the electoral college.

Halla came to America for college and spent the first few years as a rising executive at companies like Mars and PepsiCo. She fell into those same traps that so many of the American women I spoke to for this book have talked about. She didn't really get sexism. She excelled because she could be a "cool dude."

She managed the men's soccer team at Auburn University, so

she was comfortable being the only woman in the room. "I was very good at drinking," she says. "I could drink more than the best man, and I could talk about soccer, and those two things were more important than my education early in my career."

She worked for ten years in the US. She had no husband and no kids. Her career was on the fast track, but she felt something was missing. It hit her at a corporate PepsiCo event. She was used to being the only woman but found herself again and again being in a group of guys who wanted to go to a strip club. "You are this single woman and everyone is drinking and partying and you find yourself in situations that are not comfortable," she says. "I did very well playing a man, but I wasn't happy playing a man. It just didn't sit well with me. It felt disrespectful. I thought it had to do with the culture, but somewhere I started to figure out that it was more about the difficulty of being different as a woman."

She came home to Iceland. Within three years she was the mother of two and living with their father. "The boy changed me, but the girl really changed me," she says. "I had a difficult birth. She came out blue and not breathing and was taken away to intensive care. I didn't get to hold her for a few days, and during those days there was a child next to us in intensive care that died. I had one of those life-changing moments. I thought, 'When she's twenty, she is not going to face this stuff.' I made a very firm decision that my cause and my quest in life was to change this."

It was her awakening as a feminist, her "coming out" as a woman, as she calls it. "I refused from that point forward to hold back my feminine side," she says.

She's done a lot since. She's helped found Reykjavík University, she cocreated an investment firm called Audur Capital that she ran on "feminine" principles, like only investing in things you could understand. She credits this approach to being a rare firm that survived the brutal 2008 financial collapse, which still haunts Iceland. She helped change a law in the country that mandates quotas for how many women companies over a certain size must have on their boards of directors.

Here is her recipe for real change. It isn't 50/50 or anything else that depends on men. Women have to be willing to be the boss, and they have to do it *as women*, not by pretending to be men. "Men won't change this," she says. "It wasn't men who took the day off to strike. Women did. Great men supported it. And great men learned from it. But we are going to have to take charge of this journey. And we need to be the best version of our authentic selves. We can't copy men anymore. We have to be feminine leaders.

"Those values of the past are the ones that brought the entire global economy down, brought this entire country to its knees," she says. "In Iceland, women were brought in to clean up the mess."

Although she has raised a son to be in touch with his emotions and a daughter who's allowed to be strong, Halla is struck by the difference in confidence between them, even in feminist Iceland, even with a feminist mother.

"He thinks he's God's gift to mankind," she says. "I am amazed that even my daughter has a confidence gap. I am still struggling with why the inner voices of girls are so much louder and seem to drag them down so much more. Having said that, when I ran for president and came in second, she really grew a lot from seeing me take that on. She did four TV interviews on election day, and she was a star! Twitter was going nuts!"

Wait. Back up.

"That was the most enormous challenge I've taken on," she says.

Halla was not a natural choice to run for the job. She had never been in politics before. Her campaign started with thousands of people on Facebook urging her to run. "I thought, 'Oh my God, who am I to run for president?' I had to struggle with my own internal doubts, but when I went around to all the women who I thought could run, none of them had the courage or willingness to take what comes with it," she says. "I thought, 'Can I really give another keynote and say, "Women, do it!" and then I get encouraged by these three thousand people, and I say "No, not me, I have a good life"?'"

Early on, she was predicted to get just 1 percent of the vote. She got 28 percent, coming in second to Gudni Jóhannesson who got 39 percent. For a while on election night, they were neck and neck. She finished ten points higher than the polls suggested.

What explained her surge? She started talking openly about those feminine values that saved her firm from the financial crisis. She focused on the strengths of women, not that women are "better" but that they bring a different point of view, eliminating herd mentality when they have a seat at the table.

"I had all of these people with experience telling me what to do, and I finally said, 'You know what? I'm just going to fucking do this as I want. I am going to be me. I am going to run this race as I would, and that's not negative tactics, and it's not attacking people . . . it's none of that crap. I am going to believe in the future and be positive and be surrounded by girls,'" she says. "'I am going to talk about girl power. I am not going to excuse the fact that I'm a woman, as Hillary Clinton did early in her race; I am going with the woman card. I think it matters that I'm a woman.' I did it, and in forty-five days I went from one percent to twenty-eight percent."

Sitting in a hotel lobby with her for several hours, I could see many of the people of Iceland felt that way, too. They came up and hugged her, clasped her hand, and told her how they'd supported her. One man from the BBC, who was in town for something else and had been there on election night, came up to gush about how wonderful she was and how they were all pulling for her.

It was stunning to me, witnessing the ugliness of our election back home. Somehow she came across in a way Clinton could not. Part of that was the differences in the women, no doubt, but it was more likely to do with the fact that Iceland was just a more feminist country that already had its first female leader decades ago. She could run on a girl-power platform of hope and optimism.

I asked her if the negatives of running for office, the reasons other women didn't want to, wound up being worse than she anticipated. "It actually was much better," she says. "I think everybody should run. I grew from it, my family grew from it, but only after I decided to do it as me."

I cannot imagine Hillary Clinton feels that way right now.

⌘

I was so inspired by the strength of the women I met in Iceland, the easy autonomy they gave their children, and their staggering lack of judgment about their private lives. The families are heavily matriarchal, says Von-Sometime. "People here don't say, 'Just wait until I tell your *father.*' They say, 'Just wait until I tell your *mother,*'" she says.

Yet there were still confidence gaps, pay gaps, and although women didn't stay home with kids, they were expected to do more of the housework at home.

I thought back to Manne's idea of a "control." Iceland clearly wasn't it. But that march . . . showing young girls of my generation that the world simply wouldn't function without them and that they held the power to bring it to their knees. That had to be part of why Iceland had followed such a different trajectory when it came to women's rights since then. Benevolent sexism didn't seem to work there. The women mostly wouldn't divide.

And of course, having more women in power means policy is inherently more empathetic to women. I was surprised by how much Iceland's policy shifts around parental leave have shaped women's pay and opportunities at work.

Like many citizens of Scandinavian countries, Icelanders expect the government to solve problems of equality, in a way Americans don't. Part of that is evidence that it's worked in the past. Woman after woman told me the single most important piece of legislation promoting equality was the way Iceland does family leave.

Families get nine months: Three can only be used by the mothers; three can only be used by the fathers; and three can be split in any way. Families get paid a percentage of their salary during this time. If the fathers don't use their three months, the family loses it.

This policy was so successful initially that some 90 percent of men took advantage of it. But then 2008 happened. The crash of 2008 was so devastating, it factors into every cultural, business, or personal narrative I heard in Iceland. After 2008, the percentage of income paid was slashed by some 30 percent. This as the cost of living has increased substantially in Iceland. And because they were the bigger breadwinners, on average, men stopped taking leave. The family couldn't justify the income hit. Male participation fell by 40 percent and the Icelandic birth rate is at the lowest level since 1953.

Eva Dögg Gudmundsdóttir has children more than ten years apart in age and says the difference in her leave before and after 2008 was staggering. The first time she and the father shared the load and got a large percentage of their regular pay. But this last time, the money paid out was so small that she wound up taking a year's leave while her partner took none.

As such, the bulk of the work of the household fell to her. Her employers, too, began taking projects from her assuming her domestic duties would grow with a new relationship, three step-kids, and a baby on the way. She described a vicious cycle of her employers pulling back projects out of fear that she'd take over more household duties, and then the pressure to take on more household duties because—after all—she wasn't getting more projects at work and had more time. She recently broke the cycle by quitting and starting her own consultancy.

A major push is on to go back to the way things were. It's not simply that the old policy—and the near-universal adoption of it—set the precedent of 50/50 families from the beginning. It affected hiring and wages for women, too. When employers the world over see a young woman, they see a ticking uterus. In a country like Iceland, they also see six months to a year of mater-nity leave. Three months is the absolute minimum women I spoke with take, and that's a luxurious leave by US standards.

But when 90 percent of men are taking advantage of the same parental leave policy, the chance that a young man will be out for three to six months is just as great.

That said, women still take a hit for taking long leaves. One young, ambitious woman I spoke with, who didn't yet have kids, knew she'd get a nice paid leave, unlike most women in America. But she assumed she'd have to move jobs after it was over. Although jobs can't be given away, when you come back after six months, you still have to fight for your place and prove yourself again, she said.

Even "feminist" Iceland, it seems, needs policies to keep it on the rails. I'm a reluctant liberal in many ways; Gawker even once called me a "free market monster." But I came away from this trip more convinced than ever that—at a minimum—federally mandated parental leave is essential to gender equality in America.

Unfortunately, that gives me even less hope that Iceland has much to offer the US in terms of a way forward. Too much of our political establishment is locked in a struggle to take away the rights that women were already granted. We are sadly not the envy of the world when it comes to feminism. That's getting worse, not better. And much of the US seems fine with that. The stat I always go back to is that one from Pew: 40 percent of Americans believe it's bad for society if women work. Presumably that means they'll never support taxpayer dollars making it easier, even if nearly half of all American households are ones where women are the primary or sole breadwinners.

And that means the gulf between what it's like for Jennifer Justice to be a single mom and for women in poverty to be single moms will continue to widen, just like the income gap in America broadly.

There are all kinds of economists who point out why that's bad for our economy. The US economy is $2 trillion larger now than it would have been if women hadn't made such inroads over the last forty years. Women-owned businesses generate some $1.6 trillion in revenue. And increasing gender equality further could add another $12 trillion to the global economy.

Those gains have benefited and would continue to benefit men, too. But the bottom line is voters and politicians don't seem to care much.

Rights for women in America are falling more and more into the hands of states or private corporations. Individual companies are offering some of the best parental benefits anywhere in the world, even covering egg freezing in some cases. San Francisco itself has just enacted the most comprehensive parental leave law anywhere in the country, giving new parents six weeks of fully paid leave.

But if you don't work at Facebook or don't work in San Francisco, that trend doesn't help you much. As a newly elected government vows to dismantle universal health care and Planned Parenthood, there's little hope that rights for parents and mothers will become decoupled from employment anytime soon.

America has already been ripped apart by income inequality—how the twenty-first century is benefiting some while it leaves so many others behind. It seems the same is going to continue to happen with basic rights for mothers. Those who continually vote for these rights in the blue states are the ones who will get them from the states anyway, while the choices for mothers and women in red states get continually eroded.

15

The Last Place You're Expecting to See Female Empowerment

DESPITE THE COMPANY'S EFFORTS TO intimidate me, I spent much of the summer of 2015 covering the absolute unraveling of Uber China, a multibillion-dollar effort that failed spectacularly. When Uber ultimately admitted defeat in 2016, Shonda Rhimes couldn't have scripted the narrative better.

Uber had used seemingly endless cash and government connections, tactics, and lobbyists to devastate competitors in each market, and its Chinese competitor Didi Chuxing turned Uber's game on itself. Didi was the only company in the world that had deeper pockets than Uber, backed by two of the largest Chinese Internet companies and several of the largest hedge funds in the world. And while there was never any evidence of the Chinese government making life any worse for the American company in the market, Didi obviously had the home-field advantage when it came to working politics in China, if it came down to that.

And China was already the largest ridesharing market in the world by rides. In January 2016, Didi announced it had completed 1.4 billion rides in 2015, some 40 percent more than the 1 billion rides it took Uber eight years to rack up. Uber was not the largest ridesharing company in the world by a large and widening margin, despite its bravado, its scorched-earth tactics, its greed, and its valuation.

And the best part? The face of Didi in the fight was its president and COO Jean Liu. *A woman. A mother.* A woman from China handed the biggest bro-CEO in Silicon Valley his ass.

As I dusted off more and more of my China contacts in reporting this story, I was struck by how many of the C-level officers running Chinese companies were women. And how many of them were CEO, COO, CFO, or even CTO. They weren't merely the token senior woman on the team running HR or marketing. It was far more pronounced than the "Get me a Sheryl!" trend in Silicon Valley, which was still limited to a dozen or so companies.

I was particularly blown away by Yilu Zhao.

Zhao was the CFO of Qunar, a KAYAK-like company in China that has recently merged with Ctrip to create a leviathan of a Chinese online travel company, worth some $20 billion. She'd regularly come to the US to meet with Wall Street investors and analysts, and I sat down with her on several of these trips to understand why women in the far younger tech world in China seemed to be doing so much better than women in Silicon Valley. In particular, most of them were mothers.

Did they just not face the same Maternal Wall bias that we did?

Zhao's story was remarkable. She grew up in China, coming to America to attend Yale. Her goal was to be a journalist, but that didn't seem likely. For one thing, her English was laden with SAT words. For another, she was an only child of parents who had sacrificed to give her every opportunity they never had. Their dream job for her was more like lawyer.

And yet, she became an award-winning reporter for the *New York Times*. She covered education and wrote a lot about immigrant culture in the US.

In 2002 she wrote about her own journey to America, in a story that displays not only beautiful writing but also a confident, unquestioning ambition, nothing like the reticence of girls to speak up in class that Sandberg wrote about in *Lean In*.

When Zhao arrived at Yale, she was an outsider. She couldn't understand why her peers kept sprinkling the word "like" into every sentence. She couldn't take notes because she couldn't write fast enough in English. She vomited at dinners out because her stomach was so unaccustomed to Western food. And yet, Zhao confidently demanded help, coaching, and guidance from the Yale staff until she started to get As on her papers.

"My papers were always written days before they were due," she wrote in the *Times*. "I lingered after classes to pester professors with questions. My classmates lent me their notes so I could learn the skill of note-taking in English."

As she got better at English, her ambition to be a journalist returned. But Columbia Journalism School's entrance exam tested would-be students' knowledge of pop culture. When Zhao took the test, the first question was to explain who Alice Walker was.

"Because my history major had centered on works by dead white men, I had never heard of Alice Walker," she wrote. "Nor had I encountered anyone with the name Alice in the United States. Concluding that the name must be out of fashion, I inferred that Ms. Walker must be British. And who was famous in England? The Spice Girls. So I wrote in the blank space, 'Alice Walker is one of the Spice Girls.'"

She did not get in. Still, she worked harder and made it to the *New York Times* anyway. (She also got a bonus law degree from Harvard.)

When she moved back to China, for family reasons, she didn't feel she could be a reporter in the same way. So she had to switch careers. She went into investment banking at Goldman Sachs, helping take major Chinese Internet companies public before leaving to be the CFO of one. When Qunar merged with Ctrip in 2016, she and the CEO of the company left and raised $1 billion to invest in Chinese companies.

Wait, that was the backup plan to journalism the whole time?

Lemme get this straight: You arrive in America speaking such SAT-word English that you screamed you were "indignant at" the washing machine when it broke. Nevertheless, you attend *Yale*. Despite being educated only in rote learning in China, you manage to get straight As on complex, nuanced Ivy League term papers. Within a few years of graduation, you are writing gorgeous, natural prose for the *New York Times*. And then you go back to China and have a second acclaimed career, becoming some combo of Mary Meeker and Safra Catz. Oh, and you're a mother of two.

I don't know of any woman who has pulled that off *in Silicon Valley*. And in China, Zhao doesn't have the glossy clout of

Sheryl Sandberg or Marissa Mayer. She's impressive, but she's also one of many.

As I first heard her story, I couldn't help but think of Sequoia Capital's Mike Moritz, the powerful investor who'd been a journalist before he became a VC, and how he said that the reason Sequoia couldn't hire women is because not enough of them founded companies and Sequoia clearly couldn't lower its standards. That the standard was "lowered" for him, but couldn't be for a woman.

Yet in China, Zhao—a former journalist and a woman—was given the same chance that Moritz was given in the US. And she didn't feel her story was unique in China's tech landscape.

Silicon Valley Bank has a huge practice in China, and they were intrigued by this kind of anecdotal evidence of a major gender disconnect between the two tech hubs. They did a study of nine hundred or so clients across the US, the UK, and China, examining how women fared at the senior levels. The results were hard to believe for Americans who hadn't done business in the tech world in China, and obvious to those who have.

When asked how many women have C-level jobs at their company, 54 percent of US tech companies answered "one or more." Similarly, 53 percent in the UK answered "one or more." In China, nearly 80 percent answered "one or more."

I don't even think that tells the whole story, because anecdotally many of the Chinese companies I've spoken with have more than one senior woman and these women are in a larger variety of roles.

At the board level, only 34 percent of US companies said they had one or more female directors on their board. Thirty-nine percent of UK companies said they had one or more female directors. Sixty-one percent of Chinese companies had one or more female directors.

Even crazier, when asked if these companies had programs in place to increase the number of women in leadership positions, 67 percent of those in the US said no, and 80 percent of those in the UK said no. Meanwhile, 63 percent of those in China said *yes*.

It's similar to the women in Iceland being more furious with sexism than the women in America who suffer from it more greatly. Women in China have substantially higher representation at the top of corporations, and yet more of these companies have programs geared towards creating greater equality. These three stats taken together show the rebuttal of the "queen bee" myth in action: When enough senior women are empowered in an organization, they overwhelmingly support other women.

It's the good kind of entitlement. The kind white men have in America.

When Zhao was at Qunar, there were more women running the business units than men, and the entire senior finance team was all working moms. As she told me about this, Manne's words again rang in my head . . . could this be a "control group"? A place where mothers have an expectation that they can not only still hold down careers but also compete for the highest jobs in large numbers.

I got excited.

In the venture capital landscape in China, it is even more extreme, as Bloomberg reported in the fall of 2016. According to their numbers, in the US, women make up 10 percent of the investing partners and only half of the firms have any female investing partners at all. In China, 17 percent of partners are female and a stunning 80 percent of firms have at least one woman investing.

Because firms with just one female partner are twice as

likely to back female entrepreneurs, this has had a huge ripple effect on women's roles in the ecosystem. The Chinese government says that women have founded 55 percent of new Internet companies and more than 25 percent of all entrepreneurs are women.

Yes, those stats came from the Chinese government. But clearly the "pipeline" of women to sit on far more tech boards and occupy so many senior jobs at tech companies is coming from somewhere. While the percentages may not be quite that high, women are getting more opportunity at seemingly every stage of the tech ecosystem in China.

And that has the same role-model impact and pattern-matching follow-on effects that we've seen with women like Sheryl Sandberg in the Valley.

Bloomberg profiles the very press-shy Chen Xiaohong, who just raised a new $500 million fund, the largest in the world run by a woman. The largest female-run fund in the US is half that size. In total, Xiaohong controls more than $1 billion in assets under management.

Like Zhao, she was college educated in the US. But she didn't train to be a journalist. She trained to be something even less in line with Mike Moritz's beloved "pipeline" of talent. She studied to be a librarian.

Are you fucking kidding me, China?

My favorite part of the Bloomberg piece was her comments on motherhood:

> *Through it all, she raised three children. Her work habits would have been unusual, if not unacceptable, in the West. She brought her first-born son to the office every day for three years.*

She says that bringing her children helped build a bond with many of the entrepreneurs she backed. Her son did cry and disrupt meetings, but that didn't stop her. It gave her a chance to develop a more personal relationship with founders.

That pride in motherhood is so much more powerful for young career women than pretending to be a man, lying about your children, or ignoring the topic altogether. Said another VC named Anna Fang of ZhenFund in the Bloomberg piece: "For me, there were many role models, which was helpful when I started a family and was worried about how to manage being a mom and running a fund."

These women actively work to support and lift up other women:

Fang's nine-member investment team has four women and they've put money into more than 30 startups founded or cofounded by women. She is part of a group of more than 150 young female venture capitalists on a WeChat social messaging group. She's also the only woman on a five-person panel judging startups on "I'm a Unicorn," China's version of the television show "Shark Tank."

OK, first Iceland blows my mind with its lack of any stigma against single mothers and its utter inability to comprehend the concept of "stay-at-home moms." And now, China's far younger tech ecosystem has simply sidestepped the fifty years of gender discrimination and unconscious bias that still plagues Silicon Valley today?

As I dug into this more, I found several common views of why things are so different for professional mothers in China.

One is that the tech industry in China is both fledgling and a massive opportunity all at once. All sorts of people with nontraditional experience get opportunities they wouldn't have in a more mature ecosystem.

But that doesn't come close to explaining all of it. A lot of it is cultural, too. Some of it goes back to communism, when Mao Zedong said women "held up half the sky" and they were expected to work just as hard to provide for the many. They labored in the fields and historically even fought alongside men in wars. "They needed the entire population to be working," Zhao says of the 1950s era. The older precapitalist generation of women simply were never given the choice not to work, not to serve the government in some way.

And yet, even stranger than "thanking" Chinese communism for women's current success in the tech industry, the one-child policy comes up in every conversation I've had about this topic. That's not a shock because for thirty-five years it affected how one in six people on the planet were "born, live, and die," according to Mei Fong's excellent book *One Child: The Story of China's Most Radical Experiment.*

Let me say in as emphatic terms as possible: No matter how many Chinese women become C-level officers, the one-child policy was not a coup for feminism.

There are horror stories of forced ninth-month abortions, twenty million forced sterilizations, and some sixty million missing Chinese girls—killed, aborted, or seized and adopted away. (Which wasn't illegal if your child was out of status.) Pregnant women were chased down; elderly parents were jailed to force women to comply. No policy that kills that many girls is good for women. And the one-child policy's rigor and cruel enforcement over women's uteruses down to the individual community level make hard-line conservatives in the US look tolerant and hands-off.

Women's uteruses were so considered property of the state that they were basically reduced to variables in math equations. Fong details how rocket scientists—not demographers—scripted the policy, figuring they could just "up the fertility" later on if they'd overcorrected in their math. The lack of consideration for women's basic autonomy and humanity is staggering. Children were efficiently "[rationed] the same way coal and grain were rationed," says Fong.

Worse, all that suffering may have been unnecessary. Fong makes a compelling case that as it happened in other Asian countries, urbanization would have naturally decreased the numbers of kids Chinese families were having. Meantime, China's surge in growth has come less from fewer mouths to feed than from a glut of cheap labor.

The workforce had already started to contract in 2012, causing the government to create a two-child policy in 2015. But only one-tenth of the couples eligible to have a second child in Beijing have, according to Fong. City life is expensive and apartments are small. The one-child policy has essentially worked too well. Many urban Chinese feel one child is the optimal number.

Today, China is living a ghostly version of what Iceland tried to demonstrate with its 1975 walkout—what a world without enough women looks like. By 2020, China will have a thirty to forty million surplus of men, the largest gender imbalance in the world. Twenty-five percent of Chinese men will be "low skilled bachelor[s]."

Fong tells stories of runaway brides who roam the countryside collecting bride payments and escaping with the money before the wedding day. While financially devastating for rural families, it's hard not to see it as cosmic poetic justice for a country that so devalued female life that it eradicated sixty million women.

You'd think, maybe, the shortage of women in China would make them more appreciated. Not so much. The dominance of men has created a more "warlike nation" says Fong.

In 2014, a Washington Post *article [argued] that a "virile form of nationalism" has begun to creep into China's foreign policy rhetoric, which they believe has been deliberately stoked to keep the allegiance of "young adult bare branches." . . . [In 2008] economists showed that a 1% increase in China's gender ratios increased violent and property crime rates between 5 and 6 percent. . . . [And according to a 2013 study] China's bachelors had lower self-esteem compared to married men, and much higher rates of depression and aggression.*

One in four women in China are victims of domestic violence, and they have few protections. Only 30 percent of the deeds for Chinese homes include women's names, even though 70 percent contributed to purchasing them. Fong argues that this has locked women out of arguably the greatest creation of Chinese wealth in recent years.

And the policies around unwed mothers make GOP politicians look downright woke. "Out-of-plan" children are essentially a nonentity in Chinese society. Without a *hukou* registration, they can't get a job, get married, attend school, or even get a library card. Fong estimates that some thirteen million Chinese people live without this status. Even Fong was denied IVF treatments in China until she produced a marriage certificate. There is a strict adherence to heteronormative families, even as a lot of the Chinese population has become more worldly and liberal.

Despite all this, even Fong notes, there was exactly one group who did benefit from this policy: urban Chinese women like Zhao.

If you are a female born after 1980 in a major Chinese city, your chances of surviving past childhood, getting enough nutrition, and attaining higher education are significantly better than those of a Chinese daughter born in any earlier period this century or last....

Only-child females, especially, who didn't have brothers to compete with for parental resources, were the beneficiaries of the very pragmatic Chinese strategy of "raising a daughter as a son."...

... As a result record numbers of women in China are receiving a college education. In 2010, women made up half of the master's degree students in China. The country's female labor force participation is among the highest in Asia, with 70% of Chinese women either employed in some capacity or seeking employment, compared to just a quarter of their Indian sisters...

This was very much the story of Zhao. She grew up in Shanghai, and her parents gave her all the same attention, pressure, benefits, schooling, tutors, and expectations they would have given a son.

She grew up reading stories with strong female characters like Hua Mulan, a female warrior known for her kung fu and sword fighting, who takes her father's place in the army. Her comrades are later stunned she was a woman the whole time, but according to Wikipedia, "this does not change their good friendship."

When Zhao went to school, you were scored four times a year and ranked from one to 180. Everyone had a number and a rank, and everyone knew everyone else's number and rank. At school, your score was all that mattered, she said. And schools sent their best kids to compete in national competitions based on score, not unconscious bias around gender. "The schools want to win," she says. "It was harsh, but it was also fact based."

She demanded so much coaching and attention at Yale because she hadn't been socially trained otherwise. She had simply never experienced that "Lean In" thing where women are disincentivized to be smart or to raise their hand, or they may not get a date for the prom. And because, in China, men were used to competing with women to score the highest on tests, socially they got used to being equals—or even subordinate—to women in terms of achievement from an early age, she says.

Her parents put all their efforts and their money into Zhao getting a better life. Neither of them was able to finish high school because schools were closed in the Cultural Revolution. As she tells the story in the *Times*:

> *My dad was a government clerk, and my mom worked in a textile factory, bent over a sewing machine year after year in a thick soup of air filled with tiny cotton fibers. But she had a great passion for her only child's education.*
>
> *In 10th grade, I had discovered from a pirated book about American college admissions that I could apply just like any American teenager, taking the Test of English as a Foreign*

Language and the G.R.E., the graduate admissions test (the SAT was not given in China).

"Lulu, this is your chance," my mother told me . . .

Even when I was very small, my mother had told me that I could do anything and be anyone, and that smart people went abroad to study. I hadn't known there were many countries; I had thought there were only two: China and the Foreign Country. I remember wishing I had been born in the Foreign Country.

It's—I guess?—encouraging in a Trump America to see that some empowerment can come from even the most antiwoman policies. When Zhao was new to America, she even defended the one-child policy at a classmate's family's Thanksgiving dinner, where she was shocked at the size of the turkey.

How could Americans idly excoriate this policy when they had never experienced the misery caused by overcrowding? How could they speculate that only children become psychologically damaged when my friends and I had grown up very happily?

"What alternative does China have?" I shot back. "Everybody does what he or she pleases, and then have a lot of people starve?"

I would defend my government's policies passionately many times, in front of friends, professors and classmates. Growing up in Shanghai, China's richest city, I had seen a society becoming only more prosperous. People moved to bigger apartments (my senior year, my parents moved from a single room to a two-bedroom duplex), earned higher salaries, wore more stylish clothes and ate more meat.

The wounds and scars of China talked about so often in the West were not mine to see.

Part of this defense was living under authoritarian rule, the power of propaganda in China. But it was also because Zhao was lucky enough to be born into the one group of women that *benefited* from the policy. She continued to when she returned to China.

She joined the technology banking group at Goldman Sachs. She split the top duties with another woman. She remembers back when they were taking one challenged company public in America. It was a particularly intense and difficult process, where it all could have gone wrong with the slightest misstep.

She was five months pregnant and the other woman who ran the division with her was also pregnant. One of them had to do the road show in the US, crisscrossing the country and going days without sleep. Zhao volunteered because it was her second child; she'd been there before.

"Wow, you really are here for the client," one of the people on the road show remarked.

"I thought it was perfectly normal," she says. "Our job is to make the IPO happen, pregnant or not. I like the fact that I was treated equally."

I can imagine! No, wait. Having been a pregnant woman in America, I actually cannot imagine that.

"Even when you are pregnant, you still breathe and walk and live normally," she says.

It's like your body is doing something almost superhuman!

And because of the one-child policy, women have plenty of family to help them once they have kids. It's common for grandparents to move in with professional women and take a primary role helping with the kids. Indeed, Zhao says, it's frequently these new grandmothers that are the ones pushing their daughters to get back to work, to get back to contributing, to get back to achieving. *Grandma's got this at home.*

Like the women I met in Iceland—perhaps the only similarity—Zhao says she simply never saw friends with stay-at-home moms growing up. It never occurred to her she wouldn't work.

If you are an American working mom in your thirties or forties, and you've suffered so many decades of gender microaggressions that you almost turn on your heel and punch the random dude who catcalls you when you're walking to school with your kids one morning, I know what you are thinking: *This sounds amazing.*

Yes and no. (Damn you, Kate Manne!)

First off, there's still a ton of sexism in China. In 2017 a VC from a small early-stage firm in China gave a keynote where he casually said something breathtakingly sexist even by Valley standards: "Rule number ten: We usually don't invest in female CEOs."

He continued:

It's not because of any kind of prejudice. Just think about it carefully . . . besides giving birth to children, what can women do better than men? Nothing. If the company CEO is a man, but a lot of the chairmen are women, we typically won't invest in either. Why? Because it shows that the entrepreneur . . . can't recruit equally excellent and ambitious male executives.

The important thing isn't the clearly offensive thing he said. It's the way he said it: "Besides giving birth to children, what can women do better than men?" The sexism wasn't rooted in the idea that women are inherently unequal, as in the US; rather, it was a rejection of an idea that they are "better." Sounds like a typical hypermasculine reaction to female ascendancy to me.

And that exists at larger companies in China, too. One of the most aggressive things I experienced as a woman in my career was a meeting with a C-level executive of a major Chinese tech company who kept trying to grab my body as I interviewed him in a public place. I was physically swatting his hands away from me as we continued to have the conversation. No one seemed particularly scandalized in this high-end Hong Kong hotel lobby.

On a more subtle level, as I dug into conversations with high-level professional moms in China, I discovered they still had pressure to do the bulk of the housework and take care of the kids, despite there being no acceptance for stay-at-home moms in society. These women didn't have to negotiate for the right to have a career, but men typically still weren't 50/50 partners at home.

And at the end of the day, many of them still didn't have a choice. While American women may resent the "Ohhhhh, do you really want strangers raising your children?" concern trolling by the 40 percent of our country that believes it's "bad for society" for moms to work, there may well be plenty of Chinese women who wish being a stay-at-home mom was an acceptable thing in society.

If there's any thread that runs through Chinese history when it comes to its treatment of women, it's a total lack of choice. Even Zhao felt pressured to get a law degree to please her parents who had done so much for her. And Fong anticipates these urban women will soon suffer a downside of the one-child policy: Two sets of aging parents to take care of without the help of siblings, while raising children and holding down demanding careers. By 2050, 30 percent of Chinese will be over sixty. If they were a stand-alone nation, Fong says, it'd be the third largest one after China and India.

It's an interesting double-sided coin of misogyny. In America, Manne talks about how women who want to have abortions must be "punished" by misogynistic hard-liners who feel women are threatening the patriarchy by wanting to have control over their reproductive rights. The specter these people use is women getting late-term abortions.

But in China, under the one-child policy, state-sponsored misogynists were cutting babies out of women by force in their later months, in the name of what's good for society.

Oppressed women in the West have no right not to be pregnant; women in China had no right to be pregnant. Two diametric nightmares for the women living them, both with violent and moralistic undertones. But both are fueled by the same expectation that women's bodies belong more to the nation than to themselves.

⌘

As Manne said, there is no control group. A place like Iceland that has so few of the moralistic stigmas used to punish women doesn't hold all the answers; and certainly a place like China where a group of women surprisingly have benefited from the most antiwoman policy of all time doesn't either.

But what China is creating in its tech sector are new role models and new patterns. And that matters more now to Silicon

Valley than it might have a decade ago, because their companies are competing with ours. It was a Chinese company, not Lyft, that humbled and beat Uber. And the public face of that fight was a woman. A mother. That matters for China, but it matters for the US, too.

16

Back, Head, Lungs

I OPEN MY EYES, SLOWLY, my head throbbing.

Eli has wandered into my bedroom. As soon as I see him, I jolt up. No matter how quietly he creeps in, no matter how asleep I am, I somehow hear him, and it's louder than any alarm. By 2015, I was no longer the one waking him up; he was waking me up.

"Hey, baby . . ." I say groggily before breaking into a painful, raspy cough. "Want to climb in bed with Mommy for a minute?"

"Well," he says looking around awkwardly, standing with his arms pinned to his sides, ". . . actually, I'm wet."

"Why are you wet?"

"This time, because I peed."

"OK." I cough and laugh and then cough more. "Let's change you."

I pull myself up, and more than my back aching, it's my head pounding and my throat hurting. If wings, talons, and fangs were a protective mother's weapons, I felt the pain of working motherhood in my back, head, and lungs.

My entire body aches, actually. You never realize how violent an action coughing is until you've done it constantly for three weeks. There are piles of clean laundry all over my room, which I haven't had time or energy to even fold.

Megan used to take care of the laundry, but Megan is long gone. Once Evie started school three days a week, Megan saw the writing on the wall. Soon Evie would be in school five days a week, and I just wouldn't need her. She quit, and I couldn't really blame her. She got a new job with one easy baby, a shorter commute, fewer hours, and a higher salary. I doubted she had to deal with armed guards there.

And anyway, I couldn't really afford her on my own. I'd had to cut my own salary, and I was a single-income household now. In a few months, my assistant, Kathleen, would also be let go, for cost-cutting reasons. When I started this journey I had a husband, a nanny, and an assistant. I had none of these things anymore. I desperately clung to my house cleaner, Alda. I had to have someone, and she was a single mom, too. She got me.

As I lurch out of bed, I can't even think much about the day's stories, which will be published one way or another in a few hours. I'm working too hard to get the kids clothed, full, clean, and to school with lunches packed, while I stop to lean on surfaces, letting out long, raspy coughing fits about every sentence or so. I've forced down two cups of coffee before we even get out the door and brewed another one for the road.

Shower? Hilarious. I pull on jeans, cowboy boots, whatever sports bra and shirt I was sleeping in stays on. I brush my teeth and hope sunglasses will be some kind of cover to what a mess I am. I'm the only divorced mom at preschool, and it shows.

Pick the disaster of the day: The sink is broken; a smelly sludge has backed up, and I can't do the dishes until I find someone to come fix it. My upstairs neighbor's motorcycle has sprung a fuel leak overnight. My hot water heater has burst, and the garage is flooded. There are far too many of them happening lately.

It's all just too much.

I'm sad. I'm starting to think I can't actually have it all. That it's all slipping away. That on the wrong day, child protective services would be horrified if they walked into this house.

For the most part, I'm adjusting to being a working divorced mom with no childcare. It's strange, the things that I find easy and the things I find hard. Packing lunches, for instance, is nowhere near as hard as everyone's made it out to be. But for some reason, matching clean socks is my Kryptonite.

I've recently shifted from mostly running the company to running the company *and* writing two to three pieces a day. My friend former Twitter CEO Dick Costolo once told me that being the CEO is about doing whatever the company needs most from you at any given time. We changed our business model from ads to subscriptions—in part because one of our largest advertisers told us Uber was threatening to pull their business from them if they continued to support us. Our multimillion-dollar ad business had become a ticking time bomb.

With our new focus on subscribers, Pando needs me to write more than anything else. On days I write, we get a surge of hundred-dollar annual-membership sign-ups. We need that cash flow. I do most of my writing between 10:00 p.m. and 2:00 a.m. Then I wake up about four hours later when Eli shuffles in my room.

For about two months I muscled through this new reality. I slept about four hours a night, but I was doing great work. It was impacting the company; the team felt reinvigorated, and the kids were getting way more mommy time than they had ever had before. It was hard, but it was also rewarding.

I'd always been doubtful of founders who say you should run your business with a laser focus on one core metric—one "key performance indicator" or KPI, as it's called. I'd argued journalism doesn't work like that. When the KPI is page views, you produce link-bait journalism. When it's output, you don't do in-depth, reported work. Number of comments? Then you just write something needlessly inflammatory to get a response. Search ranking? You don't break news, because by definition people aren't searching for what hasn't happened yet. Social shares? You get Upworthy headlines and kittens.

You get the idea. I think of great journalism like that old definition of pornography: I'd know it when we produced it.

But finally, in this new membership world, I had found the perfect KPI: daily subscriber sign-ups. Feeling like a grown-up CEO when I realized this, I went to the Wikipedia entry on KPIs. Here's the checklist of what makes a good KPI:

- A KPI can't be expressed in dollars. Check!
- KPIs have to be measured frequently. Check!
- They are acted upon by the CEO and senior management. Check!
- They are a simple measurement the staff understands and knows how to correct for. Check!
- Responsibility for the KPI can be assigned to a team. Check!
- They impact more than one of "the organization's top CRITICAL SUCCESS FACTORS" . . . Um, probably, whatever that meant, check.
- They encourage action that helps the company's mission. Check!

As a KPI, "new daily subscribers" was perfect. Each subscriber added means we are that much closer to sustainability without ads. Unlike page views, subscribers aren't empty editorial calories. They can't be. There is no reason anyone decides to pay us ten dollars a month, or a hundred dollars a year, unless we are doing great work that helps them make decisions about their investments, their jobs, or their lives.

"There is literally nothing bad about this metric," I thought. The more it increased, the more likely we were to stay in business. And it could only be "gamed" by doing great work every single day. It was a way that our reporters could totally ethically help ensure their salaries were paid. All they had to do was do great work. Finally, it was the clearest path out of the tunnel of burning capital we'd seen yet. *Just keep doing this every day for six months, and we'll be in the black. The nightmare is over. The number in the bank just starts to increase every month.*

Once this became clear to me, I was struck by the efforts I would go to for Pando that I never would have for TechCrunch or *BusinessWeek* or any other publication. Starting my third story at 2:00 a.m. Pushing myself harder than I ever thought I could. Brute forcing that KPI up. Brute forcing the company to work. Working through sleep deprivation.

You just find a way to keep going. The human body is more resilient than our mind wants to tell us it is, right? This is all mental. It's temporary. I can do this.

If I can just keep this pace up for six months, I'll get there. We'll be profitable, and I can finally relax.

I didn't make it. We relaunched the site in June, and by September I was in the hospital.

⌘

By the fall of 2015, Pando had survived my divorce, our burn rate, nearly $400 million in frivolous lawsuits, backstabbing board members, and the largest private company in Silicon Valley history trying to put us out of business. Now we had a new threat: my lungs.

For the first time in a career filled with late nights, early mornings, unreasonable deadlines, and flights around the world, I finally reached the limits of my physical endurance. It started with a week of chest pains. That turned into a fever that wouldn't break the next week. Finally, after a week on my couch sweaty and not able to eat, having lost about ten pounds, I went to the doctor. He took a quick look at my vitals and sent me to the emergency room immediately. An X-ray showed pneumonia in three-quarters of my lungs.

I spent about a week in the hospital having a series of intravenous antibiotics pumped into me throughout the day and night, as I mostly drifted in and out of consciousness. No one brought my kids to see me. I guess everyone assumed it would have scared them to see me in that state.

This was a wake-up call. In the first generation of tech blogs, Mike Arrington had worked himself to severe exhaustion, and two of our other competitors both had heart issues. Another friend of mine running a media company, Jason Hirschhorn, had just had heart surgery, narrowly cheating death after neglecting his health.

My pneumonia didn't kill me, and it didn't kill the company. But it did kill someone else: "cool dude" Sarah Lacy. This was the last vestige of my buy-in to the "macho" founder world.

That approach had backfired spectacularly. As a result of my month or so being basically incapacitated, we'd gone from over-performing on subscriptions to underperforming. I was going to have to figure out a better way.

Particularly because so much was working about the company *finally*. We were becoming known for one clear thing: holding Silicon Valley accountable for bad behavior, fiercely, angrily, self-righteously.

A recent profile on me in *Marie Claire* showed just how far we'd come since that *San Francisco Magazine* profile that declared Eli a "problem" in my ability to build a company.

Burned so many times, I braced myself when I opened the magazine. The title and subheadline: "The Must-Read: Unfiltered, unafraid, and fiercely unapologetic, Sarah Lacy is one of tech's most influential chroniclers. You got a problem with that?"

Sarah Lacy's Twitter handle is @sarahcuda. To those who follow her incisive, sometimes biting articles on her tech news site, PandoDaily, the nickname is fitting. Lacy, after all, has cultivated a reputation in industry circles as a no-holds-barred truth teller, and in the ultra-monied, back-scratching world of Silicon Valley, the truth can sometimes bite.

Yes. Add "devoted mother to Eli and Evie" and I'm happy for that to be on my tombstone.

Pando may have been insufferable, but we were also right, and our work had made a huge difference. For the first time in my career as a reporter, not only had I found my voice, but it had found its audience. And it only came from having the freedom to do things my way and refusing to be silenced or bullied.

It wasn't a coincidence that I finally unlocked all this power at the same time I became a mother. No sooner would a onetime friend or investor turn their back on us than Eli would do something adorable. Like the day he snuck over to the dishwasher and grabbed some magnetic letters off it. He hid them behind his back, with a sweet smile, and sauntered back over to the kitchen table where I was making his lunch. He proudly put them down spelling "M-O-M."

"That's my best friend's name," he whispered into my ear and smiled.

The worst bros of Silicon Valley were no match for that kind of adorability.

I wanted to be around Eli and Evie constantly, because they made me such a better person than I'd ever been before. They bridged my confidence gap, because I found myself achieving so much more than I thought I could whenever they were by my side. That was the strength I needed to tap into now, not macho brute force.

⌘

One of the dangers of pattern recognition is faulty causality. If a CEO who works constantly builds a big company, the assumption is that this is the only way it can be done. If a CEO has any sort of healthy balance in his or her life and fails, the assumption is that he or she didn't work hard enough.

Research has shown that fifty hours a week is the max if you don't want increased risk of cardiovascular issues, relationship problems, increased weight gain, depression, injury, and a whole host of other issues. Other studies have shown that productivity declines after fifty hours per week. That means you are trading health, happiness, and relationships for diminishing returns.

So why do founders—people supposedly driven by data—continue to insist that 24/7 is the only path to success? Part of the reason that founders push themselves beyond sustainable or healthy limits is because investors demand it from them in explicit terms.

Another reason is founder anxiety. There is so much you can't control in whether your company succeeds or not, and so many variables, it's hard to know, if it does fail, what could have saved it. The Valley loves to say if you fail for "good reasons," you'll get funded again. But how can you tell if a founder failed "in a good way"? Working abusively brutal hours is the easiest, clearest way to telegraph your hustle to the world—to your employees, to your investors, and to your future employees and investors.

I guarantee you if I tried to raise money for another startup now, the fact that I worked myself into the hospital would be seen *as a bonus.*[*] But it doesn't telegraph strength and confidence to work this hard; it frequently telegraphs insecurity.

What takes strength and courage is standing up to this expectation. Samantha Ettus told her entrepreneur husband, Mitch, that she'd rather give up their alone time after the kids went to bed in exchange for him to be there for dinner and bedtime. Mitch dismissed the suggestion immediately, saying, "What message does it send to my employees if I leave the office by 5:30 each night? I can't possibly run the company and leave the office ahead of everyone else."

Ettus pushed back on him. "What if you leave the office to

---

* Shortly after finishing this book, when Pando was solidly profitable, I did actually decide to start a new company, called ChairmanMom.com. And as I expected, the fact that I'd pushed myself so hard and refused to let Pando die, even if it put me in the hospital, did help me raise money.

get home for dinner at six each night and then go back to work at eight?" she suggested. He agreed to try it for a week. *Win for 50/50 couples everywhere!*

Until Mitch got a call from his top investor. "We invest in entrepreneurs with cots in their offices, not entrepreneurs who leave at 5:30 each day," the investor said.

Mitch replied: "Well then, I will be the first entrepreneur to prove you wrong." Not only was this the right thing to do for his family, but he sent a strong signal to women and men on his team that they also had permission to be engaged parents. And guess what? The company went public for hundreds of millions of dollars.

Typically, the founders who can push back—or even have the confidence to—are the ones who have already made it. PayPal cofounder Max Levchin used to pride himself on working days on end without sleep. Once he became a dad, he developed a new system. He works all night one day a week, makes it home for dinner and bedtime every other night, and then goes back to work. Stewart Butterfield of the near–$4 billion-valued Slack brags that the average age of his developers is forty and that the office is mostly empty at 5:00 p.m.

They are well-funded entrepreneurs who've already had success, so they don't need the validation that comes with being seen to be hustling. They want to continue building companies but don't want to work the way they did in their twenties. Start-ups on average are taking longer and longer to go public or get acquired, and their founders don't want to miss eight years of their lives, let alone their kids' lives. It isn't fair to ask them to.

"You play with the tools you have, and those change over time," says Nirav Tolia, CEO of Nextdoor, who has built companies in his single twenties and is now in his forties with three kids. "Now, the tools I have are experience and deep relationships with folks I've worked with—in some cases—for over fifteen years. I have many failures that hopefully I've learned from. Back then, my tools were all the time in the world to spend on my company and an unbelievable optimism that compelled me to take huge risks. I could fail miserably and it didn't matter. I didn't have bills to pay or have mouths to feed."

And yet, his current company is valued at more than $1 billion. The company he sold to a competitor in the dot-com years never found a viable business model. He seems to be doing better with the "tools" he has now.

Examples like these matter not only because it's unhealthy for everyone but also because the expectation of 24/7 puts a mother—especially a pregnant or nursing mother—in an untenable, unfundable position. In 2011 when LA investor Paige Craig was deciding whether to fund Kiva cofounder Jessica Jackley's new company, ProFounder, and learned she was pregnant, he actually wrote on his blog what many investors think:

> *This dirty little thought pops in my head. I'm thinking how in the hell is this founder going to lead a team, build a company and change the world for these businesses carrying a kid around for the next few months and then caring for the kid after. I can't say I personally know anything about it but birthing & raising kids seems like the toughest job around. And now I have a founder who has to be a CEO and a mother.*

Craig at least was ashamed of the thought, considering himself before this happened to be a man without prejudice. And he invested anyway.

This "ideal" that keeps mothers from getting funded isn't just unhealthy, there's evidence *it's total bullshit.* A study from the *Monthly Labor Review* found that on average people who believe they work seventy-five-plus hours a week were off by a whopping twenty-five hours. "We remember our busiest weeks as typical. This is partly because negative experiences stand out in the mind more than positive ones, and partly because we all like to see ourselves as hardworking," wrote Laura Vanderkam in a *New York Times* piece called "The Busy Person's Lies."

Vanderkam writes about time management for a living and has analyzed hundreds of executive time logs. They almost all exaggerate. She once had someone tell her he was working 180 hours a week . . . more hours than are in a week. She even exaggerated her own hours, when she took the time to log them. She assumed she worked some forty to fifty hours a week, and she worked just 37.4 on average.

Like any working mom, she had days that were insane—pumping breast milk in train bathrooms, late nights and early mornings, working through vacations to catch up. Yet over the course of a year, she also got eight massages, went for long runs on the weekend, had dinner with friends, and read for a total of 327 hours.

If Vanderkam—a woman already attuned to believe people exaggerate work narratives—exaggerated her hours to tell herself a certain narrative, imagine what people in a high-pressure macho world where that's expected tell themselves.

You can do a lot with twenty-four hours in a day. A year post-pneumonia, I've found more balance in my work and life. On a heavy day, I work eleven hours. That is more than a nine-to-five job, and yet, it still gives me about six hours of sleep and six hours of mommy time. And Pando is now finally profitable.

I have another metric that tells me this is finally sustainable. I still pour myself a cup of coffee before I go wake up my kids, just as I always have before. But I have noticed I don't actually drink any of it until we're headed out the door.

17

November 8, 2016

IF YOU'VE MADE IT THIS far, you know the last five years of my life haven't been without difficulty. And yet, my children have only seen me uncontrollably cry once: November 9, 2016.

Writing this book in the fall of 2016 was an electric experience. Sexual assault, female empowerment, women's body issues, unconscious bias, and the debilitating cost of microaggressions became part of the national conversation in a way I'd never seen before.

The election campaign capped off my transformation from twenty-something-year-old who denied sexism was still a thing to thirty-something mom reveling in her momhood-given female superpowers to forty-something in-your-face, fierce, unapologetic feminist.

On that day, I felt that women in the Valley I knew all stopped judging each other and all worked to lift one another up, even if we'd had our differences in the past. My media feeds didn't have a flicker of mommy wars anymore.

But it went well beyond just that.

Via Facebook groups I connected with millions of women of different ethnicities, income levels, and backgrounds all over the country who were brought together by Hillary Clinton's campaign.

It wasn't simply a woman running for office. It was the horror show we had to watch in those final months. A disturbing reality that so many of us related to.

What elevated this election to a place where it felt as though my and millions of women's own struggle was the man she ran against. The gulf in qualifications was just the starting point. The media also played up a false "untrustworthy" equivalence between a man who seemed to lie unapologetically every time he opened his mouth and an email scandal that she'd already been cleared from. She was called weak but also too cold and unfeeling. She was criticized if she smiled too much or didn't smile enough. She was punished for things her husband had allegedly done. Her voice was too shrill. She was interrupted in every debate.

I don't know a professional woman who hasn't experienced the same fundamental unfairness. "[Those debates] were like every board meeting I've ever been in," says HireAthena's CEO Kristen Koh Goldstein. "A bunch of guys yelling over the diligent woman who actually knows what she's doing."

And then, *he won.*

Whether you like her or not, Hillary Clinton was a sacrificial lamb to sexism, and the world was throwing every sexist meme, every micro-indignity, and all the macro-indignities on her before she was going to be able to break that last highest glass ceiling.

Her most human moment to me was in the third debate on the subject of abortion:

I have met with women who, toward the end of their pregnancy, get the worst news one can get, that their health is in jeopardy if they continue to carry to term or that something terrible has happened or just been discovered about the pregnancy. I do not think the United States government should be stepping in and making those most personal of decisions.

It wasn't just what she said. It was how she said it. It shook me. I realized that "empathy" in office only gets you so far. Even a male president who calls himself a feminist is still a dude. Clinton was the first presidential candidate to actually *get* what the struggle of that very personal decision would feel like. The struggle of being a woman. The first to actually understand what it feels like when white men tell you that you do not have a right to save your own life, to do what's right for your family, or to make decisions for your own body. The first to understand that your uterus isn't communal property.

I liked Clinton for a lot of reasons, but that was the moment I got—on an emotional level—how much different it would be for women of this country to have a woman in that office.

And then I discovered Pantsuit Nation on Facebook. I watched it swell from hundreds of thousands of people to millions. I watched women pour out their most personal stories of sexual assault, insecurity, and fear of a Donald Trump America, and I watched other women tell them in the comments that they were with them, that they understood, that they were beautiful, that they had their backs.

These were people whose lives had been changed watching her publicly go through every indignity they'd experienced. It cracked us open. It ripped off the blinders. It shook us and made us acknowledge the sexism that some of us sweep under the rug so we can keep going.

⌘

The morning of November 8, I took my kids to vote. I wore one of my growing collection of agro-feminist T-shirts, and Evie wore one with a kitty wearing glasses and a pantsuit. (Yes, she just happened to own this.) Eli checked three times that I had drawn the right line on our ballot. He and Evie fed the pages into the voting machine, and then he said to the attendant, "Three stickers, please."

"I just know Hillary is going to win," Eli kept saying as we were walking back home. "She has to win. It's a have-to. 'Have-tos' are things you just have to do." Beyoncé was blaring out of our minivan on the way to school, because it was that kind of a morning.

The morning of November 9, Eli and Evie came into my room at about six, both carrying massive stuffed animal turtles and wearing urgent looks on their faces.

"Mommy, we have a *really big problem*," Eli said. "We can't find the baby turtles anywhere."

There was no better way to be woken up in the morning after a Donald Trump acceptance speech. Unlike the election, this was a "really big problem" that I could actually solve. I leapt out of bed. "I got this guys." I searched the house for every small turtle stuffed animal and proudly brought them to the front of the house where Eli and Evie were playing.

Eli was taping up flyers for an upcoming school fundraiser

on our door.* And I just sat down behind him, watching half of the duo I loved more than anything in the world industriously flyer our front door.

If I didn't have them, I wouldn't have gotten out of bed this morning. I tossed all those potential plans to move to Canada or Iceland. We were going to stay here for them. This was their home. I could keep them safe for four years. I'd been standing up to bullies the entire time I'd been their mother. This was simply the largest, the most powerful, and the orangest.

I burst into tears. Like crazy, heavy sobs. Evie looked at me, freaked out, and left the room to pretend to be a cat. She whispered to me later that she didn't know I could cry. Eli turned around smiling at first, thinking it was a comedy bit. "Why are you crying?" he asked, suddenly worried.

"I have horrible news," I choked out. "Donald Trump won."

He slumped down with an angry face before coming to hug me.

"Here's what you have to know, Eli," I said. "We are not leaving. We are not moving. And almost everyone in San Francisco voted for Hillary. Everyone you see, every day, know that they probably agree with us. This is not permanent. We will vote again in two years and then in another two years. And until then, the most important thing to know is that he is never allowed in this house. You will never be in the same place as Donald Trump. You will never meet him or have to see him. I will protect you."

The last one was a crucial point. Eli had explained his biggest fear was that Trump would make everything smell bad. Evie had explained he might come into our house uninvited

---

* As if I were likely to forget to attend, having helped organize it and made the damn flyers.

and hammer a nail through her tongue. "The spiky end," she said solemnly. I have no idea where that terrifying image came from, but these children were never going to breathe the same air as that man. Like finding the baby turtles, these were things I could control.

And that's how you recover from feeling hopeless and helpless—taking control of what you can control. Once again, my children saved me from the abyss.

The following January, Evie and I went to the Women's March in Washington, DC. I had to use the last of my airline miles to do it, and it made me a week late filing this book. But I knew we were going from the moment I heard about the march. In a sense, I knew it even before the march was announced, before Trump even won. I knew somewhere deep inside myself that if all those things happened, this was what we'd do. I knew when I met with Halla Tómasdóttir in Iceland back in the fall.

It was her description of witnessing that 1975 women's march as a child in Iceland. How it cemented for her women's equality and indispensable power. That a world doesn't function without women, and that means women have leverage. That is what I wanted for Evie. She was about to turn four, and if her first memory was being on my shoulders standing up for equality, I couldn't imagine a greater gift to my daughter.

I carried her on my shoulders off and on for nearly six miles.

"What can you see, Evie?" I asked her as she clambered up there looking through a rolled-up poster like a telescope. "Do you see a lot of awesome women?"

"No, Mama, I don't see any women," she said.

"What are you talking about? We are surrounded by women," I said.

"I don't see any women, Mama, I only see *people*," she said.

The crowd cheered. WTF, Evie. How do you get more awesome every day?

In the days leading up to the Women's March, there were plenty of examples of people trying to cause fractures from all sides—reports that white women felt alienated, debates that it had gotten too ideological, continuing resentment that a white woman involved in organizing the march couldn't understand true oppression.

But ultimately it didn't work. Five million people came together in different cities all over the world to stand up for what they believed in, and people on the march believed different things. Some voted for Hillary Clinton; others did not. In this one case, benevolent sexism *actually failed*.

But what struck me most wasn't a sense of anger—it was the love that we experienced at the airport and on the plane where we talked to women of all generations. The woman whose family gave us a ride to our hotel so we didn't have to take a cab. The women who gave up seats for Evie on the Metro. The men who helped lift her onto my shoulders. The women in the thirty-minute bathroom line who insisted we go ahead of everyone. The women who sat next to us at dinner and paid for our meal while we were in the bathroom, leaving us a note, "We've got your back." The woman I met on the flight home who did her first march at age eighteen against Vietnam. That sounded pretty badass, but she was more impressed with Evie. "First protest at three," she said. "Good for you." She took a picture of us to remember what all those little Evies could represent for the future.

That weekend I taught my daughter about democracy. I taught my daughter about the importance of the first amendment. I taught my daughter to rely on and trust other women for strength. I taught my daughter that love and inclusiveness are not just feel-good values, but that there is power in those values. Those were the first few days since November 8 that I didn't feel anger and depression about the future—I felt hope.

My daughter has never been shy about standing up for her beliefs, but this weekend she discovered her voice in a totally new way. When Evie was walking past a man with a megaphone, he—jokingly—held it out to her, and she grabbed it and led the crowd in a chant. A man asked if he could lift her up, and I said yes.

"Hey hey! Ho ho! Donald Trump has got to go!" her tiny voice blared through the megaphone and hundreds of thousands echoed her and then cheered. She hopped down and skipped over to hug my legs. "That was special," the guy with the megaphone said, and everyone cheered again. When we left the overcrowded Metro, she turned and yelled, "Girl power!" and everyone cheered again.

Watching Evie that weekend, I kept remembering what Halla told me about Iceland in 1975: *Without the march, arguably, there isn't a woman president in five years.* And perhaps without a single mother in 1980 leading the nation, Iceland doesn't emerge as one of the most feminist nations in the world today, with one of the lowest deltas in pay between men and women, two-thirds of children birthed by stigma-free single mothers, equality in parental leave that balances out the motherhood penalty and fatherhood bonus, and mandatory gender-balanced boards for companies over a certain size.

"These kinds of historic events definitely made fertile ground for us being better at this than other countries," Halla said.

It all started with a march. Where women took the time, had the courage, got over individual differences, to take to the streets and peacefully make the point that we aren't simply here to be what men want us to be. Our lives and our bodies are our own. It mattered that young women, like Halla in 1975, witnessed that as one of their first memories.

I wondered—I hoped—as I transcribed my interview with her, postelection, Could this protest in DC be that moment for America? If we do this, if enough women show up, if it's peaceful, if it's rooted in steadfast, uncompromising love and hope, in four years could we also have a female president?

Women tend to unite and find their voice in periods of extreme adversity.

In 1991 when a panel of white men grilled Anita Hill over her allegations that Clarence Thomas sexually harassed her, it seemed to be a low point for women. But when women all over the country saw the visual of only white men making that judgment call, it inspired them to get involved. That year there were only two women in the Senate. The year after Anita Hill's testimony, more women ran for the Senate than ever had before. Washington's Patty Murray said it was a direct result of those hearings, at least for her. "I just keep looking at this committee, going 'God, who's saying what I would say if I was there.'"

Michele Dauber—the Stanford Law professor who's working to recall Aaron Persky—says the bulk of her donations have been for small amounts, less than a hundred dollars, and they've come from millennial women who have never given to a political campaign before in their lives. This case shook them. "It hit a nerve among millennial women," she says. "They have come up to me crying, giving me twenty dollars and saying, 'This is everything to me.' They were cynical and jaded and had never given to a political campaign before."

Even China's one-child policy yielded some unintended feminist wins.

Leading up to the US election, entrepreneur Julie Hanna told me Trump was ultimately going to be good for women. "The same way a flu shot mobilizes the immune system, he is helping us find our voice," she said. "He will be the catalyst who helps us make a major leap forward around equality. When something is in the dark, it can't be dealt with. It has to be brought into the light. Until it's explicit, it's like shadowboxing."

Hanna and I talked about the tens of thousands of women who had come forward on social media to talk about their experience with sexual assault. Even I hadn't realized it was that pervasive, I said to her.

"One hundred percent of the women I know have experienced sexual harassment," she said. She thought harder about her career in the Valley, as she read all those women's accounts of unwanted sexual advances. "I came up with half a dozen incidents in my career, all but one in the workplace," she said. "I thought, 'Have I normalized this?' We keep it in the dark. One was with someone who was an investor and this person was one of the most powerful, well-known men at the time, and I felt powerless to do anything about it. My even telling you this is a massive shift. I would have never considered doing this."

When Trump won, I thought about tiny Halla in 1975 watching the Icelandic strike, and I reflected on my life in the South at the time. In terms of what I saw around me of female—or racial—empowerment, Memphis didn't compare well. Instead Evie would start her life crystal clear that women have the same rights as men and that we will not accept anything less.

⌘

My story is like a lot of women's. I've been lucky in some things. Other things have been a constant struggle. The things that suck about my life, suck about many women's lives. The inspiration I get from my children is no greater than the inspiration mothers all over the world get from their children. I've stood up to bullies, but nowhere near as much as women living under oppressive regimes around the world. I work hard, but nowhere near as hard as single moms living in poverty, hoping and praying their kids will be the ones to make it out.

I'm lucky my struggles were loud and public enough that I had a forum to write my story.

But while my story may not be remarkable compared to women and mothers everywhere, my resolve and my strength are also not remarkable. Don't let anyone ever tell you that becoming a mother—or even having an unrealized ability to become a mother—is a weakness or something to fear. Don't ever let your voice be silenced because it's too shrill, too bossy, too ambitious, or too anything. Take it from someone who has spent her entire life being too much of something for everybody. Just embrace the "too much" or you'll get whittled away into nothing.

One of the best pieces of career advice I ever received came, ironically, from the one person in the Valley who publicly supported and funded Donald Trump—investor Peter Thiel. It was after an early attack on me; one of the first times a senseless mob was whipped up to come after my temerity for doing my job and being a (then) young woman. "Embrace and extend," he said. "Just embrace and extend."

It's certainly better advice than changing to try to please a senseless mob.

And on days that this advice isn't enough, I ask myself, "WWE(vie)D?" If Eli has made me face difficult emotional truths with his pointed questions during "Eli Rock You," Evie has inspired me to dream of a world where girls don't have body issues, where they don't allow catcalling and leering to become normalized and steadily chip away at their sense of self-worth, where they don't overapologize, where they don't have to be good while boys are simply allowed to "be boys."

Evie laughs at herself when she does something wrong, saying, "Silly, Evie!" She will do a "booty dance" at any moment without an ounce of self-consciousness. And yet, Evie is a natural leader. When she started preschool, she convinced the other two-year-olds to all be cats for a day, only meowing at the teachers when asked a question and crawling everywhere.

Evie may be quick to apologize, but she also knows when she is owed an apology. The essence of Evie is encapsulated in an anecdote when she was just eighteen months old. We were eating on a patio area and a drunk guy walked past and accidentally kicked Evie's high chair. She stopped eating her raisins for a moment, giving him an icy stare. He apologized to her immediately. She went back to the raisins. A second drunk guy came and knocked her high chair. He didn't stop to apologize. He kept right on staggering to his table. Evie stared him down for a good thirty seconds, never breaking her gaze. She slowly finished her raisins and just folded her arms on the high chair tray, staring at him. Paul filled in her internal monologue perfectly: "I came here to kick ass and eat raisins, and I'm all outta raisins."

Sometimes I just like to sneak in her room and watch her sleep. Something so powerful, so still. It's like watching a T. rex sleep.

Frequently, when I describe Evie's amazing sense of self-confidence, her unapologetic sense of self-worth, and her sheer badass conviction, people have said, "Oh, I wonder where she gets that from . . ." gesturing at me.

I wish.

I was nothing like Evie as a child; I was like Eli: creative and sensitive, with an imagination on fire. I became like Evie by putting on a suit of feminist armor every day whether I called myself a feminist or not, whether I felt that strong or not. I needed it to walk down the street past a construction site. I need it to even have a Twitter account. I've needed it to read nearly anything ever written about me.

I became like Evie because I couldn't survive in the world and do what I do for a living otherwise. Evie has a forty-year head start on me. Imagine how amazing the Evies of the world will be in forty years if we stop calling them bossy, stop forcing princess mentality on them, and stop telling them what they are too much of or not enough of.

I still say to her every night, "I think you're perfect," and she still says it back to me. My job as her mother is to see how old she can get before she realizes how many women never feel that way. Iceland wasn't the control group Manne talked about. China wasn't either. But maybe my old San Francisco Victorian could be for a few more years.

EPILOGUE

SO WHAT NOW?

Assuming you've nodded along with my critique of all the corrosive elements of the patriarchy; that it exists inside each of us; that the guilt you feel is its most potent weapon; that the innate powers of producing, giving birth to, and sustaining life might make you phenomenal at other things. And you agree about the limited and exclusionary benefits of the 50/50 marriage; the bullshit that divorce is failure and being single means you are unwanted; the disturbing playbook that patriarchs use to discredit outspoken women; and most of all, the bizarre position women are in where the uterus is both so sacred they can't be trusted with control over it, yet so dismissed that men shouldn't pay for prenatal care and we don't deserve maternity leave, equal pay, or childcare subsidies for young children.

You are with me thus far, right? Good. So, then, what do we actually do about it?

A few things come to mind.

First, stop allowing the patriarchy to divide us. Do not engage in any mommy wars whatsoever. Let women who want to stay home, stay home. Why do you care if they love to bake and have cleaner homes than you do? Let women who want to work, work. Raise a fist and a glass to women who want to run companies and hire nannies to help them do so.

If you are a white woman, when a woman of color says, "You have no idea what real bias is," you are only allowed to say one thing: "You are right. I do not. What can I do to help you?" You have no right to get pissy about them "making you feel bad" or any such shit. Think of a dude in your office mansplaining why something that offended you *totally isn't sexism*. That is what you sound like when you say anything else in response.

Second, take ownership of your life. Stop asking permission. It is your life, not your dad's, not your partner's, not your kid's. Excel at whatever the thing is you are good at, no matter what that is. Strive to become the best in the world at *that*. And then demand the world respect it.

Trust me when I say I know this is easier said than done. I have twenty years of hatred, dismissiveness, legal threats, and real-life threats as a result of trying to do this. But I also have a house in San Francisco that was paid for by my words and people *eventually* feeling that they needed to pay me money to hear them.

Seek the 40 percent. Remember, "only" 60 percent of women face Maternal Wall bias. There are other options. Vote with your feet. Tell them—tell the world via Facebook or Medium or Glassdoor even—why you are voting with your feet. After Michelle Zatlyn of Cloudflare was told by one VC that women didn't belong at hard-core tech infrastructure companies, she went on to raise nearly $200 million from others. "Just know, it's not everyone," she says. "Associate yourself with people who do make you feel good, and want you to win because there is someone out there who will bet on you."

Believe that as a mother you deserve the basic standard of respect that most of the industrialized world has for mothers, including a reasonable maternity leave. That you deserve respect for pushing a baby out of your body and continuing the species and that it's OK to bond and recover from that before you start kicking ass again.

Look yourself in the mirror every morning and say the following: It's not just me, I'm not crazy, and I'm not a buzzkill. A world of misogynists works very hard to make you think it is you. That you are the one who can't seem to make it work. That's the lie the "opt-out revolution" was based on.

It isn't you. It's them. And even if you don't want to start your own thing, know that some 40 percent of the employment world is not like *them*. The grass may very well be greener. Try it out.

Vote with your vote. We have to stop assuming men—even super feminist men—will do the right thing. We've lived under that hope since the dawn of the patriarchy. And yes, it's gotten better in a lot of ways. But I'm not happy with where we are now . . . are you?

We need pro-woman policies, not just to conform ourselves into a pro-man world. I'm not gonna tell you your politics, but we have to look at what has worked in other places where women have more economic rights. It's fully protected reproductive rights. It's mandates around equal pay. It's childcare subsidies so that women don't have to leave the workforce for three years. It's parental leave that incentivizes men to take as much leave as women or *lose it*, so that hiring a young man is as much of a risk as hiring a young woman.

It's also quotas. Board quotas, hiring quotas, senior management quotas. Americans hate quotas because of this lie that they're an "unfair advantage." Hopefully, this book has made clear just how uneven the playing field is now. Quotas are a way of correcting for the patriarchy. If you look at the numbers of women graduating college, entering the workforce, and see that they get shaken out mid-career, you know the problem isn't "competence." There are plenty of competent, qualified women. But they face networking and confidence disadvantages thanks to the patriarchy. We have to require companies to prioritize this or they won't.

Be your own boss. Not everyone has this ability or this desire. But if you even think about it a tiny bit, find people who will push you over the edge to do it. Even if it's a sole proprietor, lifestyle business. If you have a scalable idea, and you go in with other founders, insist on being the CEO. The CEO title matters. Don't let the little patriarchy voices in your head talk you into the COO role.

If you are lucky enough to have or make money, for God's sake, invest in other women. There are plenty of amazing ones out there. If you invest in men, force them to include women and people of color from the earliest moments of a company. Research shows it's the greatest way to increase diversity as your company grows.

Do *her* dirty work. When a woman at your company makes a smart point in a meeting, amplify it and give her credit. When you see a woman get attacked on social media, take on her cause for her and fight back hard, as if it was your sister or your best friend. Sometimes we struggle to fight or advocate on behalf of ourselves, but every mom knows you don't hesitate for a second to fight or advocate for your children. Extend that mama bear ferocious love to women all around you.

I am counting on you, entitled millennials. Don't accept less. I am counting on you, *Teen Vogue* generation. You have a twenty-year head start on my generation in accepting sexism is still *a thing*. You can do what we didn't. We are here to support you, fund you, hire you, empower you, and be inspired by you.

These are just a few suggestions. I'm sure you could come up with even more. At its core it's about asking yourself every day: What's a small way I can use the awesome power of all-encompassing maternal shock and awe to destabilize my own corner of the patriarchy today?

All I am asking is that you try, not comply. Every day we can identify one small thing to do to overthrow the patriarchy. It might be stopping a woman on the street and telling her the opposite of all the bullshit she's likely heard that day. It might be choosing to support a woman-owned business. It might be standing up for a female coworker who is getting the shit kicked out of her. It might be biting your tongue when you call your daughter "Princess." (I've been substituting "President" lately.)

We can't all build massive companies that serve as role models for women everywhere and employ thousands of people. (I haven't.) We can't all write checks to struggling female entrepreneurs. (I can't.) We're not all in the position of being able to even hire or give raises to women. (I'm not.) But we can all do something to kick a tiny little dent in the patriarchy every single day.

Together, we've got this. United we mom.

ACKNOWLEDGMENTS

THIS BOOK WAS PAINFUL TO relive, to research, and to write, but it was also a rallying, eye-opening examination of what had changed in me since becoming a mother. One I had never fully thought out, let alone put on paper.

I couldn't have done it and I wouldn't have done it without the ever "YOU SHOULD DO THIS!" prodding of my best friend, business partner, and—now—*life* partner, Paul Carr. It is handy to be in love with a man who is an amazing editor. It's lottery-winning lucky to be in love with a man who can also entertain your children with an endless supply of magic tricks while you hide in a closet finishing edits.

My second huge thanks goes to my ex-husband, Geoffrey Ellis. It is one thing to decide to write a book that invites the entire world into your own story. It's another to do that to someone else, after an incredibly painful chapter has just ended. Geoff has always believed in my voice, and he shelved his own discomfort so I could write what I needed to about our marriage and our children.

I can't thank my editor, Stephanie Hitchcock, enough. She's another badass feminist warrior, and this book belongs to both of us. Her edits and guidance were invaluable in shaping a book that I was far too close to. I'm grateful Harper Business took a chance on this.

I also want to thank my agent, Jim Levine. He believed in this project since the moment I proposed it, and fought to find it the best publishing home.

ACKNOWLEDGMENTS

Gunnar Holmsteinn connected me with seemingly all of Iceland's single-mom badasses, Adam Grant read my proposal early on and gave me the confidence boost I needed to continue pitching it. And there were scores of amazing women I interviewed for this book. Thanks to all of them.

People like Pando's former chairman Andrew Anker and my former nanny Megan McQuaid didn't get near the level of credit they deserve in this book for everything they've done for me, my company, and my children. Neither did all the amazing journalists who have worked for Pando, the investors who stuck with us, and our lawyer Roger Myers who has defended us against more than $300 million in threatened lawsuits. I promise, I haven't forgotten any of you. I just had a word limit!

I want to thank my parents, especially my mother, Carol Lacy, who is still my maternal role model. I asked if she wanted to read what I'd written about her before this book was published, and she said it was my life and my story and she didn't need a say in it. That is where my empowerment came from. I know this book must have been painful for them to read. I hope they are at least proud of the mother I've become, even if they cringe at the liberal feminist I am.

My last and most heartfelt thank-you goes to Eli and Evie. I've already told you how much they've forever changed me, how emotionally insightful Eli is, and how fearlessly badass Evie is. Their love is why I've been able to achieve my dreams and keep fighting. I will spend the rest of my life repaying that favor to them.

I think you're perfect . . . Both of you.

NOTES

Chapter 1: Your Uterus Is Not a Ticking Time Bomb

20   This is called the "Maternal Wall": Joan C. Williams and Rachel Dempsey, *What Works for Women at Work: Four Patterns Working Women Need to Know* (New York: New York University Press, 2014), 127–76.

21   they see it as biology: Ibid.

21   "I have never seen effects this large": Ibid.

23   "highlighted in my evaluation": Ibid.

25   people don't consider it sexism: Ibid.

26   "genuinely good intentions": Ibid

26   "leadership positions filled by women": Kim Scott, "Thoughts on Gender and Radical Candor," *First Round Review*, accessed May 29, 2017, http://first round.com/review/thoughts-on-gender-and-radical-candor.

27   raise their kids full time: Ibid.

27   "do both jobs well": Ibid.

27   "Which nobody do I want to be?": Ibid.

28   saw it used against someone else: Ibid.

28   didn't stigmatize working moms: Ibid.

29   "may become intolerable": Suzanne Venker, "Netflix's New Parental Leave Policy Could Make Things Worse for Women," *Time*, August 5, 2015, accessed May 29, 2017, http://time.com/3986543/netflix-parental -leave-policy-women.

31   "have *been* shamed": Shonda Rhimes, *Year of Yes: How to Dance It Out, Stand in the Sun, and Be Your Own Person* (New York: Simon & Schuster, 2015), 99.

32   "price is time with your baby": Claire Cain Miller, "What It's Really Like to Risk It All in Silicon Valley," *New York Times*, February 27, 2016, accessed May 29, 2017, https://www.nytimes.com/2016/02/28/upshot/what-its-really -like-to-risk-it-all-in-silicon-valley.html.

34   a new employee gets up to speed, according to Deloitte: Christina Merhar, "Employee Retention: The Real Cost of Losing an Employee," Small Business Employee Benefits and HR Blog, February 4, 2016, https://www.zane benefits.com/blog/bid/312123/employee-retention-the-real-cost-of-losing -an-employee.

35   *allowed* would hurt their career: Trae Vassallo, Ellen Levy, Michele Madan-
      sky, Hillary Mickell, Bennett Porter, Monica Leas, and Julie Oberweis, "Ele-
      phant in the Valley," January 11, 2016, accessed April 6, 2017, https://www
      .elephantinthevalley.com.

Chapter 2: Benevolent Sexism and You

41   article for the *Boston Review*: Kate Manne, "The Logic of Misogyny," *Boston
      Review,* July 11, 2016, accessed April 6, 2017, http://bostonreview.net/forum
      /kate-manne-logic-misogyny.
43   "unlikely to come under fire": Ibid.
44   "changing circumstances and external threats": Heather Hurlburt, "The
      Myth of the Women's Vote," Project Syndicate, November 15, 2016, accessed
      May 29, 2017, https://www.project-syndicate.org/commentary/womens
      -vote-hillary-clinton-donald-trump-by-heather-hurlburt-2016-11?barrier
      =accessreg.
44   results on a national stage: Emily Crockett, "Why Misogyny Won: Ameri-
      ca's President-Elect Is an Alleged Sexual Predator. This Theory of Sexism
      Explains How It Came to This—and Why Even Many Women Voted for
      Trump," *Vox*, November 15, 2016, accessed April 6, 2017, http://www.vox
      .com/identities/2016/11/15/13571478/trump-president-sexual-assault-sex
      ism-misogyny-won.
50   "having clouded judgement": Gabriella Paiella, "Brock Turner's Childhood
      Friend Blames His Felony Sexual-Assault Conviction on Political Correct-
      ness," The Cut, June 6, 2016, accessed May 27, 2017, https://www.thecut
      .com/2016/06/brock-turners-friend-pens-letter-of-support.html.
52   "anxieties concerning women's role within the family": Kate Manne, "The
      Logic of Misogyny."

Chapter 5: Not All Moms Have the Luxury to Build a Company, but All Moms Have the Skills

79   that you can't move on: Ben Horowitz, *The Hard Thing About Hard Things:
      Building a Business When There Are No Easy Answers* (New York: HarperCol-
      lins, 2014).

Chapter 6: If You Don't Hire More Women After Reading This Chapter, You're Just Sexist

89   injuries in girls' sports: Michael Sokolove, "The Uneven Playing Field," *New
      York Times Magazine*, May 11, 2008, MM54.
90   "leave with more minor ailments": Ibid.

93   "the writer she became without them": Ruth Franklin, "The Novelist Disguised as a Housewife," *New York Magazine*, accessed May 29, 2017, https://www.thecut.com/2016/09/shirley-jackson-rather-haunted-life-c-v-r.html?mid=fb-share-thecut.

Chapter 8: The Tyranny of the Pattern

114   To a grand total of eleven: Rupert Neate, "Facebook Only Hired Seven Black People in Latest Diversity Count," *The Guardian*, June 25, 2015, accessed April 4, 2017, https://www.theguardian.com/technology/2015/jun/25/facebook-diversity-report-black-white-women-employees.

120   50 percent of the introductory computer science students are women: Bonnie Marcus, "The Lack of Diversity in Tech Is a Cultural Issue," *Forbes*, August, 12, 2015, accessed May 29, 2017, https://www.forbes.com/sites/bonniemarcus/2015/08/12/the-lack-of-diversity-in-tech-is-a-cultural-issue/#4a50e72079a2.

120   twice the rate tech companies actually hire them: Elizabeth Weise and Jessica Guynn, "Tech Jobs: Minorities have degrees, but don't get hired," *USA Today*, October 12, 2014, accessed, May 29, 2017, https://www.usatoday.com/story/tech/2014/10/12/silicon-valley-diversity-tech-hiring-computer-science-graduates-african-american-hispanic/14684211.

123   whole laundry list of them: Rachel Thomas, "If You Think Women in Tech Is Just a Pipeline Problem, You Haven't Been Paying Attention," Medium, July 27, 2015, accessed May 29, 2017, https://medium.com/tech-diversity-files/if-you-think-women-in-tech-is-just-a-pipeline-problem-you-haven-t-been-paying-attention-cb7a2073b996.

Chapter 9: "We Need a Sheryl"

131   "when we belong to a non-dominant group": Sheryl Sandberg and Adam Grant, "Sheryl Sandberg on the Myth of the Catty Woman," *New York Times*, June 23, 2016, accessed May 29, 2017, https://www.nytimes.com/2016/06/23/opinion/sunday/sheryl-sandberg-on-the-myth-of-the-catty-woman.html.

135   "It's insane": Jennifer Reingold, "Why Top Women Are Disappearing from Corporate America," *Fortune*, September 9, 2016, accessed May 19, 2017, http://fortune.com/women-corporate-america.

137   "get to the promised land or you die": Ibid.

Chapter 11: Wings, Talons, Fangs

152   why I was deleting the app: Sarah Lacy, "The Horrific Trickle Down of Asshole Culture: Why I've Just Deleted Uber from My Phone," Pando.com, October 22,

2014, accessed May 19, 2017, https://pando.com/2014/10/22/the-horrific-trickle-down-of-asshole-culture-at-a-company-like-uber/.

164 with Matthew Kohut and John Neffinger: Amy J. C. Cuddy, Matthew Kohut, and John Neffinger, "Connect, Then Lead," *Harvard Business Review*, July–August 2013.

Chapter 12: From Subject to Sovereign

177 "their jobs as clearly as men do": Sharon Meers and Joanna Strober, *Getting to 50/50: How Working Parents Can Have It All* (New York: Bantam Dell, 2009), 31.

179 man affects his behavior: Dan Cassino, "Even the Thought of Earning Less Than Their Wives Changes How Men Behave," *Harvard Business Review*, April 19, 2016.

186 "expert and he never catches up": Meers and Strober, *Getting to 50/50*, xxiv.

188 "cover she performs everything": Rebecca Traister, *All the Single Ladies: Unmarried Women and the Rise of an Independent Nation* (New York: Simon & Schuster, 2016), 41.

189 "independent of husbands and children, is revolutionary": Ibid., 27.

189 "self-supported, homes": Ibid., 10–11.

190 2014 than in 2010: Ibid., 5.

Chapter 13: The Single-Mom Penalty and the Single-Mom Bonus

197 birth age for the first time: Ibid., 17.

197 "the breakdown of the family structure": Ibid., 16.

198 a factor leading to child abuse: Ibid., 195.

198 "much living, I'm afraid": Ibid., 34–35.

206 bravely wrote about it publicly: Rachel Sklar, "I'm 41, Single and Pregnant: Welcome to the New Normal," Medium, October 29, 2014, accessed April 4, 2017, https://medium.com/thelist/im-41-single-and-pregnant-9b2da840a45a.

206 discuss who could be the father: Nancy Jo Sales, "The Baby Dinner," *New York Magazine*, November 8, 1999, accessed April 6, 2017, http://nymag.com/nymetro/urban/family/features/1375/.

210 physical abuse as the cause: Kathryn Edin and Maria Kefalas, *Promises I Can Keep: Why Poor Women Put Motherhood Before Marriage* (Berkeley: University of California Press, 2005).

Chapter 15: The Last Place You're Expecting to See Female Empowerment

235 her own journey to America: Yilu Zhao, "Destination: College, USA; Coming to America," *New York Times*, January 13, 2002.

240 "China's version of the television show 'Shark Tank'": Shai Oster and Selina Wang, "How Women Won a Leading Role in China's Venture Capital Industry," *Bloomberg*, September 19, 2016, accessed April 4, 2017, https://www .bloomberg.com/news/features/2016-09-19/how-women-won-a-leading-role -in-china-s-venture-capital-industry.

242 US look tolerant and hands-off: Mei Fong, *One Child: The Story of China's Most Radical Experiment* (New York: Houghton Mifflin Harcourt, 2016).

242 be "low skilled bachelor[s]": Ibid., 109.

244 "quarter of their Indian sisters": Ibid., 128–29.

246 "had been born in the Foreign Country": Zhao, "Destination: College, USA; Coming to America."

247 "were not mine to see": Ibid.

Chapter 16: Back, Head, Lungs

258 "truth can sometimes bite": Maria Ricapito, "The Insider: Sarah Lacy," *Marie Claire*, February 19, 2015.

259 relationships for diminishing returns: Tom Popomaronis, "Science Says You Shouldn't Work More Than This Number of Hours a Week," *Inc.*, May 9, 2016, accessed April 6, 2017, http://www.inc.com/tom-popomaronis/science-says -you-shouldnt-work-more-than-this-number-of-hours-a-day.html.

260 there for dinner and bedtime: Samantha Ettus, *The Pie Life: A Guilt-Free Recipe for Success and Satisfaction* (Los Angeles: Ghost Mountain Books, 2016).

262 actually wrote on his blog: Paige Craig, "Putting Women First," Good Angel, April 12, 2011, accessed April 4, 2017, https://paigecraig.wordpress .com/?s=Putting+Women+First.

Chapter 17: November 8, 2016

273 "'would say if I was there'": Traister, *All the Single Ladies*, 15.

INDEX

ABOUT THE AUTHOR

Sarah Lacy is the founder and CEO of Pando.com, a no-holds-barred investigative journalism site covering the tech industry. A business journalist for nearly twenty years, Lacy previously wrote for *BusinessWeek* and TechCrunch, and cohosted Tech Ticker for Yahoo Finance. She's the author of *Once You're Lucky, Twice You're Good: The Rebirth of Silicon Valley and the Rise of Web 2.0* (Gotham: 2008) and *Brilliant, Crazy, Cocky: How the Top 1% of Entrepreneurs Profit from Global Chaos* (Wiley: 2011). She's a frequent—and outspoken—guest on national television and radio. She lives in San Francisco with her two children.